Teachings From Mother Earth

Teachings From Mother Earth

Book 1

THINK INSIDE THE CIRCLE

Judith C. Stern

® PJ PENGUIN
PUBLISHING

ISBN: 978-0-9863522-0-1

Printed in U.S.A.

Published by PJ Penguin Publishing

P.O. Box 42

Marine On St. Croix, MN 55047

First Print Edition: 2015

Second Print Edition: 2015

Third Print Edition: 2015

Library of Congress Control Number: 2014960119

To Bill Moyers
for his many years giving generously in support of
enlightenment, truth and justice in the spirit of
Thomas Paine

ACKNOWLEDGMENTS

I gratefully acknowledge the help, advice, and encouragement I received from the following people while compiling this book:

Bill Moyers, host of *Moyers and Company,* PBS television, and the episode series *"Moyers: Joseph Campbell and the Power of Myth."* Bill's kind words, "Don't give up!" gave me courage.

Thank you to Rudi Hargesheimer, my dear partner, who believes in my dreams.

My adventurous parents, Frederick and Marian Stern, who instilled in me their love for wild places and a spirited attitude toward life.

Special family members: Leonard, Lisa, John, Heath, Sandra, Atticus, and Eames.

Frederick Manfred, who believed I could be a writer.

Dick Wilson, for extensive help with my first P.J. Penguin Publishing venture.

Harold and Louise Nielsen for a generous financial loan that eventually allowed me time to write.

Dick and Debbie Bancroft for a lifetime example of giving away.

Also: Harold Goodsky, Ed McGaa, Waring Jones, Freya Manfred and Tom Pope, John and Delores (Doris) DeLaittre, Roger Hammer, Therese Griffith, Joe Geshick and Mizinokamigok.

Thank you to my dear readers for giving me an opportunity to share my story with you.

Miigwech to Mother Earth for giving me life, for giving me a family, for a happy time on the best place on Turtle Island—beautiful Minnesota—land that I love.

FOREWORD

Judy Stern, my Soul/Spirit sister for decades has been totally immersed into our Ways, both Environmental and Spiritual. If any book can educate the majority society, this one belongs at the top of the list.

You don't have to be a tribal card-carrying Indian to embrace Earth Saving Spirituality, which my Lakota Sioux have miraculously kept alive against all odds and now blossoms a hundredfold. Planetary Heating, as we predicted, has catalyzed a strong involvement from our observant nonIndian brethren and now respect the power of Nature-based Spiritual Knowledge. They read our books, respect our prophecies, and most importantly are beginning to adopt our proven Wisdom down through centuries, sustaining a wholesome hemisphere devoid of the discouraging, wasteful, corrupt, too greedy society around us today. White Man has to change if we All seek to survive!

~Ed McGaa, Eagle Man, Lakota author of *Mother Earth Spirituality, Native American Paths to Healing Ourselves and Our World.*

The man who sat on the ground in his tipi meditating on life and its meaning, accepting the kinship of all creatures and acknowledging unity with the universe of things was infusing into his being the true essence of civilization. And when the native man left off this form of development, his humanization was retarded in growth.

Chief Luther Standing Bear, Ogalala Lakota

Other books by Judith C. Stern:

PJ Penguin, A Race To Save Penguin Land

Teachings From Mother Earth
Book Two
Everything Has A Spirit

Teachings From Mother Earth
Book Three
Wisdom Isn't Rocket Science

Contents

Part 1

Part 2

This book contains a lifetime of memories that Judy has now recorded from her perspective of today's world. She creates an intimate look into the America she grew up in through diaries, journals, essays and conversations, all influenced by fascinating people including Native Americans. But most of all, by listening to plants and animals, the innocent silent teachers she encounters daily on hikes through the woods: Butterfly knowledge! Tree knowledge! Sun knowledge!

INTRODUCTION

1973. Thirty-one years old. Grand Forks, North Dakota. Healthy, happy mother of four great kids. Unhappy, troubled wife. Drifting away from Christian teachings. Hungry for college education. Doubtful of value of English methods of learning.

My life is about to change. First, the prophetic dream. Next, the powwow conversion. Then, I walk into a bookstore and pick up *Touch the Earth* by T.C. McLuhan, a woman from Toronto, who gathered First Nation passages, and soft, brown-tone historic photographs, to create a vision—a vision now almost lost. I've found a new Bible. Here are people I want to be like, to think like. These are neighbors I can understand. Why? Why didn't I wish to be like my own people? What was wrong with them? Therefore, me, too. I'm not Indian.

My ethnicity is all German. My birthplace, Minneapolis. I had to know how I came to be like me, and not someone else. No Bible could teach me. No professor could answer me. No Indian could tell me. I had to find my own path, and listen to Mother Earth.

Now, at age seventy-one, I've learned that the story is as much about my people's journey from tribal Deutschland to Minnesota's forests and prairies, as it is about the Indian's 20,000 year migration and settlement across the American continents.

You, sister or brother reader, can create your own spiral of making knowledge without reading books. Go be with the wild. Find out what gives you beauty and health through the meaning you ascribe to your purpose of being. Or, begin by reading my story, my gift to you.

~ *Miigwech*, Judith Carol Stern

PART 1

Chapter 1
COMPUTERS HAVE SPIRITS
What is the difference between spirituality and religion?

University of St. Thomas, Minneapolis, Minnesota

Do I dare answer Allison's question? This *is* a Catholic school, and my job is to teach. My heart skips a beat. Here is my chance. My female brain spirals with relative replies: Should I give the students "Webster's" version—concise and politically correct? Or infuse it with personal, biased information—stories rich with my experience and wisdom? Shall I freely flay the Christian church and reveal my love for American Indian spirituality?

Years before I became a college instructor, I too was an innocent, knowledge hungry, stay-at-home, young mother like Allison. I didn't know the answer, either. I glance out the window at the buildings of downtown Minneapolis, shimmering in June summer sunshine: steel, glass, sandstone, granite; then I turn to face the silent room.

Like a reflection in a mirror, I see myself in their fresh faces and their curious expressions. When I entered college, I'd been a thirty-one-year-old mother with four small children, separated, no child support, studying applied art, American Indian Studies, and Ojibwe language in Grand Forks, North Dakota, a "hippie mama" working on a "sixties degree." Really, it was 1973, but back then they referred to any self-created liberal arts degree as a "sixties degree."

I smile softly at Allison—lovely, smart, lithe, golden-haired, blue-eyed, pale-skinned. So much like many St. Thomas girls whose grandparents have Scandinavian roots. I scan the polite, patient, twenty-seven bright College of Education students who will become elementary school teachers, hopefully in Minnesota. They'll soon graduate after student teaching and classes that include art and culture appreciation, which is my specialty: American Indian Art.

Addressing the group, I begin, "Allison wants to know the difference between spirituality and religion. Does anybody know?"

Stone silence. I'm thinking: *Gee whiz!* They've studied in a Catholic university for three years and don't know what spiritualism is? Nor, how to define religion? Maybe they can explain Christian religion, but not the meaning of religion in general? Perhaps they think of spiritualism as ghostly spirits, ancestor worship, or Halloween?

When I was young, theological terminology confused me, too. I was a Lutheran, as close to Catholicism as a Protestant girl could get, and Bible lessons were hopelessly and intentionally designed to create faith, not knowledge. Now, here I am: inwardly critical of Christian dogma that contributes to the foolish behavior that's killing Mother Earth, and wondering who will tell our children why our planet is dying right under our feet? I'm eager to share knowledge with these deserving students, yet fearful of offending any one of them—or the Catholic university hierarchy.

Looking directly into Allison's eyes, I begin, "Historically, spirituality preceded organized religions. For thousands of years, before written languages, agricultural advances, and centralized cities, humans devised mythologies about the world and their place in it. Every tribe invented a human creation story and a world origin tale. They believed everything was created by a mysterious, unseen force, and also that everything contained this force. Or simply put— everything has a spirit."

The room becomes serenely quiet. I continue, "Religions are usually highly structured organizations that teach believers to worship a superhuman deity that contains all the spiritual qualities the rest of us are not born with, but which might be earned through following written rules that were revealed to one man who actually had contact

3

with the deity, or deities."

I stop right there. I'm hired to teach art, not religion. And art is not religion, is it? Then, I hear Sarah whisper to her friend, "I'm disappointed. I thought we were going to learn about art—not culture."

Allison pops up with a new question, "I wonder how and why spirituality became religion?"

A-ha! Another arrow warms my heart. This is good! Before I can say anything, she adds more, "And I sure don't understand how everything can have a spirit. I mean, my shoes don't!"

Laughter from the class.

"You all have a spirit, according to primitive and not-so-primitive people, like almost all Asians and Africans. You, you, and you, and everything around you!" I say, noting the rapt attention among them.

Even the two women in the corner stop doodling.

"Traditional natives believe that everything comes from nature, and nature is created by some force. In Ojibwe it's called Gitchie Manito who made Father Sky and Mother Earth, but neither is thought of as a human figure. Everything is thought of as a family made by a mysterious force, all sharing original properties that remain in them, whether living or dead, but they don't completely die because all the properties go back into the earth to make more plants and animals. This very simple, basic knowledge could easily lead one to believe that something in us goes on after our body decays."

Quizzical expressions fill the room. Thus, I continue, "Your desk would be perceived of as having a spirit. Your desk, computer, and so forth, couldn't exist without earth, wind, fire, and water, or hydrogen, oxygen, iron, phosphorus, zinc, and so on. We think of these as minerals, but humans once thought of then as gifts, or magic— especially copper, gold, and iron—because everything was mysterious."

Time to move on. I focus on traditional native values that become expressed in art. Of course the students would doubt that their computers have spirits. I did, too. Making new connections, considering unfamiliar paradigms, requires motivation and time. And most of us are slow to change our thinking. But, whatever I was, I am no longer.

I instruct students to prepare art materials for our project. While they cut butcher-block paper, mix paint, and distribute it all, I gaze out the window again.

A few blocks away on Nicollet Mall, Mother would take me shopping and treat me to lunch. She had three beautiful sisters. Joyce was a women's clothing fashion buyer for Young Quinlin and later for Bjorkman, across the street. Both were the finest lady's apparel stores in Minnesota. Young Quinlin Tea Room featured a round pool with a fountain circled by real tropical plants. Gorgeous models slinked among linen-draped tables on thick carpet, wearing the latest styles. Sweet Grandma Myrtle was eighty when she lost her balance, toppling into the pool—horrifying everyone—especially herself, a grand, dignified, richly dressed lady who always wore gloves. Poor Myrtle! One day I brought a tablet to sketch fashions, and dreamed of being a fashion designer.

Adjacent to Young Quinlin, Aunt Lorraine managed Amluxen's, an ornate fabric emporium with mahogany woodwork and chandeliers. She supplied me with exotic samples of foreign fabrics, thus I lost interest in baby dolls and used a sewing machine to sew for big-girl dolls. Later, Lorraine worked in the state capitol as an accountant.

Aunt Alice and Uncle Bud were contractor/builders for lavish Edwin Lunde homes for the rich. He also built the University of Minnesota Arboretum building, a timber-frame, Tudor-style landmark near Lake Minnetonka. Mother was our Girl Scout leader, an accountant for Harry's Restaurant, saleswoman for Childcraft books, Avon cosmetics manager, painted landscapes, sewed our clothes, loved fishing, cooking, and taught me canning. Dad's Aunt Ethel owned a florist shop/greenhouse apart from the much larger one the Stern brothers owned in North Minneapolis.

Luckily, in the prefeminist fifties, I had role models and stories about tough German ancestors—Mary and Minnie, widowed with four girls who prospered, running a big farm, owning a resort and Priebe's Dining Hall at the Minnesota State Fair.

Dad had a Lake Street used car dealership. He changed to a Desoto/Plymouth dealer. Later he began Lakeland Realty, and finally an awning manufacturing company. Always in sales. Always hunting or fishing, frequenting piano bars—singing, telling stories. He disapproved of Aunt Joyce who married a writer and had artist's parties, gathering on the floor for poetry, beer, and hardboiled eggs (German-American beatniks). Uncle Warren had a play performed at Theater St. Paul. They had hard times and asked my dad for a loan, causing a fight between Mom and Dad. My plan to become a beatnik ended.

Mom prayed hard about this and everything else—reading her Bible, Billy Graham books, and historical biographies. Dad avoided church, followed all sports, and read newspapers for hours. He was gone too much according to Mom's complaints. I didn't care. He atoned for his bad ways by treating us to many upscale restaurant dinners—places with shrimp cocktail. My older brother, my only sibling and my best friend, liked steaks.

When I was a teen, I learned a family secret. Handsome Harold got Aunt Lorraine pregnant before marriage, and her furious father arranged an abortion. Later, they married after she changed from Lutheran to Catholic. The abortion left her sterile, so Harold left her for a Catholic who gave him children. She couldn't marry again due to Catholic laws. I often heard Mother moan, "Pooor Lorrainy!"

Years later, Mother's prayers couldn't save Lorraine from dying from cancer, or Dad from self-centered extravagance. She divorced him, but their love never faltered, and she remarried him five years later. (Don't ask me if he became a "new man.")

Being a sensitive, observant child, I concluded that Bibles, laws, and many adults fail to provide common-sense guidelines—a conclusion now firmly entrenched in me. My festering feeling that institutionalized injustice in all forms of manmade power was contributing to misery and suffering of women everywhere has been confirmed. I had to mature to know how.

At eighteen, I married my high school boyfriend, became a mom and member of the PTA, Jaycees, Ladies Aid Society, Teacher's Wives Club, and neighborhood coffee clubs. My husband was a deacon in our Congregational Church, and I taught Sunday school. When he received a fellowship to pursue a doctorate degree at the University of North Dakota, Grand Forks, we crammed four kids into a new Ford wagon and headed west to become flatlanders—a fond term for prairie dwellers. We moved into student housing on the edge of a cornfield, away from the famous flooding Red River, among many future friends. Fate, or chance, would intervene to change my life forever.

Allison stands by my side, "The art supplies are ready for the lesson." Her eyes shine. They remind me of a garden rabbit I surprised one night with my flashlight. Her spirit is strong. I discovered my spirit many moons ago—on the Dakota prairie—seduced by midnight stars, damp sweet grass, burning sage, gentle people, and thundering Lakota drums.

Chapter 2
ON THE WINGS OF AN UNSEEN SPIRIT
COMES THE DRUM
What is a Powwow?

Devil's Lake, North Dakota

"Carnival tickets cost two dollars each for adults and fifty cents for kids. The powwow is free," said the fat-faced lady in a monotone voice as she made change in the ticket booth, which displayed a poster of a carnival Ferris wheel and words underneath: Devil's Lake, North Dakota. Spirit Lake Indian Reservation; July 28–29, 1972.

"What powwow? What's a powwow?" I said, surrounded by four excited kids.

She jerked her head while handing out tickets. "Over there."

I raised one hand to shield my eyes, and peered into a fiery ball of sun setting on the western horizon—a celebration of reds and yellows cavorting over the prairie, rolling away in grassy waves to the ends of the earth in all directions broken only by gullies lined with cottonwoods, scrub oaks, and pin cherry bushes that protected precious streams. Against the blazing sky, I spotted a black silhouette; a huge oval-shaped canvas roof on poles, open to all sides.

The kids tugged at my sleeve, "Come on, Mom! Let's DO it!"

"That must be the powwow," I murmured to myself, as children pulled me along toward the merry-go-round, tilt-a-whirl cars, penny arcade, and candy floss booth—new delights at every turn.

After all the rides that everyone else loves—which make me sick; after the steaming, puffy fry bread laced with honey and washed down with Coco Cola; after nobody won at the beanbag toss game—night fell. Gaudy but gay neon lights flipped on, filling the hot, dusty air.

8

My brain grew pleasantly numb from the silly artificiality of the carnival—a little oasis of mindless, frolic, and fun. The antique calliope cranked out tinny tunes; while our clothes, sandals, and hair became coated with fine black soil that turned to mud in the creases of sweat on our sun-browned bodies.

Indian families filled the crowd, some dressed like us in T-shirts and jeans, and others in calico cloth shirts or dresses decorated with beads and ribbons, like costumes.

I steered the children toward a fence that separated the carnival from the cooler surrounding grassland. Through the gate, and into the starry night we walked toward the canvas shelter, following a strolling couple—fascinated by a gal in a dress that swayed and jingled, and her guy with a black-and-white feather twirling atop his head.

We timidly chose a place to sit on sweet prairie grass near the back of the tan open tent. About two hundred natives circled the enclosure, facing the center, which was empty except for two large drums and some men milling about, talking. We watched and waited like everyone else, although I felt slightly uneasy. Seeing no other "white people," I wondered if we were really welcome, though I didn't catch anyone looking at us.

As night deepened, the air grew chilly—the scent of damp grass permeating the air with rich, earthy odors. I shivered with enchantment as we huddled together, scanning the immense starlit sky behind us.

"Children," I said, "Look! Isn't it marvelous how clear the sky is?"

"Look, Mom! The big dipper!" whispered Leonard, oldest son.

"Oh, Mommy! A falling star!" cried out Heath, youngest son.

"Quick! Make a wish!" I whispered, embarrassed and amused, for his voice was young, but loud. Two heavyset Indian matrons smiled down lovingly at my awestruck, blue-eyed blond. I smiled back and felt much better. We all relaxed, my dark-haired, brown-eyed daughter, Lisa curling up by me, Johnny searching for the little dipper.

9

Loosely strung around the canvas-top interior, bare electric bulbs bathed the fascinating scene in an eerie yellow glow. A wispy breeze rose, sweeping through the tent, gently swaying the lights. I'd never been to an outdoor religious revival meeting, but I'd seen them in movies. The spectacle I was about to witness was the exact opposite of Burt Lancaster in *Elmer Gantry*.

At one end of the tent, costumed Indians began gathering, but nothing else happened. Looking around, I saw that we were like peas out of a pod among all the dark bodies with black-haired heads, narrow brown eyes, wide cheek bones, smooth-skinned complexions or pockmarked faces, alert poses or bent-at-the-back posture, men with barrel-shaped chests: Quiet people with a gentle, conservative demeanor, who spoke in soft conversation. Sounded like English spoken with an upward inflection at the end of each sentence as though every statement was a question. A Scandinavian influence? The Dakota could have learned English from Northern European immigrants, or Canadian—French-Scotch settlers from the Pembina region, for we were only one hundred miles south of the border, near Devil's Lake. Later, I heard a conversation in Dakota which incorporated these melodious rhythms.

Men began to seat themselves around the drums. Still, nothing happened. There seemed to be no consideration for time at all. In the moonlight, babies slept peacefully next to grandmas. Adolescent girls stole glances at favorite braves. A group of gleeful boys played hide-and-seek among parked cars and trucks. They ran to a tent post where a long-limbed, muscular fellow stood wearing a faded white cowboy hat cocked low over one eye. A shiny silver button on his hatband held a short black feather. A beaded pouch dangled about his neck. One of the lads touched it—running his fingers across the red and blue seed beads trimming the sides, then he playfully swung around the man's legs. The kids all clung to his tight jeans and tugged at his vest until he

10

laughed, reached into his vest pocket and gave each boy a coin, and sent them on their way. He leaned back against the post, folding his arms, which made the tattoo on his skin bulge over his muscles. I thought the popular cowboy was rather impressive, but I soon forgot about him when I heard an announcement coming from the area where people gathered—a man's voice telling one of the drum groups to begin a song. The drummers picked up their sticks and began to wail loudly in high-pitched tones, slicing the night with sounds I didn't know men could make.

"*Ai ai ai ai yi yi yi yi, ya ya, ho, ho, ai ai . . . .,*" sending shivers up and down my spine, into my fingertips, electrifying my body, penetrating the deepest fiber of my being.

Then, seven men began to beat the drum.

"*Boom, boom, boom, boom. BOOM, BOOM,*" again and again the drum lifted the earth, let it go, and lifted it again, over and over, along with the "*Ai ai ai,*" and deep guttural chants, not fast or slow. Out of the drum rose, stirring reminders of ancient times on earth. Rhythmic vibrations crept through the ground, into my bones, blood, and being—the being that beats with one heart connected to the cosmos. A path of energy flowed through that tent on the wings of an unseen spirit. I was seduced by amazing feelings—an instinctual awareness of something in me that had been lost, or misplaced. A willing captive I was!

The children sat transfixed. No doubt about it. Those rhythms, those strange people—feared, loved, or pitied, misunderstood or misrepresented, lazy or wise, those all around me knew something that was missing in my knowledge.

My daughter, Lisa, gave me a look of delight, and oldest son, Leonard, his wide brown eyes glowing with excitement, had made another discovery. The middle son, Johnny got up on his knees to see a procession of dancers enter the circle in twos, threes, and fours, while

11

youngest son, Heath, stood up to peer around his brothers. First to enter were a couple of elderly men carrying flags. Then more men, followed by adult women, young men; and lastly, young girls—some holding the hands of a few wee toddlers who tried to dance. About fifty dancers paraded by.

Most men wore a hair ornament shaped like a roach of spiny stiff hairs in a row down the back of their head, with a twirling feather on top. Vests were stitched with seed beads in geometric or floral designs, or embroidered with bright thread, or trimmed with ribbons. Under the vest might be a ribbon-shirt: a pullover type of blouse of plain or printed cotton, with a V-neck opening for the head, a pointed collar, long sleeves, and streams of ribbons sewn on the chest, back, and sleeves. Leggings were mostly short—a few long; but all seemed to be plain colors and unadorned—unlike the breechcloth flap over the leggings, on front and back, which were usually decorated like the vest. They all wore beaded moccasins of elk or moose hide, and wristbands of fur, grass, or metal. All carried something in their hands made of natural materials, maybe a pouch or eagle feather. Many had a neck scarf. I didn't see any masks, face paint, animal skin garments, long eagle feather headdresses, or scalps!

Women wore ankle-length dresses and shawls simply cut, but elaborately decorated, mostly calico prints or solid cotton with satin or grosgrain ribbons, but one was navy-blue wool with white seashells. They wore beaded moccasins on their feet and beaded barrettes in their hair, which was pulled back from their face in a bun if one were a matron, or in braids if one were a maiden.

These were slow, traditional dance steps with men and women holding their backs and heads straight and tall—eyes forward. The women's dipping up and down caused the fringe on their dress and shawl to sway, or the silver cones to tinkle. Every costumed person danced. But as the night went on, they took turns dancing in groups—

all men, all women, or young or old. Now and then, the whole crowd was invited to get up and move around the circle. I was too shy, even though I wanted very much to try.

The oldest son went to the car to fetch jackets and a blanket. My sleepy-headed children were nodding off quickly. The continuous beat of the drum cast a mesmerizing spell upon all of us. I sat very still, my poncho draped over my shoulders. I was filled with awe, feasting on the perfumed air—wet prairie plants mingled with faint campfire smoke.

The onlookers without dance regalia didn't join in unless it was an intertribal dance, which included tourists. I saw no tourists, other than ourselves. One disheveled intoxicated man was quickly whisked away when he sought to enter the circle; otherwise I saw no evidence of liquor. A speaker with a microphone would announce each dance, or report a child separated from his parents, or tell about available food, or about up-and-coming events, including more powwows in other states. He spoke in English and Dakota. I wondered how many Dakota people knew their language, and where they lived, and who still cared about their rich traditions. What jobs did they have? How many had been converted to Christianity, and which kind? A Lutheran Indian seemed like a weird anomaly to me, but I knew there were Catholic ones.

The fetching chap in the white cowboy hat sat on a folding chair in the drumming circle, holding one hand to his ear and beating the drum with the other; while a beautiful Dakota maiden in a pale-blue aqua costume stood a few steps behind him, bending her knees to the rhythm and trilling her voice with a handful of other women.

The repetitious "tom-tom" tones had a hypnotic effect on me, like a peaceful spiritual reality. Yet the stimulus of exotic sensations also excited me—rawness, simplicity, and earthiness, mingling easily with people so different than me, so far from home; or was I really removed from those strangers?

Why was I drawn to everything I was experiencing—so much so that I didn't wish to go home? Fighting with myself to remain awake, I nonetheless lay down, heavy with thoughts. I imagined that it was one-hundred years ago; that no pioneers had yet crossed the tall bluegrass expanse on their westward march to the Rockies and the Pacific; that grizzly bears terrified the people, and bison roamed over every rise; that gardens of corn, squash, and beans grew on river bottoms; that teepees were home. I began feeling jealous! Oh my! What freedom they had! What beauty! Yes, there was much to feel envious about, or perhaps I was naive—prone to romantic notions.

Pulling my wool blanket about me, using my arm as a pillow, I tried to rest. The drum boomed on, but I failed to notice that the people were all going home—driving away toward the darkened carnival and the road back to Fort Totten. Only a few young drummers remained to sing and drum by the light of a blazing fire shooting sparks into the clear, cool night.

I rolled onto my back, folded my arms under my head and gazed up at billions of stars, recalling that my mother-in-law, a sweet, generous, well-educated woman, had died the previous summer while traveling alone, visiting historical sites featuring the 1862 Sioux Uprising in southern Minnesota. After visiting the pipestone quarries, she drove away on the highway and later crossed an intersection where she had a head-on collision with a Catholic priest who was entering the road. They were both killed.

Two weeks after that tragedy, I experienced a colorful, vivid dream. The memory of that made a chill creep up my legs. I shut my eyes and pulled the Hudson Bay blanket over my head, trying hard to remember all the details: Edna appeared to me in her living room, holding a small, square cedar box with the lid open, allowing me to examine the contents. The chest had seen many seasons, and stored an unusual array of Indian items: fetishes made from pipestone, wood, animal hide, stones, leaves, and shells. "This is for you," she stated mysteriously, "Take it." Without saying a word, I accepted her strange gift, thinking that she must have gotten it during her trip, wondering why she gave it to me.

Months later we learned that Edna's estate gave enough money to my husband to return to college to earn an EDD (Doctor of Education). He chose the University of North Dakota where he received a fellowship and a job working in rural schools, including St. Michael's at Fort Totten and Fort Yates at Standing Rock Reservation, which gave me an opportunity to do some volunteer work with natives and learn about their culture. At UND, I became involved with a group creating an alternative school for the children of some college teachers who shared open-minded goals that led to many rich experiences.

The powwow drum stopped. I sat straight up, watched the guys leave, checked the kids slumbering in the car behind my blanket, then lay down. A chord had been struck in my heart that would need strumming forever.

Chapter 3
THE POWER OF THE WORLD WORKS IN CIRCLES
Have you seen square shapes in nature?

University of St. Thomas

"We're going to learn about the importance of symbolism in American Indian culture," I say, standing at the blackboard with chalk in hand and turning to draw a large circle for all the students to see. "I want you to learn how they think—not just what they do. Let's avoid the quintessential Thanksgiving Day Indian lessons with happy natives giving food to save the pilgrims who then all share a big feast and live happily ever after. This simplistic, stereotypical perception, which is often the only information elementary school children receive about Native Americans, fails to inform students about the indigenous people that still live in or around Minnesota. Teach kids about their own history; how natives are connected to it; and how life changed, or remained the same, when Europeans arrived. Isn't it far more exciting to learn that such and such happened right in your own area—places we can still visit, connect to and study?

"In Minnesota, we have Ojibwe, or Anishinabe, people who were forced out of the East by westward expansion. Then the Ojibwe fought for new territory with the Dakota who were here, and still are in the South. Indian means from East India, a name derived from an enemy people. However, Indians do still use the term themselves. But if you want to be proper, use "First Nation," as a general term, and then the tribal name in their language."

I then teach my class to use maps to show original and current language areas, reservations, and territories for the United States. This isn't art, but it is culture; and I've discovered that most of these

16

learners know very little about indigenous people. They've not gotten beyond the Thanksgiving stories of their childhood!

"See this book in my hand? If you only read one book about Indians, read this one: *Black Elk Speaks*, written by John G. Neihardt, who interviewed, then wrote the life story of Black Elk, an Oglala, Lakota holy man who lived in the 1930s in South Dakota."

Pointing back at my chalk circle, I continue, "Black Elk describes the significance of circular shapes, thus I will read some of his words from this book: '. . . everything an Indian does is in a circle, and that is because the Power of the World always works in circles, and everything tries to be round. In the old days when we were a strong and happy nation—and so long as the hoop was unbroken, the people flourished. The flowering tree was the living center of the hoop, and the circle of the four quarters nourished it . . .'"

Addressing the class, I ask, "Have you ever seen square shapes in nature?"

No replies.

"Have you ever seen a square flower, bug, lake, river, sun, or moon?"

Some listeners shake their heads "no."

"The Indians didn't see any, either; and when Black Elk was forced to live in a square log cabin, he said it was a bad way to live."

I show them pictures of Indian dwellings from across America: an igloo of ice, a pueblo of rounded corners, a *kiva* constructed of stones in a circle, a Dakota teepee, an Ojibwe wigwam, and an Iroquois longhouse, all shaped by curves rather than angles.

"If you look at a globe full of countries, water, and place names for everything, you see how we now imagine our earth. But it wasn't always this way—for thousands of years, people didn't know the rest of the world. Natives were more concerned with survival than geography and commerce, and their immediate concerns shaped their worldview. Without knowledge about engineering and technology, they were always at the mercy of nature; therefore, all their thoughts and actions centered around propitiate behavior to appease Mother Earth and Father Sky. Such appeasements took on varying forms all across vast North and South America, creating different cultures with unique traditions. The Mayan people from Mexico and the Incas from Peru both developed survival systems that gave them luxuries the Ojibwe and Dakota learned about much later. Often such riches also led to misery and inequality among the people, whereas the Canadian and northern plains dwellers lived a more primitive lifestyle, but practiced a more democratic socially free ethic. Moral precepts are subject to change for many reasons, but one of them is surely availability of food, and another, attitudes about how nature works."

I then pose a question to the class, "What do you think when you hear the word circle?"

"The sun, moon, earth."

"A baseball."

"A plate."

"My ring."

"A circle of friends."

I stop them there, "Wait! A circle of friends is good—it's a concept, rather than an object. We are conceptualizing with symbols. We imagine our friends as a circle. Objects are just objects without meaning unless we assign symbolism to them. Why don't we use the term, 'a square of friends'?"

"It just doesn't sound right?" says Carolyn.

"Because we don't stand or sit in squares when we gather. We usually arrange chairs in a circle, or sit in a circle," replies Rita.

"Why?" I ask.

Rita says, "Everybody can be seen and heard. Nobody gets stuck in a corner, or in the back of the room."

18

"Then why," I ask, "why are all the classrooms in St. Thomas arranged like this? And all the church interiors, too? Think about it!" Pause. "Circles symbolize much more than shapes, and have since art began. Circles with colors and numbers represent ideas—like equality and wholeness. The Dakota, Lakota, and Ojibwe think of the earth as a sphere with four colors comprising the interior—fire colors: red, yellow, black or blue, and white," I say, while drawing three more circles within my circle on the blackboard. I then instruct the class to use paper and crayons to do the same.

"The natives drew two lines through their circle, creating four equal quadrants, so let's draw a new circle with four quadrants and colors. Can you think why they chose those colors? Why did they choose four sections instead of three? While you are drawing, concentrate on these questions. Then, create a third picture of the earth as you imagine it. Compare your work. The young children you will teach will learn that there are several ways to conceptualize our common home— the earth, or Mother Earth."

That term, "Mother Earth" was like a foreign idea to me when we moved to Grand Forks. I never heard my mother use it, nor my teachers, nor anybody I knew. It wasn't in any geography texts, or in the Bible. It sounded as odd to me, as "a square of friends" sounds to Carolyn. I wondered: Would any of these students ever feel comfortable calling their planet "Mother"?

Chapter 4
BUCKS AND SQUAWS SIGNS MUST GO
Why are you chopping down the bushes and pulling up their roots?

Grand Forks, North Dakota

One sunshiny July day, my oldest son ran in the house, excited by a discovery. Opening his fist, he revealed small round stones about the size of pearls. He'd caught them in his butterfly net while searching the bottom of a stream that ran through the campus.

"Look, Mom! Each one has a hole in the center! Why? What are they? Are they bones?"

His playmates came to inspect the treasure. His brothers and sister stood in the circle gawking.

I said, "They look like bone beads that turned to stone—beads that could have been strung around the neck of an Indian. They could be over five hundred years old, which means they're older than contact with white traders who brought glass beads that replaced ones like this. Perhaps we should take them to a professor of archeology."

After a long time, we received a phone call from the expert we had deposited our precious stones with, and he verified that they were indeed prehistoric. However, he never gave them back! No problem—Leonard simply found more in the stream—beads that we kept."

The stream, lined with trees, plants, and bushes ran clear, feeding birds, bugs, and small mammals. The two older children played there alone, while I brought the younger ones along to explore and picnic. Once four-year-old Heath fell in the water, and Lisa saved him.

One afternoon, we went for a hike, following a sidewalk across a road bridge that traversed the stream, when we came upon an alarming sight. Men in work clothes were devastating the trees and plants along the creek, using chain saws, axes, shovels, and picks.

Shocked and sickened, I stood like a statue, unable to find my voice. Glancing down at my sons pleading, sad face, then back at the "plant bullies" wielding their axes, I managed to utter, "Stop!" They didn't hear me. One man turned to warn us to "move back."

I yelled, "Don't do this! Please! Look at all that dirt you've exposed. You're creating bad erosion and ruining the stream. Why? Why are you chopping down the bushes and pulling up their roots?"

"Well, just a darn minute now!" he snarled, "Hey, guys! This here lady wants us to quit our work—says we're spoiling the ditch!"

They respectfully stopped for a few minutes—long enough to hear me repeat my concerns—then, went right on with their destruction! A pickup truck nearby had UND written on the side. I knew where the construction garage was, so we all huffed on over there to complain to a supervisor, who listened sympathetically and even agreed to "look into it."

The next day, we went to check the site, and no more damage had been done. Ha! The stream was saved! I'll never know why those men thought their idiotic actions were necessary.

That small victory was monumental for me. My marriage was turning from bad to worse, and my will to change it was crippled by fear. Instead of a new beginning, we were growing further apart as he spent more and more time "at the office," which friends said was a lie. His deceased mother had wanted me to get a college degree and offered to pay for it, but he'd refused to give me permission to use the money. I went to a doctor who said I suffered from "cabin fever"—a common winter prairie malady caused by being indoors too much. He suggested I join a club and get out more; then he saw my bruised arms. I told how he'd come home drunk and beaten me up so badly the bed slats broke. He told me to see a counselor. I couldn't bring myself to go—couldn't imagine raising four kids alone. I'd only had one job in my life, at a Dairy Queen store during high school. Also, my husband threatened me if I talked about going to work or college—strange behavior, since his mother had a master's degree in education and had taught her whole life. To make things stranger—his doctoral thesis, which I was typing, was about the self-actualizing of the individual! The more I typed, the worse I felt!

A teacher's conference in another state promised to be a fun time. I said I could get my mother to watch the children and go along.

He said, "Who you? What would you have to talk about?" Then he laughed.

I was so angry at that mean bully, I stormed out the door and headed for Interstate Highway 29 to hitchhike home to Minneapolis! Right away, a rusty pickup truck stopped. Panic! Out jumped a hairy, weird hippie, stinking high on marijuana, who slipped and fell on top of me. Brushing myself off, I peeked in the cab of the truck. The driver waved his arm and sneered, "Ya wanna jump in, honey? Ha, ha, ha!"

I ran! I ran toward home. But the kids wouldn't be there yet, so I walked toward campus, crying and confused. Lonely, too, because I was too ashamed to confide in my new female friends, all college career women and (gulp!) feminists. I *knew* what they would say.

Somewhere near Union Hall, I collapsed under an arching oak tree—feeling like the weight of the world had pushed me into the dirt—like a dried-up acorn, small and withered, I was afraid to confront the obvious changes my life desperately needed. I didn't even think of turning to God—he certainly hadn't helped the other women in my life who also had "men problems."

My yellow T-shirt clung to my back, soaked by perspiration. The afternoon heat baked the earth, turning grass into scratchy straw that itched my bare legs below my cut-off blue jeans. Removing my red bandana from around my neck, I lay it out flat to dry away my tears.

"Aho!" An arm thrust from behind the tree trunk abruptly snatched

it away! Wheeling about, I saw no one! Rising up, tip-toeing around the tree, I watched in amazement as a funny Indian fellow ran to hide behind another oak, where he held out one arm, waving my bandana.

Trying to decide whether to laugh or yell, I walked toward my mysterious, mischievous man. But when I almost closed in on him, he popped out and danced about, waving my scarf, all with a gleeful smile.

Thoroughly vexed by such a roguish imp, I could only surmise that he was either crazy, harmless, or both. Obviously an Indian, he displayed none of the noble characteristics I liked to ascribe to his race. His teasing was maddening; his demeanor ridiculous; and his dress deplorable. His ratty T-shirt and blue jeans were thin and patched. His tennis shoes had holes in the toes. His hair was long, dull, and uneven. He was slight of build, but appeared strong, and was undoubtedly nimble!

"What are you doing?" I blurted out, "Give me that bandana!"

Saying nothing, he only beamed more brightly—continuing with new silly dance steps, teasing me to chase him. His face was young, smooth, with almond-shaped black eyes. His nose was too wide, yet not nearly as wide as his big mouth.

Feeling more amused than threatened, I walked right up to him, but he scampered off! I gave chase! He let out a loud, "Whoop!," stopped in his tracks, and did an about-face! I almost crashed into him! Above his head, he wagged the red cotton prize. I reached up high.

He skittered away. Off we went around the oak trees, avoiding a few bemused students who cheered me on. He halted. We faced off eye to eye. I hastily snatched the item of contention, while he laughed boldly, falling down on his knees, his back, then sitting up to look at me.

Moved by his merriment and delighted by his fanciful antics, I too fell into chuckling, and soon, gales of laughter flew from both of us!

"You are crazy!" I said between laughs, "Really nuts!"

"I know," he said, "What's your name?"

"Judy," I stammered, catching my breath, "My name is Judy. What's yours?"

"Brady Barber," he replied in a gentle voice.

"Are you a student here at UND, Brady?"

"Oh my gosh! I forgot. Where did I put it?" he said, looking around, "I have to find my notebook. Oh, I left it over there," he said, as he left. He returned with a beat-up spiral beige notebook with smudged writing all over the cover. He sat down again; this time— yoga style—with legs folded and tucked close to his body; his back straight as an arrow. (Pardon the pun!)

"What classes are you taking?" I asked him, curious about his notebook.

"Oh some of this, and some of that. Maybe I'll become a teacher, but I really like philosophy. I'm always scribbling down thoughts in this book. Do you know anything about Greek philosophy?"

"Nothing," I murmured, finding it ironic that an Indian wanted to learn about Greek culture, surprised that my "imp" had academic desires. "Nothing but what I learned in high school, like Homer's *Iliad* and the *Odyssey*, and a little Plato. How about you?" I asked, noticing that he was clean, and didn't look very different than the hippies, some of whom needed fumigating.

Brady spoke about Plato and Aristotle, while I secretly wished to ask him about his background, "Where are you from, Brady?"

"Fort Totten."

"Really? We went to a carnival there in July—that is—my four children and I, and . . ."

"YOU have four kids? Wow! I wouldn't have guessed it. I thought you were a student."

"Mothers can be students, too, you know."

24

"Oh, sure they can. You've probably already graduated."

"From high school. I'd like to go to college, but I'm not sure what I'd study, and anyway . . . never mind. I better get home. The children return from school soon, and the youngest needs to be picked up at nursery school. He goes three afternoons a week so I can type my husband's papers. He's working on a graduate degree."

Brady said, "I hope we can meet again. I promise to not tease you."

"On the contrary—you'll never know what a gift you are. Thanks for teasing me!"

I left him looking puzzled.

One month later, we had a Halloween party for friends and neighbors, a costume party with a keg of beer, my homemade baked beans, steamed raisin brown bread, coleslaw, potato salad, and bratwurst. A guest brought brownies baked with marijuana, unbeknown to me. Like a polite hostess, I ate three, and felt unusually jolly when a professor asked me what I was majoring in. I listed the canning of fruits and vegetables—mostly tomatoes and dill pickles, the changing and laundering of diapers, the cutting and sewing of clothing and curtains." Then the room went dark. Someone standing behind me had reached around and was covering my eyes.

"Guess who?" said an unfamiliar voice.

"*Hmmm.* Can you give me a hint?"

"Where is your red bandana?"

"Brady!" I squealed as I wheeled around—"Brady Barber! How did you get here? So good to see you again."

"George brought me. He's a friend of your husband. I didn't know I was coming to your place. Quite a surprise!"

I couldn't stop giggling. Brady looked at me funny, then at the plate of brownies, and said, "Say, have you been eating brownies?"

"You betcha'—they're better than mine!"

"George made those—they're full of marijuana."

"Really? Oh my gosh!"

"George and your husband are always smoking dope together, but then everybody seems to be trying it these days—even growing it," Then, Brady chuckled, "George let me lick the dough off the beaters. He licked the bowl." We laughed.

After one o'clock a.m., only George, Brady, the Johnsons, and the Clarks remained in the living room, talking. The conversation turned to stereotyping of Indians in North Dakota—the UND logo with a cartoon character of a stupid-looking native, the rednecking insults of some good old boys, and some negative newspaper coverage. Brady said that an old motel had an offensive sign on a billboard that used the words "bucks" and "squaws." It made him mad.

"Let's go take it down—right now!" someone cried, "It's nearby."

"Ya—let's do it—I'll get a chain and we'll hook it to my bumper, the other end to the sign, and we'll rip it down!" said another.

I protested, "Someone in the office will hear you. You'll get caught!"

"No we won't, because you can detract them. Pretend you need a room."

"I can't do that!"

"Well, don't you want to help Brady here—our buddy?"

Everybody was looking at me.

"I'll just ride along, and help if I'm really needed."

Brady beamed, and we all ran out and piled into George's Ford sedan, and drove the few blocks to the down-and-out seedy motel on the end of town where we turned out the car lights, cut the engine, and sat peering at the door.

My husband said, "I'll go inside first, to see who's working, and come back and report."

"Why don't you just distract him, or her, yourself?" I pleaded.

"No!" he whispered, "Only a pretty woman will do."

The car was so full, I had to sit on his lap, so I got out and he went in while George told Brady to fish under the seat for a chain.

The report was: "One guy with the radio on. The sign's far enough away from the motel, so I doubt he'll hear anything." The chain came out, and I went in—my heart pounding hard, convincing myself that it was my duty to right a wrong on behalf of a good cause.

"Do you have any rooms left?" I asked as loudly as I could, as a scrawny clerk with wire-rimmed glasses shot a look at me.

The phone rang, and he called out, "Just a moment, please. I'll be with you in a moment. Excuse me."

"Don't hurry! Take your time! No problem!" I called back. I heard a clanking sound outdoors and glanced at the clerk, but he sounded like he was having an argument. Sweat began running down my neck.

Rip! Crash! The man angrily slammed down the phone. He cocked his head toward the door, listening. Panic!

He jerked his head up, "I clearly heard a crash outside."

I clapped my hands together, "Darn flies! You'd think the bug season would be over. I clapped again. "Gee, nice guy like you, but sort of sounds like you've got girlfriend problems. Too bad—a nice guy like you. I'll wait if you want to call her back."

With a frown on his brow, he stared at the open door. "Did you hear something fall out front?" he asked, cocking his left ear, as though to hear more clearly.

"No, no—it's getting windy outside. Storm coming, they say . . ."

More noise, "Bump, bump, scrape," then quiet.

"Maybe I better go have a look," he said in a worried voice.

"But you've already made me wait this long, so perhaps I'd better go out and check on my kids, then I'll come back and tell you if any thing's amiss. Okay?"

"Well, okay. Sorry about the delay. That's real nice of you. I'm just filling in for the owner tonight, and I wouldn't want any trouble."

"Don't you worry about a thing!" I assured him, making a hasty retreat to the getaway car—ready to take off—with a square plywood sign flat on top of the Ford, being held down by hands reaching out of all four car windows. George drove with one hand, while I moved the stick shift to change gears. "I hope we're not going far!" I excitedly said to my laughing gang of co-conspirators. Then I told them about the lucky phone call.

Not far at all did we go. I watched speechless, while the guys whisked the ugly "bucks and squaws welcome" sign down our basement stairs, into the corner by the washing machine, flat against the wall, where it remained until we left North Dakota.

Chapter 5
THINK IN CIRCLES, FOURS, AND COLORS
Why did Natives choose red, yellow, black, and white?

University of St. Thomas

The struggles of the St. Thomas students seated before me are a mystery. Not all come from rich families and, even if they did, wealth never guarantees a trouble-free life. I can't know the hopes and dreams of each one of them. I can only try to inspire them to think creatively—not "out of the box"—a current phrase for a tired, very old idea. No, I'm teaching them how thinking in circles works. It is the basis for American Indian philosophy. Circles move, flow, curve. Boxes, squares, angles, all are static. Over time, often things that move and change have more power. This was no mystery to natives.

The spirits of Black Elk and Brady Barber circle my head as I speak. "The Dakota and Ojibwe of Minnesota chose a shape to symbolize their understanding of how nature works—a circle. They also chose colors to symbolize values they respected. So why do you think the natives chose red, yellow, black (or blue), and white as significant colors for the circle? Look at your drawings and think about the earth as a sphere, supporting plants and animals, rather than a geography map divided by countries and connected by roads. What meaning might the indigenous peoples have assigned to the four colors?"

No reply.

I ask, "Which color would you choose for summer or spring?"

Sarah says, "Would spring be green? But, there is no green on the circle. Would summer be yellow?"

"First, there are four directions: East, South, West, North. East is the first, and the color is red because light, or each new day, comes from the East. Yellow represents the South because spring winds and warmth arrive from there. Black or blue comes next because dark clouds and rain come from the far West to nourish the land and grow the plants. White, or winter, is last. White brings rest, peace, and snow, which turns to water in the spring, and begins the circle all over again.

Allison asks, "Why aren't blue and green used?"

"If you think about the earth long enough, you'll understand the color choices. My Indian mentors never answered a question of mine directly. And back in the seventies, there were few books that revealed spiritual traditions; consequently I had to figure such things out by myself, and I'm glad! My sense of discovery was delightful. Mentors always gave me a hint, and allowed me to ponder for days, or months, until I got the answer on my own. It's like solving a puzzle. Don't be in a hurry, like most Americans. And remember, learning doesn't stop when you get a degree. My college education is a tool that gave me lots of information, but I really learned how to think when I pursued knowledge about alternative cultures. Take a class in anthropology to understand yourself better in relation to others. Or, sit by a tree and think about blue and green!

"I have a new question for you. Why do you think the circle is divided into four quadrants? Why not two, or five?"

Tom raises his hand, "Because there's four directions?"

"Yes, but there's more significance than that. Like shapes and colors, numbers are also meaningful. Four is an even number, and any even number can be divided by two to achieve balance. Can you think of ways that nature works in fours?"

Allison says, "There are four seasons, and I've read that there were four main elements: earth, wind, fire, and water."

"Good! Any more examples?"

The room is silent, so I continue, "There are four stages of life;

four races of man and women—red, yellow, black and white; four kinds of creatures: those that swim or creep, those that fly, the two-legged, and the four-legged." I pause, and add, "I'm sure you can think of more if you use your imagination, but you have to think in terms of nature."

"Let's all take a ten-minute break. Who will pass out some papers for me?"

Allison comes forward, "I'll help you."

"*Miigwech!* That means thank you, in Ojibwe."

Chapter 6
COMPLIMENTS HAVE UNEXPECTED MEANINGS
Why let precious topsoil fly away?

Grand Forks

Brady and I would talk about the big questions: Why are we here? What's the meaning of life? He didn't teach me any mysterious secrets of the Dakota, however, I learned a lot of wisdom from my small philosopher friend. The children loved his teasing ways; the girls on campus sought his attention; the professors respected him; friends surrounded him, for his generous ways were exemplary.

A bitter cold winter arrived. He wore a tattered, old, brown parka with a pocket large enough for his notebook, and we'd sit on a bench in the sun—the snow glazed and glaring around us, watching students scurry by, going from one class to another. His sparkling dark eyes, big toothy grin, Dakota brown skin (some Irish within), his quiet warmth—all gave me solace when I was desperately unhappy and frightened.

"Judy, I think you should just take a class and see how you like it. Don't be afraid. You'll do just fine."

"But I don't have any money of my own. My husband won't pay for any classes. He said so. He says a woman's place is in the home. He laughs and says, 'Ya gotta keep women barefoot and pregnant!'"

"Let me talk to Professor King. Maybe he'd let you monitor one of his English classes. Would you like that?"

"Sure, but what about the children?"

We sat thinking some more.

I said, "Maybe if I'm only gone for an hour at a time, my oldest son could watch the younger ones, but of course I'll have to wait until summer when they're out of school."

Brady said, "Maybe I could baby-sit for you," but his tone was not enthusiastic.

"Oh thank you, but no. You don't want to anger my husband. He sure wouldn't want you there."

Brady looked at me, frowning, but I couldn't meet his eyes. I was recalling the time I'd signed up for a night class and on the way to the car to go to my first evening, he threw a paper bag full of garbage at me. I cried on my way to a gas station where I stopped to clean myself off. I completed one class in political science, and then quit because the pressure from home was stressful. I did write a thesis in which I advocated an amendment to the United States Constitution, stating that all citizens have a right to clean air, water, and land. Soon after, I was surprised to learn that Gaylord Nelson, US senator from Wisconsin (1963–1981), founder of Earth Day in 1970, had the same idea, which I found in the congressional record. He said, "The economy is a wholly owned subsidiary of the environment, not the other way around."

My idea was pretty good after all! Returning to full-time motherhood, I canned my pears, tomatoes, and peaches; washed diapers, clothes, rugs; and cleaned, cleaned, and cleaned again.

My neighbor Clair, from Cavalier, a teacher working on a master's degree, and a strong women's liberation supporter, invited me to join the Grand Forks Scotties curling club, although I knew nothing about the strange sport from jolly Scotland. It sounded like fun, and I learned that it was indeed! I loved curling with Clair. I can only compare it to bowling on ice.

Our club hosted the US Women's Curling Association bonspiel; spirited contests between hearty Western rural women who played outdoors in below-zero weather, and arrogant flask-carrying, mink-wearing babes from wealthy Illinois suburbs with heated rinks.

Traditionally, curling is a genteel, polite competition in which winning is second to sportsmanship; however, the haughty ladies of Chicago's North Shore were coldly reserved—rarely spoke to us. It IS possible they were simply numb from the freezing, unheated corrugated metal building in which everyone's breath hung in front of their faces. Those highland lassies didn't hang around to chitchat after a match—hurrying off to the Holiday Inn in a waiting limousine.

The championship match was scheduled for Sunday afternoon, and the banquet party for Saturday night, at the modest Westward Ho Motel where poolside festivities were planned without any thoughts of actually swimming. Norwegian knit sweaters and wool slacks were the normal attire.

Ya, you betcha, the beer-drinking North Dakotan—Minnesotans sat at round tables near the food, don't cha know! And the bourbon sippers sat apart, facing the edge of the pool. The defending Illinois champions were in position to win again; and their leader was unpopular, to say the least, yet I was shocked at what happened.

An ample, ruddy-faced gal from Grafton, North Dakota, turned to three others at my table, and burst out, "Let's go!" Jumping up hastily, they surrounded the lounge chair of the unsuspecting skip, hoisted her up by arms and legs, and swung her into the air—bourbon glass and all! Her body plunged into the calm water that splashed on her horrified teammates, amid cheers and roaring laughter! Clair and I chuckled all the way home.

On Sunday, the dried-out curlers had their quiet revenge. Without a word, they won the match, untied their curling shoes, donned tall, sleek leather black boots with high heels, grabbed their gorgeous long mink coats, their trophy, and ran out the door to a long, black sedan with the motor running. They hit the road heading south. *Touche!*

I must confess that, although the Chicago curlers were unfriendly and rude, there was something about their style that I liked. I wrote to my mother to have her mail her used beaver fur coat to me. It was incredibly cold—so cold that the children had to cover their faces against frostbite when they walked only one block to school.

I had never been anywhere except Canada and Colorado on camping trips. I wondered what it would be like to go to New York City and stay in a hotel, eat in a five-star restaurant, and attend an art opening in Soho. Mother's father had taken her by train to the White House to meet President Hoover. Grandpa took his four daughters to Florida, Cuba, California, and New Mexico where they stayed in the La Fonda Hotel. I have her match and menu collection, and black-and-white photographs. Yes—there was life to be savored beyond a miserable marriage. Someday, I'd buy me a pair of tall, sleek black boots, too.

A warm spring day arrived. I pulled on my scuffed up leather hiking boots and crossed Highway 81 into a cornfield. Nothing but pitch-black soil for miles. So dry that my boots didn't sink in. March winds had come, but rain hadn't yet followed. I played my hiking game—set your sights on a feature on the horizon, and walk toward it as straight as you can. I could cover four miles that way! Clouds formed in the west. A raw wind began to flutter my scarf, and within an hour the sky grew dark—not from clouds, but from dirt! Stronger and stronger gusts pushed me along like an unseen hand moving me—across open plains. God was lifting the topsoil from the earth, swirling it away, obscuring the sun, stealing the shadows, pushing me harder. I stopped to lean against a tree and watch. The prairie was flying away—airborne, disappearing before my eyes. God's labor going. God's work of thousands of years squandered! Was this God's doing, or man's, or were they one and the same? The grit in my mouth felt rough on my tongue. My squinting eyes grew sore. Hunkering into my jacket, I rolled my scarf around my head. Peering through a slit, I began to walk toward home, against the force. I could have waited out the windstorm, but I figured it would begin to rain.

The next day I spoke to a local resident in the grocery store who just laughed when I said my car, house, hair, and everything had been covered with fine dirt. She said, " Oh ya! Every winter and spring we get 'snirt' storms—snow and dirt. They turn the sky black! It's always been that way. Yup—since I can remember. Ha, ha."

I replied, "Why? Why let precious topsoil fly away like that?"

She shrugged her shoulders and walked away with her grocery cart.

"Always" may have begun with the tilling of the soil for the farmer, but not for me. I was appalled and distressed when told it was more economical and efficient to plow in the fall—more important than leaving stubble or plant cover that could add nutrition in lieu of expensive commercial fertilizer. The rows of sausage-shaped white metal tanks on wheels that sat on the edges of towns and lined the fields were for fertilizer, insecticides, and herbicides to control weeds and insects, and replace the nutrients that had blown away! It seemed to me, they were killing the soil, polluting the water, and fouling the air—and becoming addicted to methods that would eventually make them like "junkies"—dependent on chemical companies who set the costs of their products. And nobody could ever replace that rich tillable soil.

The hippie movement, the civil rights movement, the women's movement. In 1973, all were in full swing. Everything seemed to be moving, but me. Clair agreed with me, when I told her I believed my most important role was being a mother, and I didn't mind being at home. In fact, I felt lucky because, throughout history, women's lives had been ones of drudgery or factory work. She argued that women deserved more than less drudgery and a clean workplace. Women's rights should include equal pay for equal work; shared property rights

36

and no-fault divorce laws; nondiscrimination for job opportunities; representation in congress and government; and, with the advent of birth control pills and abortions, a freedom to choose options for one's own body. She even said women should be paid for the housework they did!

When I wasn't typing my husband's doctoral thesis, copying it from handwriting on a yellow legal pad, since computers were still being perfected—when I wasn't hunched over the typewriter in a corner of the bedroom—I thought about Clair's words, and about what I was typing: The Self-Actualization of the Individual, an examination of how people learn and develop to their fullest potential! Quotes from educators like Piaget and Maslow's hierarchical steps to knowledge.

Vito Perrone, Dean of the School of Education at the Harvard Graduate School, supervised UND College of Education graduate level teachers. They created the New School to upgrade North Dakota's public school system. A related endeavor was the Open School formed by the same teachers for their own children. Children of all ages chose their own subjects, progressed at their own pace, and helped each other. The parents were the instructors. One of my children attended while I volunteered to lead nature hikes with plant identification. Clair and I secured a grant for money to build a Tibetan-style yurt on campus, and to study Asian art and history with the kids.

Brady told me about a poster in the Union Hall that advertised a series of free lectures on Native American culture. I was able to attend a few of them, after which my curiosity grew enormously.

My husband was working with schools at Fort Yates, and teacher friends taught at Fort Totten near Devil's Lake where Brady was from. Very early one morning, Brady and I rode with my husband to Fort Totten where he dropped us off and continued on to Fort Yates. There were many "Indian schools" in the Dakotas, but these were not like the old boarding schools that I would one day learn about.

That day was a real eye-opener for me. I planned to be an observer, but a teacher soon asked me to help in her English class, with some pupils who were about twelve years old. They all had old textbooks with stories they were to read aloud to me. She left the room, while I stood in front, examining the bored, tired demeanor of the mostly Dakota boys and girls. They reluctantly opened their books to the page I chose, then closed them after I selected one girl to read to the others. She knew the words, but read with such a soft, disinterested monotone, nobody listened to her. Then I called on a boy, who performed the same way. Several students were absorbed in drawing little pictures in notebooks, so I peeked at them and saw that they were very good pencil line drawings of horses, Indians, and cartoons.

The stories in the text were nothing they identified with; and words meant less to them than pictures. So I changed my assignment and asked a boy to stand and tell me a story about his drawing. Everybody sat up and took notice. The boy was embarrassed because he thought I was punishing him, and notebooks began disappearing all around the room! "Please keep your notebooks open! I see some very good sketching and, instead of reading from the text, perhaps we can make up some stories of our own. Your pictures inspire me to want to know more about them, so who wants to start?"

Everybody looked at poor Bill again, so he began to tell me about his horse. The kids listened politely. After a few more stories, I asked them to write down their stories to read to each other. But before they began, I picked up the rejected textbook, turned to the neglected story, and read aloud with as much feeling as I could muster. They all listened. When I finished, I said, "Read your story aloud with feeling, so your listener will be excited and want to hear it. And try to write it with a surprise at the end, so they'll keep listening!"

They were about to resume writing, but the regular teacher came back in the room—a signal for all the students to slap shut their notebooks—which they did! She looked at me holding the text, and said, "Well, did they give you any trouble? I see they're not reading?"

"They're a wonderful group! Some very good artists, too!"

"Artists?" she said, doubtfully, looking at the smiling class, as I slipped out the door.

Later in the day, feeling good, and comfortable, I spoke with two girls in the hallway about school life. Before departing, I told one of them how pretty her jacket was—that I really liked it. She was extremely uncomfortable, turned red-faced and looked at the floor, saying nothing. Her friend seemed embarrassed for her, too. We parted, but I had a strong sense I'd said something wrong.

While Brady and I waited on the school steps for our ride home, he explained that while my compliment made one girl feel good it could have made the other one feel bad, so I should have said nothing, or complimented them both. He also said that real traditional natives gave away an item that someone else liked or wanted. Brady told me, "In the old ways, that girl would have given you her jacket!"

I felt terrible. Brady laughed at me. Then, he told me he had been invited to teach a class at the school. He was so excited, and really nervous.

"How can *you* be nervous? You're an Indian!" I exclaimed.

"Yes, but they said I could decide what to teach them. What do you think?"

I said without hesitation, "For God's sake, give these kids a good reason to be here! Make learning relevant to them!"

We sat watching the icicles drip on the pavement, enjoying the scent of spring in the air; the warmth on our faces; when out of the old-fashioned red brick schoolhouse, walked a stooped, elderly woman. She stopped when she saw Brady. She wore a navy-blue dress and sweater, dark socks, and worn brown shoes, and her hair was neatly combed back in a bun. Her face was creased by many ages, but her eyes were clear and bright when she saw Brady greet her.

He introduced me as some students came out the door—they greeted Brady. The woman snatched at one of the kids to make him stop, and berated him, "I saw you in class! You weren't listening again! You have to listen to the teachers and learn! I went through hell in white schools so I could learn! The nuns beat me with a hose if I spoke Dakota. I had bruises all over my body, but I learned!" Tears welled up in her eyes.

The group looked embarrassed, but Brady put his arm around her and walked her down the street. The kids left. Startled by her blunt confession, sickened by the nuns' cruelty, amazed that she rationally justified the nuns' behavior as having some benefit, I sat in disbelief.

Chapter 7

SPIDERS HAVE AS MUCH RIGHT TO LIVE AS WE DO

Where does equality begin and end?

Grand Forks

Mother phoned from Minneapolis to make sure everybody was doing "well". She was doing just fine. I told her what she expected to hear: about school, our social life, and the children.

"Have you chosen a church yet? It's been a long time and the kids need to be going to church." Her tone was warm and motherly.

"We've been pretty busy, and we just haven't worked it in yet. The kids and I have been taking Sunday rides to learn about North Dakota while Dad's at his office. We go to parks, farms, museums, and things like that."

"Well, you could do that in the afternoon. What about church?"

"I type on the thesis all morning while the kids watch cartoons on TV, then we go have fun."

"Oh, I see," she replied, dripping with disappointment.

When we hung up, I knew I'd given her something to worry about, but I wasn't going to lie. The truth was, I didn't miss church, and was beginning to question teaching religion to children before they had an opportunity to think for themselves.

That Sunday afternoon, I led the children in a line across the open, dusty cornfield on a hike. While they kept an eye out for gophers, I recalled the "snirt" storm that blackened the heavens, and the lectures about Indians that stressed their love for Mother Earth, and thought about my feelings of kinship for their beliefs. Then, my father's voice came to me, as he lay in bed on Sunday morning when I was a child, "I don't go to church because I'd rather be outdoors, like when I go

41

hunting or fishing. But you and your brother should go because it makes your mother happy." Dad's attitude agreed with me, because I wanted to be outdoors all the time, too.

Easter was different. Easter and Christmas brought all the relatives together. Including me, a smiling, skinny little girl standing on the top steps of Our Savior's Lutheran Church, in a new fluffy pink dress with a pinafore and a straw hat. Mother had sewed my dress; but the best part was the rabbit that brought the basket waiting at home, full of hard-boiled eggs—pink, blue, yellow, and green; chocolate eggs and jelly beans; and sticky yellow marshmallow chickens.

After the service, Dad drove us to Grandpa Stern's greenhouse and florist shop where the dank, earthy aroma of row after row of lilies, azaleas, begonias, daisies, geraniums, and petunias drove me wild for want of summer and made me lonesome for sweet green grass and trees that swayed in the breeze.

We drove home with a huge regal lily. Home to Mom's fancy ham dinner, and often, the first strawberries of the season from California, served with angel food cake and whipped cream that came off the top of the milk in the bottles the milkman brought to our door, all enjoyed by loving family members—women in the kitchen, gossiping over food and dishes; men in the living room, telling fishing stories. I curled up low in the corner of the living room listening to the men boast about their catch—none more than my dad.

Those Northwoods stories were part of an annual ritual in preparation for the coming seasonal fishing opener in Minnesota, and Canada. The dining room table was cleared, and the men, boys, and I moved in with the maps of canoe country that Dad spread out on the table—smoothing out the creases, finding a pen to point out routes and destinations. The names of the lakes, rivers, and camps were magic to me. I knew them. I knew where the campsites were on Namakan, Quetico, Beaverhouse, and Lac La Croix. I could picture the Loon

River portage and the shallow, treacherous channel full of hidden boulders and flitting dragonflies. I could feel fish biting on my minnow. And mosquitoes biting my flesh.

The condition of motors, rods, and reels was discussed. Also, the cost of a license, the limit for fish caught; for walleye, bass, northern pike, and my favorite—lake trout. (We rented a boat from the resort until years later when Dad bought his own.) Lots of speculation about when the ice would "go out" often led to bets waged on the date—bets for a six-pack of beer or a bottle of whiskey.

I understood that spring ritual, and the roles of the participants. Mother and I also prepared to go up north. She sewed our summer clothes and filled a box with new games—books and toys for rainy days in the cabin at Nelson's Resort on Crane Lake; while I helped clean the house, bake cookies, iron clothes, walk to the store, and plant the flower garden.

To me, spring was a renewal of life. With joy, I watched the wildflowers pop up in the woods, and the buds on trees become leaves. And on Easter Sunday at church, I sensed that aspect of celebration, but never understood the purpose for which Jesus had died for me. The brass trumpets and choir songs brought tears to my eyes; I sang out with joy in my heart, but I didn't know why Jesus had to suffer. The bunny tradition was definitely better than the dead Christ story.

I'd always been confused by the relationship between God the Father, the Son, and the Holy Ghost, and Mary the Mother, and Mary the first one that saw Jesus after he woke from the dead. Also, which one was human like me, or spirit or ghost, and when were they all one? Sometimes I felt guilty that I didn't appreciate God's suffering for me, but that was because I didn't understand sin, either.

Every night I prayed, "If I should die before I wake, I pray the Lord my soul to take," in English (and in German, my parents' ancestry). Mom and Dad never accused me of sinning, and I had no

43

reason to think I would die in my sleep, and having a "soul" was never explained to me! I learned that you just do some things because they had always been done that way.

That thought reminded me of the North Dakota farmers who cleared their fields of all ground cover every fall, like their fathers and grandfathers, even though they knew fertile topsoil was blowing away.

The children and I stopped our hiking to rest in the shade of an old cottonwood tree near a farmhouse. I asked them if they missed going to church, and they replied that they missed their friends at the church, but were happy to have made new ones. They didn't really miss anything else. I didn't ask them what they understood about their Christian teachings. Perhaps they thought like me when I was young: that as I grew older, such things would become clearer. Adults had ways of knowing things that children didn't. I had to trust them.

We ate our sandwiches, chips, and juice, and decided to stop to eat cookies on the way back home. Walking along, I thought of all those starving Chinamen, (for whom I ate every last bite on my plate), and Africans, (who had plenty of wild game to eat), and whom I suspected were perfectly happy with whatever beliefs they already had, but I didn't know what those beliefs were. I just remembered contributing to missionaries so they could go change the savages to think like us. But no one ever told me how they thought. I guess it didn't matter.

When I was small, there were other things I hoped would become more clear. Why did we sing of glory to Christian soldiers going off to war to kill enemies when the Bible said killing was sinful? If God loved and cared for all the world's children, why was it all right to kill some, but not others? Did all of God's commandments also have exceptions to the rules? If the whole world had one god, (the Lutheran one, of course), and if some didn't even *know* it was their god, it didn't seem fair to fight them before they even had a chance to become a

Lutheran! How could there be only one book as a source for one god with one truth for everybody! So much about the Bible contradicted itself. How could all those contradictions be true at once?

My father said derogatory things about Jewish and Black people. Lutherans said things about Catholics, and other Protestants, even though I was told they all had the same God! The "love one another" doctrine didn't extend very far afield. Even Lutherans used God's name in vain. The same god used to "damn" things, was the one I prayed to at night! Not much respect there! How strange that God was invoked as often in violence, as in love. As a little girl, my worst dilemma was all the hypocrisy displayed by adults.

Now I was a mother myself, struggling with the moral teachings of my children, unlike generations before me in my family who apparently didn't question Christian theology. Or did they? Becoming a mother and a Sunday school teacher didn't automatically enlighten me. Quite the contrary.

Of all the questions I had, one burned brighter than all the rest. That night, after the children were asleep, I reached for my Bible, an Oxford S.S. Teacher's Edition, a hand-me-down, crumbling at the edges.

In the light of my bedside lamp, I propped up my pillows and began examining the index in the back, searching for words that would lead me to my answer. I wanted to know God's instructions for how we should live on the land. How did he want us to care for it? Surely something that important would have a story to elucidate me. If I couldn't understand Christian doctrines, perhaps I could at least understand biblical influences on American attitudes about the land.

First, I was amazed at all the brutality and violence I was finding. I realized I really hadn't read the Bible since my confirmation classes; and then, I read only what I was taught; and, as a Sunday school teacher, I used a workbook and followed it. Neither experience had plunged me into the horrible, dark, sick, sinister depths of biblical revelations. Fascinated by all the bloodshed and gore, I got out of bed to make a pot of tea, returned, and settled in for a long night.

My eyes were sore by the time I had my second revelation. Researching for explanations concerning man's interactions with our shared planet, I was stunned when I concluded that the teachings of scripture have actually contributed to, and encouraged, changes that are proving so harmful to the earth. Clearly, man's activities have been blessed, and sanctioned by the Christian God. God may have made the soil, but he commanded his children how to dominate it. Also, "his children" were the Christians for whom it was intended, not the American Indians, women, and Africans who were treated like slaves or property.

After a poor night's sleep, I went to the library and checked out *Silent Spring*, a book published ten years earlier by Rachel Carson, which described environmental changes due to man-made pollution. She had studiously presented findings about pesticides, herbicides, and much more. She warned about a poisonous, toxic earth that would cause cancers and silence animals, especially birds. Very scary stuff.

Housework, hiking, reading, and typing continued day after day, as I did my volunteer work for the children's school. Then one day in September, I read an article in the *Grand Forks Herald* newspaper. Headline: Indian Teachings Aid Environment. Edith Whetung, a native from Ottawa, Canada, said in her speech, "White society, guilty of misguided approaches to education of Indians, has suffered from its failure to learn fundamentals of Indian wisdom." She also told her audience, the Canadian Association of School Administrators, that: "European philosophers from the eighteenth century: Locke, Montaigne, Voltaire, and Rousseau recognized the contribution of

North American Indians and were influenced by it."

That article impressed me. Feeling motivated to someday learn what those men had discovered, I clipped the story from the paper to save it.

Showing the article to Brady, he asked me, "So, when are you going to go to college? Professor King told me you could sit in on one of his English classes—Creative Writing. Would you like that?"

"Oh yes! I'll talk to him myself."

Soon after, a group of hearty outdoor enthusiasts organized an overnight canoe trip on the Pembina River, a lush, tranquil waterway traversed years before by rugged fur traders and Indians. During a shore break, I removed our gear from the canoe to retrieve our rain jackets from the bottom. A friend named Bruce Hovland (His nickname was "The Hoover Machine") asked me why I was unloading the canoe.

I replied, "Because my stupid husband laid our rain jackets under our stuff packs to keep the packs dry. Now, the jackets are wet, and it looks like rain, and I have to dry them out so I can wear mine."

"I don't get it," he said, "You're much smarter than him. Why aren't you the one going to school?"

I glanced over at Brady who had overheard Bruce's remark. That elfin mug of his wore a grin as broad as a canoe. I looked away and said nothing to Bruce.

Around the campfire that night, I told everybody I was going to monitor King's class that fall, knowing that my husband would be surprised; knowing that a public announcement would make it more difficult for him to stop me; knowing that, in the past, shaming him for hitting me had worked—for a while. (In the past I had told his best friend, who intervened on my behalf; but in Grand Forks, I was on my own.)

I clearly remember everything about that classroom—sitting at a desk by a window—watching autumn leaves swirling around red oak trees, listening to Dr. King talk about poets and poetry, taking notes and feeling like I was part of something wonderful. Instead of reading Betty Crocker, I was reading Robert Frost.

I'll never forget a small incident between myself and a Native American student who sat next to me across the aisle. A hairy spider was crawling along the floor between us. I thoughtlessly raised my foot to kill it, but the girl stopped me.

"Don't kill it! It's not hurting you, is it? Spiders have as much right to live as we do. Let it go," she insisted.

Others had turned to hear her lesson, then returned to the lecture. I smiled nicely and thanked her for teaching me. But I really thought she was going too far. After all, insects caused humans all sorts of grief, like killer diseases. Where does equality begin and end? What does respect for animals mean to me, or to Indians?

We always read the *Minneapolis Tribune* on Sunday mornings. A report in November 1972 by Finlay Lewis told about, a takeover of the Bureau of Indian Affairs (BIA) headquarters by a caravan of Indians calling themselves the Trail of Broken Treaties, men and women who went to Washington to demand fair government treatment on reservations and in cities. A young group from Minneapolis led the March. They were aggressive activists known as the American Indian Movement (AIM).

Older tribal leaders were wary of the influence of the new city warriors who threatened their cozy relationship with the government that could cut their funds. The militants ransacked the BIA building after discovering thousands of files proving mishandling of Indian affairs over one hundred years.

In December, Jack Anderson's reporting included, "The startling story can now be told how Indian activists used a police escort to help smuggle stolen government documents out of Washington." Further, "With motorcycles roaring, the police rushed a forty-car Indian caravan through the city. The ceremonial escort was eagerly provided by the harassed officials at the BIA, whose building had been ransacked by the Indians."

Further, "The police, as they whistled traffic to a stop to make way for the Indians, had no idea that they were unwitting accomplices in the biggest document heist in history."

Anderson went on to say, "For the Indians had discovered in the BIA's files documentary evidence of bureaucratic bungling, neglect and outright chiseling."

The Indians spirited away thousands of papers wrapped in sleeping bags in car trunks and a chartered bus. Only when the Indians were far out of town did the FBI realize what had happened. Then they organized a "nationwide dragnet to retrieve the incriminating documents."

Meanwhile the angry president's men in the White House promised to force hundreds of Indians out of the building. However, college-educated Russell Means, an Oglala Sioux from the tribe of Crazy Horse, had found incriminating data on Washington officials, which changed the attitude of White House aides who then agreed to negotiate with the Indians over their grievances. Meanwhile, Indians were stashing documents all over the nation, after splitting up in Cleveland.

I thought, "Wow! The lovers of Mother Earth and defenders of defenseless bugs also have warriors fighting for tribal rights and better living standards for all natives."

In the library, I found books about contemporary Indian life, including *Our Brother's Keeper* by Edgar Cahn; and a pamphlet produced by the Minnesota League of Women Voters, "Indians in Minnesota." Both were full of sad, bleak statistics about education. As

I turned out my bed lamp and rolled over to sleep, an idea came to me.

I could study for a degree in education (since I already knew that topic after all my typing), and also study Indian culture. Then, someday, somehow, I could teach on a reservation.

First, I needed to enroll (would I be accepted?); second, I needed time and freedom; and third (most difficult), I needed to get money. I hardly slept all night.

The next morning I saw the children off to school, packed the four-year-old into his red wagon, and pulled him across campus to the office of Elgie Raymond, a kind, older Lakota man, a student advisor and counselor. My son played on the floor while Elgie gave me forms to fill out and a list of spring semester offerings.

More afraid than excited, I returned home, washed the breakfast dishes, put in a load of clothes to wash, made the beds, played with the baby, put him in bed, then sat down at the kitchen table with a cup of Earl Gray tea, a pen, and all the application forms. I poured over the class selections. I wanted to learn everything, but whenever possible I decided to choose based upon the instructor, for I knew that was more important than the topic.

After I was accepted as a student, Clair found a day-care facility where little Heath could go for part of the day; and Len, the oldest boy, could help out after school.

Predictably, when my husband saw money missing from the joint checking account, he reacted violently, which only hardened my resolve to get through school. I had lots of encouragement from my friends, and the words of my college educated mother-in-law, who had passed away, "You must go to college. The people you will be associating with will all be educated. You'll be happier, too." She wanted to pay for it, but she died, and my husband got the money.

It wasn't easy. I signed up for: Chippewa History, Indian Arts & Crafts, American Indian Spiritual Philosophy, Intro to Biology, Intro to Psychology; and two graduate level courses: North American Archeology, and Great Arts Cluster. I added two summer classes: Physical Geology (a trip to the Black Hills), and Advanced Topics in Geology.

I was scared to death when final exams came—even had to switch from tea to coffee. Failing my Intro to Biology test, I sat at the kitchen table, sobbing, late one night when the phone rang. It was Husband calling from Fort Yates.

"What's the matter?" he said, sounding puzzled.

"I failed Biology." I cried.

"What? You failed something? *Ha, ha ha!* You mean Miss Perfect can't do it all? *Ha, ha, ha!*" I could imagine a cynical sneer on his face.

I hung up on him and grabbed my biology book and began reading all night long.

I talked to my biology instructor who agreed to let me retake the exam. I explained that I'd taken on too much, but I could do it.

In the end, I received very good grades. Indeed, Mother phoned from Minneapolis to say, "I received a letter from UMD addressed to "The Parents of Judy Stern." Inside is a formal note card that says, "Congratulations. Your daughter is an honor student!" and "Her average is A."

There was no stopping me after that.

We reclaimed our rented-out house in Minneapolis and settled into a new routine: all the children in school, Dad back to his teaching job, and Mom at the University of Minnesota for evening classes.

Brady Barber surprised us with a visit on a perfectly beautiful autumn Sunday. We were so thrilled to see him that he agreed to spend the night. He proudly opened his scruffy canvas back pack and presented us with parsley, pretzels, whole wheat bread, and moldy hot pepper cheese—all given to him freely from a co-op near the university where he was taking a class in dance.

During dinner, he told us stories about his summer hitchhiking, about his new class, and how he survived by dumpster diving, and how it was terrible how much good food restaurants throw away. He said he was heading back to Devil's Lake, to his home at Fort Totten. I told him about my studies and packed his bag full of good food.

We hugged him "goodbye" and said we'd see him when he came back to the big city.

Two days later, I took the big chunk of moldy cheese out of the refrigerator, unwrapped the cellophane and began to trim the edges, wondering if it had been in a dumpster, considering that I really should discard the whole thing.

The phone rang. It was from Grand Forks. Brady was dead. My heart fell. They didn't know yet why he died, but would call me back later. I hung up, grief stricken, then remembered the cheese. Was that it?

I stood staring at the cheese—fuzzy blue mold on fractured white solidified rotten milk; small red flecks of squishy hot peppers. Is that what killed Brady? Did I have a chance to save him by warning him not to eat foul food? Should I try to call his mother and tell her that I knew why he collapsed? I threw the sinister poison in the garbage, scrubbed my cutting board and my hands, and went out for a walk to soothe my shocked body.

That night I wrote in my journal, remembering Brady, tears flooding my eyes as I wrote. This is four lines from that writing:

He appeared unexpected
And left for unknowns
Nothing possessed him
Mother Earth—his home

The next day we learned that Brady had collapsed while running on the reservation, from an undetected heart disease.

I would have to find another Brady Barber with whom to share my deepest thoughts and dreams. In my heart, I knew that was impossible, however I was eager to meet new people.

In March of 1973, the country in turmoil, I began college. News headlines all across the nation were focused on Wounded Knee, South Dakota, where American Indian Movement protesters were occupying that town to draw attention to grievances that hadn't been addressed after the BIA affair in Washington.

On one side were 200 AIM members and supporters with few weapons. On the other were 300 fully armed FBI officers, local white people, and Dick Wilson, Oglala tribal president, whose rule of fear had intimidated most of his tribe.

Wounded Knee had been the site of a massacre in December, 1890; 470 troops of the Seventh Calvary Regiment murdered 106 men and 225 women and children who were starving and had illegally left the reservation to find food. After unconditionally surrendering their few hunting weapons, four Hotchkiss repeating machine guns mowed them down. A blizzard blanketed the prairie before the slaughtered bodies could be buried, but later they were thrown into a mass grave marked by a plaque commemorating the bravery of the soldiers at the Battle of Wounded Knee.

The 1973 Wounded Knee standoff continued for several weeks with AIM leaders Russell Means and Dennis Banks as two prominent leaders. One year later in January, a much-publicized trial took place in the US District Court in St. Paul, Minnesota, with William Kunstler, defense attorney, who was in Wounded Knee during the occupation. In a *Minneapolis Star* article dated January 8, 1974, he said, "Today is a struggle for Indian rights far greater than any I have been involved in before."

In that same paper, in March 18, 1973, director of Indian Studies at

Bemidji State College, Gerald Vizenor was quoted, "AIM has been punching away at the issues of legal and economic injustices, but so have many educators and lawyers and politicians and writers," and, "The problem is not one of information, but rather a way to bring about institutional changes that will free tribal people from poverty and cultural invalidation." Also, "Where people have lived without justice there has been violence. Tribal people have lived for centuries without justice. The violence of the American Indian Movement is the problem of the white-dominant society. It is not the problem of tribal people; white people have created the need for violence. Yesterday was a good day to negotiate, because tomorrow may be a new confrontation."

The years 1972 and 1973 were transformative years for me and the Native Americans, but also for the entire nation. The Richard Nixon presidency (1969–1974) continued the turbulence of Lyndon Johnson's (1963–1969) leadership during the war in Vietnam.

In June of 1972 I was golfing with Clair when we learned about the break-in at the Democratic National Committee at the Watergate Hotel, a Nixon-inspired scheme to steal DFL information. After years of antiwar rallies, massive protests, (including the shooting of six marching students at Kent State University in 1970, the year of the largest demonstrations in American history); after continuous White House lies and intrigues that divided our nation, and our families, many of the younger generation turned to the beliefs of Oriental religions.

I wasn't looking for another religion, and I considered those who turned to wearing turbans, veils, or whatever, to be an extension of the extreme behavior of some youth as expressed in rock music. I felt that if extreme behavior was necessary to stop the war and bring peace, it was fully justified to counteract the far more extreme behavior of the warmongers and profiteers from death.

Nixon once said, "When the president does it, that means that it is not illegal."

I had been taught in school that monarchies had been left behind in Europe. Perhaps my teachers were wrong.

Chapter 8

FEATHERS DESERVE CEREMONIES, TOO

Which plant or animal would you choose?

University of St. Thomas

"The people of all native cultures share certain characteristics, and one of them is an intimate relationship with the plants and animals that provide them food, herbs, housing materials, clothes, and lessons about how to live. Some are revered more than others, but all are respected. Many, many stories still exist that illustrate how children learned behavior from animals who did foolish or wise things—especially wild animals," I explain to the students.

"The Algonkian tribes identified themselves by their clan membership. They would say, "Hello, my name is Harold, and I'm from the Turtle Clan. If we did that, what plant or animal would you choose?

"You can learn much about a student by doing this simple game. Now, make a name sign by folding your square of cardboard in half, and writing your name on one side.

"Now, if you could choose one plant or animal that you feel close to, what would it be? Think of ones that are wild, not domesticated, and preferably that live in our geographical area. Perhaps you recall a special tree in the yard where you grew up, or maybe an experience that inspired you, or you may have had a powerful dream.

"On the other side of the cardboard, write your plant or animal name. And, while you are thinking, consider how, and why modern civilization has abandoned our reverence for many vital living beings. We even behave as if we can live without them." I pause one moment.

"Native American art forms reflect a continuous instinct that

56

shows native dependence on harmonious relationships with that which sustains them. Most depictions include plants and animals.

After a few moments the cards have names on them, so I ask for volunteers to explain their choices. Heather raises her hand.

"I chose wolf. I don't know why, but I've always felt a deep interest in wolves. They seem so family-like, and contrary to their reputation, they are peaceful and usually don't bother anybody."

"Wolf is a wonderful choice. Wolves do exemplify tight bonds in the pack, and cooperation for survival, also cunning, and freedom. The Ojibwe needed a cooperative spirit because they were often faced with starvation in harsh winters and didn't have the preservation methods we now enjoy. Oh, also, wolves have never killed a human."

Dan raises his hand. "I chose a bear. Bears are strong and fierce, yet playful and comical. I saw one on a canoe trip once, but it was far away and ran when we paddled around a bend."

"*Ahhh*, yes, bears are good defenders of territory, and their young. The grizzly was the most feared animal on the northern plains. Did you know they once lived as close as the Pembina River Valley in North Dakota? Bears are omnivores, but mostly they eat plants and roots, thus the natives who saw them digging up roots thought of them as healers, because so many roots had healing properties. And, if you could see a bear without its hide, standing up, it would resemble a human figure, with five-digit fingers and toes!"

Bao has a turn. "I chose an elephant because I'm from Laos and Thailand, and elephants are a revered symbol in those lands."

I respond, "You will have to teach me about elephants!"

After Bao, the choices include hummingbird, horse, willow tree, iris, tiger, butterfly, robin, daisy, rose, fox, and more. Last to volunteer is Allison, who decides she likes eagles.

I ask her to explain her choice.

"I grew up in a rural area by a river, and there was an eagle nest

57

nearby, in the top of an ancient white pine tree that had lost its top, perhaps due to a lightning storm. Our family was lucky to be able to see eagles return each year and make their nest even bigger. Those nests are huge."

I ask, "You mean it's still there?"

"Oh sure. My parents still live by the river."

"What are the habits of eagles that you observed?"

"They are very strong and edge out other birds. They also fly higher, and can see for very long distances. They may be smarter, too."

"Are these behaviors that you admire?"

"Yes."

"Eagles are deeply respected by natives all over North and South America, and their feathers are symbols of power—often worn in the hair by leaders of a tribe. If a feather falls to the ground during a dance, everything stops until the feather has received a ceremony, and it has been restored to the one who lost it. I have seen this happen more than once. A special drum song accompanies one man who dances around the feather four times, then picks it up. A person has to earn the honor of having a feather, and know how to care for it."

Allison looks at me wide-eyed. She surprises me, "Do you have one?"

"Yes, I have been honored to be given four eagle feathers."

I'm relieved when nobody asks me how I earned them, because it would be inappropriate to share those stories in a public classroom. On the other hand, I'm eager for people to learn about Indian ways, or alternatives to Christian dogma, and our consumer society.

Later in the class, we work on a project called, "Pictograph Rock Drawing," or learning Indian ways to convey messages, which includes the use of animal drawings.

"The Ojibwe had no alphabet. They made symbols on rocks, tree bark, and animal hides, a practice that was worldwide. Some drawings recorded important events; some were decorations on objects; some gave directions or warnings; and some appealed to unseen spirits, such as water spirits who control safe crossings, or passageways.

"Do you recall the canoeing trip slide show we had in which I showed pictographs from Lac La Croix, Quetico Provincial Park, and Superior Provincial Park in Canada? We saw the red symbols at Agawa Rock on Lake Superior.

"Indian drawings were like prayers, or appeals for good fortune. The animals depicted were usually the ones they hunted for food or clothes. Some symbols are universal in nature, like circles and spirals which I saw in a museum in Tende, France, where hundreds of such rock drawings were found in caves or in the open.

"Remember that pictographs are surface drawings made with red ochre from stones they ground and mixed with fish oil; and petroglyphs are etchings carved into stones, like those found near Jeffers, Minnesota.

"The prehistoric nature of rock art leaves us to speculate about the meaning of each drawing; however, often repeated figures or shapes can be understood, even if we can never know what was in the mind of the artist at that time.

"My goal here is to teach you about human-animal relationships, not meaning in spiritual symbolism, but you can find books on that topic.

"There were also pictograph messages on birchbark and buffalo hides, but spoken language and songs were mostly used, and Indian oratory was often very eloquent.

"Let's take a break before beginning our pictograph project. If anyone has a question, please feel free to come up and ask me."

Most of the attractive young students begin chattering with friends. Others scurry out the door, heading for the vending machines, leaving me to myself.

All but one. The woman named Allison. Seated close to me, I notice her rise from her seat. She approaches me in a hesitant manner, as though unsure of something, or uneasy within herself. Like her lovely long blonde hair draped over her shoulders, her arms hang freely, relaxed, like her trim lanky body.

Her eyes look off to one side as she stands at my desk, deliberating.

Patiently, I wait, hands folded in front of me, curious about the woman's shy manner, watching her face flush with embarrassment—a most becoming tinge of red in her cheeks.

Finally, her sincere blue eyes meet mine. She calmly says, "I don't have any Indian blood in me, but I have a strong desire to know more about Indian ways."

I reply assuredly, "I'm not Indian, either, but that doesn't matter if you have a sincere heart and lots of patience."

"I am sincere. Are there any ways to know the things you learned beyond this class?"

"Certainly! Libraries, museums—both are great resources. Also, computer sites. I provide each student with a list," I tell her, smiling with encouragement.

"I know that," she begins softly, "But would you meet with me sometime—just to talk? About native ways?"

Such an earnest expression! Such gentle strong energy! Such eyes! I consider her proposal, weighing my obligations, wondering what she wants to know; yet concerned about the appropriateness of meeting a student alone. Then I remember. I'd once made the same request, and life is a circle.

Chapter 9
ENERGY KNOWLEDGE CANNOT BE PURCHASED
Don't you think that continuous taking without giving back is sheer craziness?

Loring Park, Minneapolis

I'm going to meet Allison at a coffee shop across from Loring Park, a few blocks from the university. Such a shame it would be to sit inside on a fine, glorious spring day. I leave a note in the bistro, telling her to find me on a park bench by the pond. Resting my hands on my lap, I close my eyes—tilting my face back, feeling the sun's warmth upon my white skin, the noisy antics of ducks flitting upon the water—quite comical; the smells of sweet lilac blossoms, sprouting grass, new pots of petunias and geraniums waiting in boxes to be planted. My garden has just been seeded. Sixty-five heirloom tomato plants started in April are now safely in the ground.

For many years autumn was my favorite season. Now it's spring. Beginnings appeal to me more than endings, yet all seasons are beginnings when we live in cycles—even fall.

My Sierra Club backpack contains a book, *The Great Unraveling*, by Paul Krugman, op-ed columnist for *The New York Times*. It's about "losing our way in the new century," a brilliant book about bad leadership and deceit; economics and politics.

Iraq and Afghanistan remain occupied by the US. Our economy is in a shambles, and the public's memory is so short and uneducated that we learned nothing from the horrors of the Vietnam War. Knowledge doesn't just make people good, it can make us deceitful and sinister.

Growing older, it's harder to avoid cynicism, and feel hopeful. My son said, "Why bother to vote? I did last time. It didn't do any good."

If this generation loses hope, who will be the next creators of beauty? The keepers of the earth? My grandchildren?

Soon, Allison joins me on the park bench. She apologizes for being "a little late," but I tell her not to be concerned, that I haven't worn a watch for many years, and living on "Indian time" relieves stress.

"Thanks for coming," she says, catching her breath, "I'm done with classes for the day, and I don't have to work until tomorrow night."

"Where do you work?" I inquire as she sits next to me in the sun.

"In my dad's office—computer work. I don't have to worry about being fired," she laughs, "He pays my tuition."

"Sounds like a good situation," I say, thinking how lucky most of the St. Thomas students are to have loving parents who spend their money on their child's education. After I returned to Minneapolis from Grand Forks, I had to paint the outside of houses, while taking the children with me, to earn another year's tuition.

"I am divorced," she says, "And have two children to support, so I'm anxious to begin teaching school. I've been working nights while my totally great mom baby-sits. Sometimes it's hard to get my homework done."

"*Ahhh!* Two children? I overheard you talking about them."

Allison tells me about herself. I realize we do have some things in common, and I can feel comfortable sharing with her.

"I agreed to meet with you," I begin, "Because just over thirty years ago, an older, wiser woman met with me in a park, for the same reason. I too was curious about native traditions. She was teaching a class at St. Kate's in St. Paul. Our group of students formed a strong bond, despite our differences in age and background, and went on to enjoy several adventures with our unusual teacher."

"Who was she? Can you tell me about her?"

I reach for my thermos and pour us each a cup of steaming hot honey-lemon tea. Six downy ducklings appear. Moms with baby strollers move back and forth in the distance, while the sun warms our spirits, and we settle in for our first long afternoon together.

"She called herself Mizinokamigok. She had been named Island in the Universe Woman by a Naushbwadsway, a vision holder of the Ojibwe. Early one evening in the spring of 1974, we sat together on my red-wool blanket, under a gigantic, nodding cottonwood tree on the campus of the University of Minnesota. Below, we saw the Mississippi River carrying melting snow and ice chunks downstream. Dandelions, sticky new grass, and robin songs heightened the air of expectations that stirred in my heart. She had agreed to be a mentor to me. I felt excited, grateful, serious, and resolved.

"Earlier on, up in North Dakota, I had found my direction, but with Miz—that's what we called her—I found a guide who could help me along the Good Red Road."

"So she was an Ojibwe Indian woman?" Allison appears excited.

"Yes, she was ordinary in appearance, not old nor young, was large boned but average in build, had a roundish face pleasantly featured, with creamy skin the color of a café latte—smooth and youthful, with narrow expressive black eyes and waving charcoal gray hair that fell on her shoulders. She dressed simply, in slacks, T-shirt and tennis shoes; however, she usually wore one of her special sweaters that she designed for herself and for stores—unique creations rich in color and imaginative shapes."

"Wow!" exclaims Allison, "Did you ever get one?"

"Yes, indeed. Eventually, I sold them for her. I think she liked to think of herself as a designer; but to me, she was my teacher.

"Miz was far from ordinary, not only with her design abilities, but with her teaching methods. She had a strong bearing—that of a person in command—purposeful and thoughtful, demanding attention.

"During a lesson, she sat still, looking down, folding or unfolding her hands, gesturing a little, listening. She used words sparingly in a crisp, or quick pace, followed by long intervals, during which I waited in anticipation for the next words.

"Her face could suddenly soften, or become quite animated, or break into a quick grin or a muffled laugh. Then, just as quickly, she could return to controlled, concentrated emotion. She communicated more without words than anyone I'd met up till then. Her body and eyes did most of the talking, asked the questions, became amused, or even made me 'shut up!'

"She often responded to a statement with, '*Ahhh*,' which, according to the pitch, meant several things. The higher it was, the greater the affirmative. She created a presence by using quietude. She felt that making noise was for those who had nothing to say in the first place. It became clear that to exercise one's ego, only demonstrated one's weakness. Now, Allison, I gave her gifts, for her teachings, which occurred in a group or with me alone. I think it would have been difficult in a large class."

"I suppose so," says Allison, "But how did she teach you?"

"Her primary method was to ask me a question, and wait while I worked on the answer, which might be immediate or weeks—even months. I'd call her on the phone or meet with her and if my response was satisfactory she'd say, '*Ahhh*' followed by another question. If I was far off, I'd get a, '*Hmmm*' and silence. I don't think she said more than eight whole sentences in any one session. I often just rattled on, letting her respond to my meandering, like a branch floating on the river, bumping into things that would change its course.

"She was an extraordinary teacher, in that she taught me how to teach myself. In fact, she taught me very few direct lessons. I did not sit there and hear one line of wisdom after another."

"You mean," asks Allison, "she didn't tell you about secret rituals, or stuff like that?"

"Oh my, NO! I learned about a belief system with cultural habits that and traditions.

"Miz created situations, or suggested them, which gave me the option of utilizing or rejecting them. Whatever happened to me was my choice, and therefore my responsibility, and my joy. She was the disseminator of clues to a magnificent new mystery. With the solving of one riddle, she would send me off to solve another one.

"No, Miz never called herself a shaman, or used that word, but she did eventually introduce me to one. I didn't ask about secret medicine societies. Nor did I feel like an anthropologist. I wanted her respect, so I respected her privacy.

"You see, Indians believed you had to earn knowledge and know how to use it. You had to show and express an interest before you were taught, because knowledge could be used for good or bad. Only those who deserve to know, should know. Sometimes, answers require a very long time. Sometimes, there are no answers. Sometimes I think there should be fewer questions.

"She helped me see things in new perspectives. I know now that she simply helped me find what was already within myself, and is in most anybody, if they recognize it.

"The things she talked about were not unlike good old common sense—simple ideas that sounded foreign to me, which made me think, 'Why didn't I realize that before?'"

Allison chuckles, "Oh, I have that happen all the time. I think our parents raise us with best intentions, but some of the stuff they pass on to us can actually be bad for us, like bad television and junk food."

I nod in agreement, "Yes! Talk about dumb decisions! We have so much we don't even need, compared to what we do need."

Allison says, "I know. It's all so complicated. People are so darn stressed out. And for what?"

"Wisdom lies in simplicity. The most profound teachings are also the most simple ones. Simplicity is like honesty—like the term—the simple truth. People who share, live simply, honorably, and honestly, if given opportunity.

"Complications obscure essentials, create confusion, and encourage justifications for actions or thoughts. We wouldn't have to sort through so much junk if we didn't make it in the first place."

"That's for sure," replies Allison, with a long sigh, "My parents work so hard to have two large homes and all sorts of big toys, but we never ate meals together; and we each had our own TV to watch different shows, and just having a conversation hardly ever happened." She thought for a minute, "Did you say that you met Miz in one of your classes?"

"Yes. One of my anthropology teachers at the University of Minnesota told me where to find her. Miz had been raised far up north at Nett Lake Indian Reservation, or Asabekonezagaiganing; had married and moved to the big city. She taught Ojibwe Culture first at St. Kate's in St. Paul, and later at the University of Minnesota. Outside of the classroom, she had a small group of Indian and nonIndians who met informally with her on a regular basis in their homes. I also met alone with her every week or two."

"Sounds real cool!" Allison coos, "Were you like counterculture hippies? My mom has a picture of herself and Dad. His hair is really long!"

I laugh, "Dear me. No. I was a thirty-two-year-old mother of four. One classmate of mine was a bookstore owner. One was a school teacher. Another was a General Mills executive, and another a journalist. Most had finished college long before I got started, and I was in my first year.

"However, we were all highly influenced by the times—the counterculture movement, as you called it. There was a sea of people like me, who questioned the norms and values of the leadership."

"I've seen documentaries," Allison adds, "about the 1968

Democratic Convention, and old movies with Woodstock musicians and political protests. I think it would have been fun for me."

"It wasn't fun for disenfranchised blacks, poverty-ridden Indians, women without many protections, Asians fleeing to the US from Laos, and children in bad schools. Many thought only old white men were not suffering, and they were making the rules for all the rest."

"I see," Allison murmurs, "Martin Luther King died for his people."

"Yes," I say, "And many went to jail for their beliefs—some for a lifetime."

"Did you think Miz could teach you something to solve the problems?"

"*Hmmmm*," I pause, "No one person could do that. She was like a stop on my journey—a temporary island in my universe, a go-between, a connector, a mentor, a messenger, a junction in my path. I'd met several Indians when I lived in North Dakota, and one was a special friend, but he died. Miz was the first one who took me under her wing. All did not go smoothly. More than once she became angry at me, and I very puzzled by her. Trust and intimacy require time and understanding. Patience and earnestness overcomes obstacles. I didn't want her to be my personal counselor—listening to my problems. I was working on a vision—a way to transcend day-to-day occurrences. My college degree would help me raise my children. It was like a stepping stone in a creek. My goal was more far-reaching than that. Miz represented my connection to the whole ocean."

Allison and I sit in silence, while I pour more tea into our tin cups, checking the sky for the sun's position, amused by the antics of two silly red squirrels.

"At that time in my life, I was, above all, a woman searching for a heightened kind of strength and courage. I'd been deeply damaged spiritually in a bad marriage, and was in the process of bringing energy into myself, trying to find the means to protect my children.

"I was scared because any attempts to save my marriage were failing, and I had never been really employed in my life."

"I can identify with that feeling, except I had my parents, and two children!" Allison offers, "I get tired a lot."

Nodding, I say, "I have always felt that no matter how tough things are, they're always much harder for someone somewhere, a thought that helps diffuse self-pity. And Miz taught me that if I believe that someone needs me, I can focus on them and become a giver of my energy. Then I am not thinking only about my loss which is a sure way to lose energy. Miz was teaching me that the choice of giving energy is a tricky one, and also that not everyone deserved to have my energy.

"Miz had a heart condition, and she actually used her mind to help control it, so I couldn't take too much of her energy. She could not giveaway indefinitely.

"Remember that I said Indians valued certain kinds of knowledge?"

"I do remember," replies Allison.

"Miz once told me that it doesn't matter how many credits you accumulate to get knowledge. That's all you get in the end—credits.

"She saw the gathering of energy as a kind of knowledge. Unlike things, knowledge would never go away. It is deep—coming from experience—experience earned in exchange for sacrifice and giving away. Giving and receiving is not a gain or loss equation so much as an exchange of energies. I believe that the idea is to become so strong that one can give away and remain strong, like a rock on a seashore, like a root that reaches deep into the desert, like the shell on a turtle.

"In agreeing to mentor me, Miz had chosen to give away a measure of herself; and I in turn, gave back to the best of my ability. Eventually, I was able to sell many sweaters for her!

"Yes, Allison, I learned that energy knowledge cannot be

purchased, nor found in books. One must learn it experientially through observation of nature. It is free, pure, and abundant—like all that the Great Spirit gives.

"Remember that I taught you that everything works in circles and fours?"

"I do," Allison says.

"Well, nothing is really "free," because we live within a circle, which means that everything "comes back," thus humans need to reciprocate. All of life gives and receives naturally, except humans, who need to learn how from the other animals and the plants, in the way that Miz's people have known for centuries. Don't you think that continuous 'taking' without giving back is sheer craziness?"

"Of course it is. 'Do unto others as you would have them do unto you,' is the same idea, isn't it? All humans know that is a universal concept. Don't they?"

"That's a wonderful rule if people use it, but so much of it can be only partially helpful. What if somebody hits you? Should you hit them back? Oh, it's a real good rule, but it . . . well, maybe some other day we can talk about this."

"Do you need to get going?"

"No, I'm fine. How about you?"

"Let's stay awhile longer."

"Okay. I should say, all this stuff about energy and giving away was at first personal. I thought of it in terms of family and people relationships. Only years later did I realized that all life works in such a way. The lake constantly gives away to survive. Everything in nature sheds, dehydrates, erodes, erupts, and so on. Why? So that cycles are maintained. Everything is always accommodating something else— making space, moving over, nourishing, sacrificing. As Miz said, 'It's not how much you giveaway, but what you have left!'"

Allison and I sit quietly, contemplating. I wonder how she may be interpreting my story in a helpful manner. I sometimes responded to Miz in ways that surprised her. I wonder what my curious student thinks.

She turns to me, "Do you have an Indian name? We talked about plant and animal names in class, and I thought perhaps you did."

"I have three: one that I gave myself when Miz asked me what I would choose, and one that my Ojibwe language teacher gave me years later. I chose Mang, or Loon, because I saw that he can fly, swim, and walk therefore connect unlike things. My teacher, Rose Barstow, called me *Aabitawayi'ii Ikwe*, Halfway Woman in Ojibwe— my learning was just that. Since my vision quest Dayshun calls me *Mememgwaa Ikwe*, Butterfly Woman."

"I'd like to have an Indian name some day," Allison murmurs as we prepare to leave the park to the ducks and squirrels.

Chapter 10
YOUR ROOTS ARE IN EUROPE
How can I earn a living and help Mother Earth?

Nett Lake Indian Reservation, Minnesota

Miz wanted our group to experience a giveaway ceremony at the SaGiBahGah Days powwow held each spring by her band, the Boise Forte Ojibwe at Nett Lake. She arranged a weekend trip, while we planned a giveaway breakfast to acknowledge her, by honoring her people.

None of us knew exactly what was expected of us, yet we all felt aroused at the tantalizing prospect of playing a role at the powwow. After all, we were just a bunch of sincerely nosy *"wasichus"*—white folks—a negative term used by natives. Would they really welcome us? We had to trust Miz.

Each summer my father had taken our family to Nelson's Resort. We would leave the city, drive 300 miles north to the small lumber town named Orr on US Highway 53, then we'd turn onto County Road 23 for another thirty miles to Crane Lake on the Canadian border. But our group was going to the Indian Reserve, situated ten miles west of Orr. Dad never took us there.

The only Indians I'd ever met were the ones who worked at the resorts on Crane Lake, and at Campbell's Cabins on Lac La Croix in Canada. Father liked to tell how Johnny Ottertail, a fishing guide and trapper on La Croix, had saved his life. Dad never wore a life vest, even though he fished on a lake every summer weekend of his charmed adult life. He couldn't swim one inch. His story recounted how he was alone in a canoe on Lac La Croix when his boat overturned in rough waters. He was strong enough to hang on until

Ottertail arrived from shore and rescued him. Dad always ended his tale with, "I sure was lucky!" Yet, he never changed his ways.

Before the trip, Miz and I met again on campus at the University of Minnesota, where I became a student after a summer of geology classes at Grand Forks. We spread out my red blanket in a wooded corner on the West Bank, above the swirling rush of the Mississippi River. Like spectators of a great event—spring break-up, we watched ice floes bump and grind until they disappeared out of site. Then, our imaginations followed their trail. All that snow runoff would join the Minnesota River at nearby Fort Snelling, and about thirty miles south of that, would join the St. Croix River, where all three rivers would mingle mud, stones, sticks, fish, and bones, then continue on to the sea at New Orleans in Louisiana.

I let out a sigh, then told Miz, "I feel like I'm on a path, and I'm not sure where it's taking me; but I feel that it's the right direction—like a river."

"*Ahhh*," she replied, "Yes, well, that's how we are. We don't always know why we do what we do at the time."

"Also," I continued, "I'm trying to trust my instincts, yet I have to be a responsible mother. I'd like to be an artist; however, I'm planning to be a teacher, so I can raise my kids. Being an artist is only a dream, right now."

"*Hmmm*. Does there have to be a contradiction? Maybe you can do all of them?"

"My friends say I'm a good artist because I'm creative, and I should follow my heart; but things are not good between my husband and me, and I'm afraid I may one day be the sole supporter of my family. I certainly can't count on making a living at being a sculptress."

"*Hmmm*, hard choices to make," Miz says, looking down.

"I also wonder how I can earn a living, and help Mother Earth? My parents think I should sell real estate. They couldn't understand that, in the Indian way, buying and selling that which the Creator gives freely, is crazy."

"Well, the world has changed, and I suppose you could earn a good living that way."

"I don't want to. It sounds boring. It's just a functional occupation to fill an artificial need—like all sales. Don't we all know when we need something? Thousands of people spend their lives playing a game—trying to out-hustle each other, trying to convince others they need things they don't!"

"You sound pretty cynical."

"I would like to have a job helping people have things they need."

"Not everybody agrees what people need."

"I think it's rather clear!"

"You do?"

"Sure. It's whatever the Indians needed—plus flush toilets."

"Flush toilets!?" Miz looks into my eyes, astonished!

We broke out laughing, as she added, "There isn't an Indian who would disagree with you about that!"

"Think about it!" I said, "The Ojibwe never needed health insurance. They never went hungry so they could pay their premium."

"Ha, ha, ha. That's true."

"And, before Europeans arrived, no man ever went to jail. There weren't any. Now, more are imprisoned in America than any place on earth. Jailing people is a for-profit business, just like medicine."

"*Ahhh*, that's true. Well, you can choose what you sell to others, something that makes them feel good, like sweaters."

"Yes! You have time to reflect and relax while you're working at your loom at home, and you love making them, and making people happy. You create good feelings, and do no harm. Don't you think it's so sad that people spend their life in a job they hate? I suppose they don't see a choice, and have to feed their family, and keep silent if the factory is polluting the water, yet, they get sick from drinking it. That's wrong.

"When I lived in North Dakota, I saw farmers dumping chemicals on their land even though Rachel Carson warned against it. Our government banned some of them in the US, but allowed them sold overseas, and we import food from those very countries. Many of our corporations bribe our government officials—legally, because we call it lobbying—with money for their campaign war chests—amounts that are obscene. . ."

Miz shakes her head, "I think citizens should be able to trust the leaders they choose, but even good men become swayed by a bad system."

"Oh, Miz, I think they *are* the system. A system is only as good as the men and women in it. I think Thomas Jefferson would turn over in his grave if he could see how elections are monopolized by television."

"Wow! You sound angry."

"I am! As long as everybody's making choices based on money, I don't see much hope for reversing the environmental mess we're in. I mean, how do you make people care when they're only worried about their own day-to-day problems? I'm afraid they'll only wake up when *their* well is poisoned; or *their* son dies of cancer; or when they can't swim in *their* lake. People are so self-centered! Why is that? I'm really no different, I suppose. Except that I do try to consider the consequences of my actions upon the earth as a whole."

I stood up and walked around long enough to release some tension in my body, while Miz calmly watched the river.

When I sat down, I found two crunchy oatmeal cookies in my pack, and offered one to Miz. She smiled, handing me a red apple. After a time for silence, she softly said, "What do the animals do?"

"They don't stuff themselves till they need weight reduction clinics! They don't foul the air with acid rain. Most of them seem to do their job to insure that their offspring will flourish. But people are different."

"That's for sure. Why?"

"It must be because our brains are bigger. We can make more trouble for ourselves. And we do it. That's for sure. What do you think?"

"We make it not just for ourselves, but for others—including the animals," Miz said, "By the way. Don't include *all* people in your accusations. Millions of people on the earth, including most American Indians, aren't guilty of the things you're talking about. Remember THAT when you get upset. Look at your own people first."

After the usual ranting and ridiculous accusations, Husband agreed to be with the boys over the weekend, while I brought my daughter along to the powwow at Nett Lake. She was a beautiful, energetic twelve-year-old who could pass for an Indian with her brown eyes, olive skin, and chestnut hair that fell down her back. We shared hair and skin color, but my eyes were hazel-green.

Leaving Minneapolis we joined lines of cars full of happy vacationers heading north. Some were pulling fishing boats with two motors on the back, one large one to get to the fishing hole, and one small one for trolling. A Southern friend of mine, who once visited Minnesota, remarked that he thought Minnesotans were very clever to have two motors on each boat, in case one failed!

The tiny one-street town of Orr, nestled between the shore of Pelican Lake and a railroad track, was the last stop before entering the Nett Lake Reservation. It felt strange to me, to be heading in that direction. However the Orr Cafe was a familiar, friendly, favorite place, and I'd promised Lisa we'd have lunch there. We seated ourselves on stools at the cafe counter, sniffing the sweet scent of home-baked sticky pecan rolls, fruit pies topped with sugary crusts, and my favorite, soft fudge cookies with dark-chocolate frosting. Mom always made them.

We ordered pea soup and tuna sandwiches with chips, cookies, and water. We were having a great time being out on our own. Lisa was interested in all the fun stuff hanging on the walls, mostly the stuffed fish. A local man and woman sat next to us, bent over their coffee mugs, apparently listening to us.

The man turned to me. "Goin' fishin?'

"Not this trip."

"Too bad. A shame! Good fishin' up here."

Lisa piped up, "Look, Mom! That one's a walleye!"

"That's right, I agreed," encouraging her, "What's that one?"

"Oh, that's a northern pike!"

"Right-o! How about that one over there?"

"It looks like a sunny, but it sure is big."

The man sat up straight and declared, "That's a crappie. See his belly?"

"Oh look, behind us. There's one more, Lisa."

"*Hmmm.* Is it another walleye?"

"I think it's a lake trout like Grandpa caught. Only his is bigger."

"Bingo!" cheered the man, making Lisa giggle with delight. "I can tell that you two are fishermen!"

"No!" exclaimed Lisa, "We're fisherwomen!"

I thought to myself, *Ahhh—she's learning!*

Lisa told the man, "Grandpa and Grandma are at Nelson's Resort, but we girls are going to a powwow today, and we're going to camp out. Kali will be there, too. She's another girl my age."

The woman looked at the man, "Oh say, I think it's SahGiBaGah Days!" Then she looked at us, "You will have a good time! Be sure to have some fry bread. It tastes best when it's right out of the hot fat! You'll like the dancing, and all the colorful costumes. We went to a powwow at Lake Superior once, had a cabin near Gooseberry Falls; and we ate smelt at the Green Door in Beaver Bay. Say! If you like fish, you should try their annual smelt feed. Right honey?"

She turned to him for affirmation. She got it.

"Ya, you betcha!"

I followed Miz's directions, driving away from Pelican Lake toward Nett Lake, famous for its wild rice. A narrow dirt road zigzagged through the wilderness, overshadowed by lofty needled pines, arching white birches, and mature sugar maples, each tree a source of useful sap. We passed by two funky signs from the '40s advertising Ma and Pa resorts. We passed a woman planting a garden outside a modest, neat cottage. We passed a deer in a frozen pose. And a shack falling down—returning to the earth in a heap of rotten logs under curled-up stacks of faded asphalt shingles. What stories could be told about that place?

By the time we joined our group, late-day sunbeams cast mysterious shady shapes over the tents we erected in a grassy grove of spindly pin oaks. Miz chose the spot, which was adjacent to the simple frame house of an Ojibwe medicine man. She was instructing each of us to present him with a gift we'd brought from home. One by one, we shyly approached the strange fellow seated on a straight-backed woven lawn chair, not far from his front door. He wore a crumpled, but clean, blue long-sleeved cotton shirt, khaki pants, and leather boots. His head was bare. His shaggy hair matched the color of his twinkling eyes— black. His darkened skin was wrinkled into peaceful lines telling me he'd lived a good long life, and I wondered with intense desire, just what secrets he held in his mind, for he appeared so ordinary.

Our turn to give arrived. Lisa and I carried a large box of good used clothes and set it down before him, feeling that perhaps he'd resent our handouts; however. Miz had assured me that I should give it to him. Lisa opened the box, and I removed the top item, a thick, sturdy, gray tweed wool sport coat.

I turned to him, "*Aaniin, nimishoomis!*" (Hello, Grandfather.) "*Miigwech!*"

"*Boozhoo!*" (Hello) he replied, grinning at me.

Handing him the coat, I said, "Please accept this small gift. I appreciate your kindness in letting me camp on your land. Perhaps you know some others who would also like some items in the box."

"*En, en, miigwechiwi!*" (Yes, yes, thank you.) His face was beaming!

He stood up, nodding "yes" as Miz told him to try it on. She thought it looked great. "Look, it's perfect!" she said, "He really likes it!"

I didn't think it fit that well, "Perhaps it's a little long?"

"No, no!" Miz insisted, "That'll keep him warm in the winter. That's a good practical gift, and it looks like new."

Everyone stood around smiling as the medicine man proudly showed off his coat, an expression of glee painted on his face.

Lisa whispered to me, "He likes it, Mom." I looked down at her. She was happy, too.

Grandfather removed his jacket, and sat down, folding the coat on his lap, holding it, running his dry, boney fingers across its softness.

I glanced at Miz. She looked at me as if to say, "See? I told you he'd like it."

When everybody had their tents in place, we formed a circle and sat down to check supply lists and duties, since our giveaway gesture was to feed breakfast to the entire community on Sunday morning at the recreation hall. Everything seemed to be in order.

It was growing dark, and some of us wished to go for a short hike, so we walked up a road just to peek around. Miz had disappeared. We thought perhaps she had gone to visit her mother or friends. Little could we have guessed what she was planning for us that evening.

We hadn't wandered far, when a drumbeat sounded in the distance, behind us. Our backs straightened. We halted, turned, and listened, our heads tilted toward the rhythm on the wind.

"The powwow's beginning!" someone shouted, "We don't want to miss the Grand Entry! Let's go!"

"I have to stop and get my shawl," I excitedly exclaimed, scurrying along, "But I'll catch up with you soon." Lisa continued with the group as I popped open the trunk of the car, opened my suitcase, and grabbed my shawl—fine-spun aqua rayon with silk embroidered flowers—fuchsia pink and pale yellow. The edges dripped with long fringe. Then I changed my top. I had sewn a special shirt, like the ones I saw at the Fort Totten powwow worn by the men, and similar to the dresses of women who danced. It was aqua-colored calico covered with tiny pink rosebuds — ribbons of blue, yellow, and white stitched horizontally on the front and back, with other ribbons hanging down. I wore blue jeans; however, if I'd planned to dance, I'd have brought a proper skirt, too. In my hair I wore an ornament of polished pink shell, ivory bone, and one wood bead, stained purple. It jiggled when I walked.

Hurrying through the dusky, dark forest lit only by lighting from the powwow, my sandals springing lightly on a pine needle path, I came out onto a clearing where a small, but growing, mingling crowd moved about, a mixed bunch of natives and whites, the old, the young, and babies.

Brimming over with enthusiasm, I expected to see a big-top tent, or a canopy. There were none.

I moved toward the drumbeat, past cars, pickup trucks, blankets spread out, and lawn chairs. The warm spring night air smelled ripe with wet grass, balm of Gilead trees, crushed moss, and, yes, horse dung!

Where was Lisa and my group? I stopped at the gathering at the edge of the powwow circle, which was defined by a low weathered, split-rail fence and tall wooden posts strung with bare light bulbs, mostly concentrated near the only entrance by the announcers booth.

The Grand Entry was in full glory: A few male elders carrying flags, veterans of World War II, came around dancing. Warriors of recent wars, some in blue jeans and T-shirts, came dancing. Grandmothers, young mothers, and children in a rainbow of colors, came dancing. All moving slowly in a clockwise rhythm, moving quietly in unison, in great contrast to the loud "*boom, boom*" of the drum, and the guttural wailing of men's voices—those voices that once again sent shivers through my body, setting my mind in a trance, just like in North Dakota.

"Hey, Mom! Here you are!" Lisa said, tapping my shoulder.

She and Kali led me to our little circle of *wasichus* surrounding Miz on the opposite side of the fence. Miz's eyebrows rose when she saw my shirt, "*Ahhh!*" she said in a high-pitched tone, "*Ennn!*"

Dancers dressed in categories: men's traditional, men's fancy, women's traditional, women's fancy. Between rounds, the announcer, or anyone who wished to speak, used the microphone at a wooden table to broadcast news, offer prayers in Ojibwe, say words of honor about someone alive, or departed, or to give a speech, such as the one exhorting the grave effects of alcohol. A very long speech!

The tone of the powwow was relaxed, free, and unstructured. No discernible leader; no specific time schedule.

Anyone could join in the intertribal dances. My friend Bill and I followed a dancer whose style I admired. Her back was held firm; her eyes focused forward, very dignified—unlike me, trying to watch my feet, and not trip over them. When I finally learned the steps, the song ended. Feeling disappointed, I returned to the group.

Fantastic, sweet smells drifting by my nose made my tummy growl. Bill, Roger, Kali, Lisa, and I went in search of fry bread, maybe some chili or a squaw dog (hot dog). All booths had handmade signs: pizza, ice cream, hamburgers, hot dogs, chili, pop, and coffee. We admired beaded jewelry, birchbark baskets, T-shirts, newspapers, posters, books, and more. Lisa picked out a beaded barrette for her shiny hair.

We found three fry bread vendors in a row. Bill stopped at the first, but I steered him further, murmuring, "Her bread looks cold and gray." At the next one, "Oh, oh. Those little golden clouds look cold, too."

"I'm just hungry," protested Bill, "I'm taking the next one!"

A fat Ojibwe lady waited by her electric cooker full of hot lard, with blobs of white dough ready, and a deep pot of honey on the table.

"We'll take five pieces," I said, "We like it hot out of the cooker!"

"Me, too!" she grinned, revealing a gap between her top two teeth.

The cook, who appeared as if she ate half her product, adjusted her bib apron over her ample bosom, plopped raw dough into the fresh smelling, sizzling lard. Without a word, we admired the bouncing blobs hissing, popping, puffing up above their oily pool in culinary magnificence, teasing our twitching noses and salivating mouths.

Carefully, she turned each fry bread with a long-tined fork, until they were golden brown, like giant amber jewels. She flipped them onto a pan lined with absorbent tan paper, then set them on napkins and proudly handed one to each of us.

An invention of the gods! A pastry all crinkled with fissures, like an old woman's cheek. I dribbled honey on mine, while Lisa tried powdered sugar and cinnamon. Crispy on the outside, and airy within, the aroma was doughnut-like. Hungrily, I took a bite, ignoring the bee nectar dripping around the corners of my mouth, while I tried to pour

81

hot black coffee with sticky fingers.

Laughing at our greedy appetites, Bill said, "Croissants in a Parisian café couldn't be any better!"

The cook laughed appreciatively, while we all said, "*Miigwech!*"

We moved on to the chili booth, and then bought ice-cold apple juice. Walking back to our group, the stars above seemed as close as the treetops—shining as brightly as the joy in my heart.

"Miz has been waiting for you!" Jack said, "She wants us to dance together," he said nervously.

Everyone appeared anxious, so I said, "That's fine. We can join an intertribal dance."

"You don't understand! She wants us to dance alone! Without her!"

"Fine," I said, "We can do it without her."

"No, no! She said just our class—NOBODY else. It's an honor dance."

"You mean—just our class? Nobody else? No other dancers?!"

I heard Miz's commanding voice behind me, "You dance to honor the Bois Forte tribe!"

I was stunned! The fry bread in my stomach turned into a heavy ball of lead. I could only imagine how silly I'd look. What if I tripped, or stumbled? No one had told me about this custom. I wanted to flee, more than I wanted to honor anybody!

We all huddled together like a flock of scared turkeys in a thunderstorm. None of us eight "wannabes" had powwow experience, except Bill, a blue-eyed, sandy-haired Ojibwe-Swede from Pine County.

I began practicing my dance steps in place, since I'd have no one to copy or follow. Slipping my sandals off, I left them by the fence. The damp grass and soft dirt felt reassuring under my warm feet, easing my fears. I didn't have time to consider what I'd done to bring myself up to such an unlikely event in my life.

Like a mother duck, Miz herded us through the entry in the fence, into the arena, empty except for the two drum groups of men in the center, watching us with blank expressions. I looked away. I quickly glanced back at Lisa and Kali, Roger's daughter. Both of them giggling with delight! I shot a look at Roger. He grinned. I grinned back, and we shrugged our shoulders, as if to say, *They're not worried about us—why should we be?*

Miz gave a signal to the announcer, an elderly gentleman wearing a red ribbon shirt, holding a microphone. I have forgotten his exact words, but he said something like this: We have visitors who are students of Mizinokamigok in the Twin Cities, and they have come to honor the Bois Forte Band by doing an honor dance this evening, and hosting a breakfast on Sunday morning, to which you are all invited.

He finished by announcing which drum would perform the song.

Boom, boom, boom, boom!

Ay, ayy,aiiiii!

The heartbeat of the drum reminded me to have courage, as we nervously entered the circle clockwise, the circle that suddenly seemed the size of a football field. On my right beat the drummers. On my right sang the singers. On my left sat the audience—watching. I couldn't look at them—watching. What were they thinking, behind those dark faces with black eyes—watching?

Did they think we were nuts? Or, did they see good people doing a good thing? Perhaps they didn't know what to think!

Boom, boom, went the drum. *Tap, tap*, went my heart.

Together, we moved in a small mass, like an unsure, awkward evolving growth, wanting to expand, but confined by hereditary rules clutching us all together. Yes, I felt more like a slow-hopping frog than a graceful, flying loon on the wing.

Boom, boom, went the drum. *Tap, tap*, went my heart.

Around we went once, bobbing up and down in rhythm. I thought, *Forget yourself! Concentrate on the beat! Let go! Relax! This is fun!* The ribbons on my shirt danced. The seashell in my hair jiggled back and forth. Rhythm grew in my body. Harmony stole my fear and drew it skyward.

Boom, boom, sang the drum. *Tap, tap*, sang my heart.

Dipping gently, swaying slightly, I felt shy, but courageous. Stepping simply, planting my toes and the balls of my feet, I felt cautious, but bold. Moving repetitively, respectfully, I grew natural and confident.

By the third time around, shifting one foot before the other, my brain and my bones became one. Soon, I felt euphoric, like I was flying. Flying among the stars, gathering them in my arms, sprinkling them like charms. I *was* the sky. I *was* the earth. Blood rushed through me like a river awakening ancient vibrations, like dead senses rising out of a tomb of lies and logic. A bear of stars appeared and disappeared. A butterfly made of moonbeams scooped down and fluttered in my hair. Rainbows shimmered in the crowd.

Boom, boom, soared the drum. *Tap, tap*, soared my heart.

The fourth time around, Mother Earth cradled me in her strong arms.

Then, . . . *THUD!* The drum stopped. Such silence! I stole a peek at the faces in the crowd. I couldn't read them. However, I could sense many positive vibrations.

After we all walked out of the arena to join Miz, I saw smiling, kind expressions aimed at all of us.

Feeling higher than a cloud, I anxiously sought out Miz's attention. I told her, "*Miigwech!* Thank you. Next time, I won't feel so shy!"

She put on her "teacher's face" and bluntly said, "*Ah ha!* What do you mean? Not everything has a next time! You may never do this again!" She said it with such finality.

Immediately deflated, I fell out of the sky, out of the moonbeams and butterflies, and stood like a tree stump, absorbing her words. The others were all around her, flushed and excited, but the stark truth of life was upon me, "You may never do this again."

And I haven't. Well, not exactly like that.

On Saturday morning, I hiked down the road and back. When I reached the powwow, it had already begun. Since arriving at Nett Lake, I'd been searching for a face in the crowd—one that I'd seen only once before—in an elevator at the University of Minnesota.

It was men's fancy dance time. Perhaps the man was in the circle. I'd heard him speak Ojibwe in the elevator. When we reached our floor, I cheerfully said, *"Gi minoa-ya ina?"* (You feel good?) I was eager to use new words I had just learned. We exchanged information before parting, during which I told him I sewed ribbon shirts for powwowing, weddings, and deceased natives who deserved the finest in their coffins on their trek to the spirit world.

I handed him my business card which had my name, phone number, a bear symbol, and the word, "designer." The man's name was Harold Goodsky, but his friends called him Dayshun, from Nett Lake, and he was in his last quarter of studies in social work.

Through the mail, Dayshun ordered several shirts, trading for money and wild rice. I thought he'd be at the powwow.

Sure enough, he was fancy dancing—making a mighty impressive figure in full Ojibwe regalia, wearing a floral woodland-patterned, black velvet beaded vest and breech flap. His shirt was as he'd ordered it: red cotton with black, white, and yellow ribbons across the back, down the arms, on the collar, cuffs, and one long streamer that fell over his heart. As he moved a deer tail roach on his head, and an eagle feather bustle on his back fanned in and out. Indeed, so much of his costume was intended to be in motion, that his bobbing this way and that, his jerking his head about, bending deep at the waist, reminded me of the courting ritual of a prairie chicken.

The dance ended. He came over to greet me, "*Boozhoo!*"

He reminded me of a big bear with his strong demeanor and bodily presence—tall, thick skin—the color of dried oak leaves in the fall, narrow eyes—penetrating and dark, a rounded nose, a mouth set in seriousness, but not hard.

"Welcome to Nett Lake! Come and meet my family," he offered.

There stood the whole bunch—smiling, all wearing my shirts.

I said, "You all look beautiful in your powwow outfits."

"Thanks a lot. We really like your sewing."

We talked together. I invited them all to breakfast on Sunday morning, then said I was going to get up real early to go fishing before breakfast."

"Fishing? For what? Do you have a boat?" Dayshun blurted out.

"No, but I have a rod and reel, and . . ."

"Harvey and I can take you out for an hour or so," Dayshun said, looking down at the little guy who approved, "And I'll bring bait."

The next morning, we met on the dock at Sugar Bush, their home, and set off in an aluminum boat for the end of an island where we dropped the anchor and fished, and talked while silly seagulls entertained us.

Dayshun said he was going to school so he could return to help the kids, but he may never actually get his degree, because many of the natives would think he was "uppity" and would turn against him. He said there was a lot of jealousy and judging that went on in many Indian communities, but it was mostly a few bad apples. He said he'd been a founder of the American Indian Movement in Minneapolis along with Dennis Banks, George Mitchell, and others, who were "sick of police harassment," that they organized a foot-and-car patrol with church funds to pick up Indian kids off the streets before the police took them—intervention to help troubled teens. Harold and George left AIM for social work, while Dennis and others continued on a more radical, political, national agenda with AIM.

We each caught a walleye. Dayshun said that a giant fish lived in a bay on Pelican Lake—soooo big, it had been mistaken for a log!

"Have you ever eaten smelt?" I asked.

"Nawww. They're no good. Only you immigrants—you Scandinavians like to eat them because they remind you of home!"

"I'm not Scandinavian. I'm American, and my heritage is all German."

"What's a nice German-American girl like you doing up here? I saw you Friday night doing the honor dance. Why'd you do that?"

"Because I hope to learn all I can about your culture, and Miz gave me a way to give thanks for the sharing."

"What do you want to know about my culture? What's wrong with your own?"

"It's sick. I'm a wannabe and proud of it! My own is sick."

"*Ho, ho ho!* Is it now? Well, I don't know. They're an awful lot of 'skins' trying to be white guys. Do you know what we call them?"

"No, what?"

"Apples. Red on the outside and white on the inside."

"*Hmmm.* If I'm white on the outside, and red within, what's that?"

"*Ho, ho!* I don't know," he laughed.

We fished quietly for a few minutes. He looked at me, "Why do you think your culture is sick?"

"Well, I figure that Western societies, especially the American one, don't understand their relationship with the earth, or what their progressive attitude is doing to it, and without a healthy earth we are not healthy humans. So, what good is all the logic, intelligence, information, computers, and all the rest, if we're all sick?"

"*Hmmm.* Go on." Dayshun murmured, staring into the water.

"I see it as a universal problem, since we all breathe the same air, drink the same water, and catch the same fish! It's so simple, I just don't understand why people don't all see the connections." I paused, "Now, *you* people are so tuned into such thinking that it's like eating or sleeping."

"*Hmmm*. Perhaps you give us too much credit. Most of us have lost it, or become so assimilated into white ways that we've forgotten the old ways ourselves. There's a lot more Catholics and Protestants here than traditionalists."

"What are you, Dayshun?"

"Oh, I believe the old ways. I speak my language, but most don't. I wish they'd all learn it again. Heck, most of the people here will stay home and watch television before they'd attend the powwow. It really makes me sad. Hell, it makes my heart bleed."

"But you're getting a college degree. I admire that. It's great that you can also use your new skills to teach old ways, too."

"I don't want to become too different. Maybe someday I'll get that degree, but I don't ever want to live in a city, or apart from Nett Lake. These are my roots, and will be for my kids too, and so I have to be here to teach them the good ways. You whites move all the time and pay no attention to where you are. You're roots are in Europe. We are part of this soil. Our bones are buried here. The spirits of our ancestors walk here."

"Do you think I was silly to dance like that last night? Do you think native people might resent my caring about their ways? I mean, I don't want to take anything from anyone, but if everyone doesn't learn some alternative thinking patterns pretty soon, we'll all perish together on this earth. What do you think?"

"I think you are beautiful, and what your group did was also beautiful. I'll bet you gave some folks a few things to think about up here—seeing you people so fired up about Indian ways and all. To see you value those ways helps them see them with good value also. They aren't so sure that they're old ways are good anymore, but you and I know they are. Give them time, and they'll wake up. Meanwhile, they're still enough old ones around who remember, and a few who practice, and they just need the youth to come back—and ask. You're a good example to them."

"But I don't want to be, or tell anything to Indians—just to my own people."

"That's okay. Do it."

Now that was a big challenge. Could I accomplish such a big goal? How would I ever find the time? Could it match my passion and energy?

That morning, the Nett Lake Community Hall bustled with activity. Bill Skelly, our main chef, rose to the challenge of cooking for most of the community. A long line of appreciative people lined up across the room, waiting for us to serve them flapjacks, scrambled eggs, fried bacon, buttered toast, jam and jelly, syrup, pitchers of orange juice, and pots of hot coffee. I waited on Dayshun's family, relatives, the old medicine man wearing his new tweed sport coat, people I'd seen dancing, beating the drum, or making speeches.

One of Dayshun's friends told me I was lucky to have the best fishing guide on the lake; that fish were becoming scarce, and I was lucky to be taking home five nice walleyes. Then he said, "Dayshun's the best duck-hunting guide in these parts, too!"

After the powwow ended on Sunday, I had lots to think about while Lisa fell asleep in the car on our way home. A strong memory haunted me. After my mother-in-law's death in a two car accident involving a Catholic priest who also died, she appeared to me in a vivid dream, offering me a cedar box full of Indian charms and fetishes—beads, pipestone, shells, herbs, feathers, bones. My circle was moving. My path led me on, and on—as though I could watch myself in an unfolding drama that I did not write.

Chapter 11

LIFE IS LIKE A ROAD MAP

Do human animals have more problems than
other animals because we think more?

University of St. Thomas

Allison is not among the students today. I begin the class by saying, "*Miigwech*, or "thank you," in Ojibwe, "Thank you for allowing me to have the honor of sharing my knowledge with you." I look down for a minute of silence, then continue, "Everything is a gift in the view of the Ojibwe, and that includes learning. However, not all learning is beneficial, nor equal. Indeed, it seems to me that the old time natives were better at prioritizing knowledge than most of the rest of us.

"This book in my hand, *Touch the Earth* by T.C. McLuhan, is a compilation of quotes from speeches given by Native Americans. I'm very fond of this small publication. It was the first Indian book I bought in North Dakota, and feels richly imbued with wisdom. I'll read a passage from a speech given by Young Chief, of the Cayuses, at a treaty signing in Washington Territory, before signing away their land:

I wonder if the ground has anything to say? I wonder if the ground is listening to what is said? I wonder if the ground would come alive and what is on it? Though I hear what the ground says. The ground says, It is the Great Spirit that placed me here. The Great Spirit tells me to take care of the Indians, to feed them aright. The Great Spirit appointed the roots to feed the Indians on. The water says the same thing. The Great Spirit directs me, Feed the Indians well. The grass says the same thing, Feed the Indians well. The ground, water and grass say, The Great Spirit has given us our names. We have these names and hold these names. The ground says, The Great Spirit has placed me here to produce all that grows on me, trees and fruit. The same way the ground says, It was from me man was made. The Great Spirit, in placing men on the earth desired them to take good care of the ground and to do each other no harm . . . .

"You can teach elementary school children," I say, "about the ways Native Americans communicated without books. First, they were gifted orators who made many eloquent speeches without a script. Many were extremely fine artists, perhaps because they relied on original dreams and visualization. They thought in pictures or symbols more than English people. During the winter, tribal elders told the same stories to the children generation after generation, serious and funny tales that taught morals, entertained, and bonded the tribe's identity. Each tribe had their own stories, characters, and geographical places where the narrative took place, a certain rock, river, valley, and so on. This method bonded not only the tribe's people, but the people to the land. Natives felt related to everything."

I ask the class, "Do you know any stories about your ancestors and the land they lived on?"

A few hands go up. They tell from which country their family immigrated, but few know much more.

"Do you have anyone in your family who is the story-carrier for the past, so future generations know where they originated?"

A few have someone who did a genealogical chart.

"Perhaps such things were more important to natives because they couldn't find it in a book or a computer. They had to remember. Some tribes used hide painting, like the Lakota. Some used birchbark, like the Ojibwe. Some made objects out of stone, clay, wood, or plants. Symbolic drawings recorded certain events, gave directions, or warnings and communicated without an alphabet."

92

Following my lecture, I announce, "For the remainder of this class we will do a project you can do with your young students. We'll pass out paper, and each of you will draw your chosen plant or animal about seven-by-ten inches, then paint it red or black, cut it out, and make a story about it to tell the others later. Don't write it down. Next, we'll make a rock cliff on the wall using butcher-block paper. We'll draw a river on the floor with birchbark canoes and Indians paddling by this dangerous rapids. We'll pretend that we are in the canoes. Each of you will take turns pasting your symbol onto the cliff, and telling your story while in the canoe. Tell the children that the Indians didn't tell the meaning of their cliff symbols to anybody, and they remain a secret today."

Kathryn raises her hand, "You said before that some of the pictographs on overhanging rock cliffs were prayers to water spirits who controlled passageways. But, perhaps it's none of our business to guess what another person's prayer is. Perhaps we should just respect such drawings, and let them be a mystery."

"What do the rest of you think about Kathryn's suggestion?"

"Makes sense to me," says Sarah. Everybody nods.

"Reminds me of the Indians who protested the digging up of bones," says another, "Yeah—and bones on display in museums," says another.

I stop them, "Wait a minute. I think you're all correct, but here is what I was told when I was a student in archeology in Grand Forks. A Lakota woman from Turtle Mountain sat next to me every day. I asked Yellowrobe her thoughts about the digging archeologists did to discover things. She said she didn't like it, but since the Europeans had done such a good job of obliterating their culture, she had no choice. She hoped to reconstruct the past through her university studies."

At the end of the class I check the fall weather out the window.

93

Allison and I have a second meeting scheduled for later today.

Allison arrives at Loring Park with a cell phone glued to her ear. She snaps it shut, hustles over to the bench, exclaiming, "What a splendid autumn day. Oh, you have a blanket over your legs."

"Yes, I have trouble keeping my left foot warm, but I want to be outside even if it's chilly. When I was little, my physically fit mother bundled us kids up and rolled us out the door into the snow. Our neighborhood gang of rosy cheeked chums had no TV. We went ice skating on Mud Lake, built snow forts, had snowball fights, slid down steep hills on sleds and toboggans, and went skiing at Wirth Park. We only went inside to eat. Then we continued playing after dinner in the dark."

Allison tucks her phone away, "I was just talking to my son. He and his sister are in grade school. Now they're watching TV. I told them to go out and play, but Mother worries about them, unless she goes out with them."

"What's she worried about?"

"Oh, you know. Some kidnapper might get them, or some pedophile. I don't know. I guess that we have to be more careful these days. We have a real nice neighborhood, but we don't know everybody. We're all too busy working, I suppose. Trying to get ahead, or keep up!"

"So you use a cell phone to stay connected?"

"Yes. But it won't always be this way. I'll get my own place and have more time after school is done."

"Miz taught me some things about connections that seem like simple knowledge, but I've come to see that those things are important, because how we frame our thinking shapes our attitudes and actions."

"You mean like thinking positively?" Allison asks.

"*Ummm*. No. I mean, thinking realistically. You see, we are taught that life is like a linear progression, but if one studies nature, one can see this is not so."

Allison shrugs, folds her hands, and says, "I don't get it."

"Well," I begin, "Many years ago, Miz led our group to a powwow up at Nett Lake. Before the powwow, we had a session at a nice spot overlooking the Mississippi River." I pause. "As I recall, I was wondering if human animals have more problems than other animals because we can think more.

"She said that, 'These answers will come to you according to where you look for them. You may have to look far and wide, and for a long time.' Miz found a pen, reached for my art sketch book, and opened to a clean sheet of paper. She drew a circle in the center. She made a dot in the center of the circle. While pointing the pen at the paper, she spoke slowly. She said, 'Everything works in a circle, but not directly, nor predictably. You have your own circle. That is your life. But it is not alone.' She then moved the pen far outside the circle and made another dot. She said, 'You are in the center, then you are far outside of it.'

"Then she made a dot on the other side of the sheet, saying, 'There is someone you've never met, but you will. Here's another dot for someone you already know. Maybe it's a son. Here is a place you've been. Here is a place you're going.'

"Soon, she had drawn dots and more dots all over. There were eight dots in the center, but I don't think she was counting."

"Miz said, 'Now listen to me.'

"She leaned close, and I hung on every word. Eye to eye. Energy high!

"She said, in a low voice full of gravity, 'Your life, and the meaning it has, lies in how you choose to connect all those dots.'

"Then, she began connecting the dots. She drew lines like arrows, all over the paper, connecting some, and not others. They went in all directions, and seemed to have no pattern.

"Miz leaned close to me again, her narrow black eyes growing wide, penetrating mine. She taught me, 'Life is like a road map. You will travel many roads and cross many intersections. Some more than others. The dots are the intersections,'

"At first, I was quiet. I said to Miz, 'Isn't that rather chaotic? I mean, my life looks like a mess! *Haha!*' We both laughed hard.

"After we settled down," Miz cautioned, '*Ahhh*. Don't forget the circle! You're only looking at the lines! The circle always pulls you back inside. You are the one who leaves it. Don't ever forget your center.'

"I said, '*Ahhh*. Now I see! There IS harmony, then?'

"Miz narrowed her eyes even more, and pronounced, 'Well, that's up to you.'

"Then we fell quiet. She said no more after we folded the blanket and walked to our cars in the parking lot."

Allison says, "Wow, she gave you a lot of energy that day, didn't she?"

"Yes, she did," I mutter, nodding my head.

I thought to myself, words that hung heavily on my mind, *Don't ever forget your center.* I felt as though I had, and I felt as though I had let myself down, but I didn't tell Allison that. I would tell her about all the good times between the difficult ones.

"*Miigwech*," says Allison, her straight blonde hair rippled by the growing wind, her eyes watering with emotion, "I had no idea there was so much to learn about Indian art, and now, there's so much to learn about how to live. Why aren't we taught lessons like circles and lines, connections and centers in school? It makes so much sense to me. I'm going to go home and write it all down."

"Oh yes, my dear. Go write it down—if you must."

"Well, shouldn't I?"

"Next time, next time. I'm going to have to go now." We fold my blanket, and walk to the street, to our cars.

"Goodbye," we part cheerfully, "Have a nice evening!

I begin to walk away, then turn and yell after her, "*Gigawabamin wabang!* Or, I'll see you tomorrow."

"*Gigawabamin wabang* to you, too," she cries, laughing.

Chapter 12

NATURE CANNOT BE A FOOL

What happened that caused differences in beliefs between Indigenous and Anglo-American tribes? Why would two disparate cultures that share the same land mass interact so differently with the earth?

Loring Park

"Which hand? Choose one!" Allison quips, both arms behind her back, a funny grin on her face— reminds me of the joker in a deck of cards.

Playing her little game, I reply, "The left side."

A jug of amber maple syrup drops into my mitten. She chuckles.

"*Oooah! Miigwech. Ziinzibaakwadaaboo* (maple sap). *Owa* (That's good.)"

We settle onto a park bench bundled up like furry bunnies in a hole, ready for the oncoming winter.

I tell Allison, "Sarah's Table Chester Creek Cafe in Duluth serves a small jar of REAL maple syrup with each giant blueberry-nut pancake. *Ummm*—that's good."

"I love Lake Superior. Do you go to Duluth often?"

"Yes, but I haven't always loved the North Shore."

"How could you not love it? You love nature."

"When I was two years old we began vacationing at Nelson's Resort on Crane Lake, back before Voyageurs National Park. Nothing made me happier than when our family was together fishing.

"One year Dad's business was bad. We went instead to Two Harbors and rented a room in someone's home along Highway 61. In the morning, as my parents slept, the friendly owners invited me to their kitchen for cocoa where they peppered me with questions which I

98

answered. Dad woke up. I heard, 'JUDITH! Get in this room now!' He promised me a good spanking when we got home, for speaking to strangers. My trip was ruined. I was scared, but he forgot all about it. No spanking."

"Gee whiz, while I grew up," says Allison, "there were so many kids in our family, we hardly went anywhere. One summer Dad got a bonus from work and took us all to Lake Superior to camp at Gooseberry Falls and Temperance River. One night we slept in a quaint log cabin near the Gunflint Trail, went out water skiing, then to Sven and Ole's for pizza in Grand Marais. To me, that area is my favorite."

"We're certainly shaped by childhood experiences. My children don't camp much—preferring a gym for exercise. One coaches hockey. Hiking was very important to me. I usually hiked five miles per day. I even hiked from Two Harbors to Canada on the Superior Hiking Trail at the age of sixty. Now, my ankle's bad, but I hope to improve."

Allison says, "I've never even been to Canada."

With regret, I recall my Albany River trip. I tell Allison, "I think the fated trip to Osnaburgh House on the Albany River killed my kids' desire for wilderness fun. Everything went wrong! However, strangely, it became another dot on my map of life with meaningful memories."

Allison wonders, "Where is it? Why did you go there?"

"My husband led canoeists from New York on a ten-day trip, leaving me to maintain the base camp till he returned, my choice. We were on the Albany River in Ontario, a great river like the Mississippi. Our base camp was about 300 miles south of James Bay, near Osnaburgh Lake and the Albany Outfitters, and an Indian reserve.

"The kids and I were having a grand adventure. The boys caught fish all day long, huge northern pike and tasty walleyes for supper.

Then the thunder gods unleashed a torrent of rain that forced us to vacate our island and paddle back to the outfitters. Man, that was one scary day in fast, high water, pouring rain, and hidden rapids. With Lenny paddling in the bow and me in the stern, our single aluminum canoe piled full of soaking wet gear and three other wide-eyed shivering kids clinging to the gunwales, we made it.

"Meanwhile, the outfitter's kid was sick with chicken pox and their machine storage building had burned to the ground, sealing my decision to leave early. Dad could hitchhike home!

"Prior to our departure, I drove to the Mishkeegogamang Indian village to find Lorraine. She agreed to sew and bead a leather pendant for my neck. I asked her to bead a loon image in the leather circle. Curious natives gathered around us. They laughed when I requested an owl pendant for my friend, Roger. I thought I'd mispronounced *gookooko'oo*, owl, but I hadn't. Some tribes believe a superstition that an owl is a messenger of death. However, we white folks think big eyes and bushy eyebrows are for wise professors and wise owls. Navajos and Athabascans were discouraged from attacking Southwestern Pueblos, if scary stuffed owls were displayed around their village. Navajos migrated down the western coast of Canada, leaving behind the Athabascans who spoke the same language, and probably also feared owls. In the Southwest, the Apache and Hupa split from the Navajos."

Allison joins in, "Native migrations. Pioneers moving. Immigrants fleeing. Reminds me of the Norwegians; the Protestants, founding new churches in America. I'll bet the Indians wish that whites had learned how to get along with each other and stayed home! Across the ocean. What if the American Indians had invaded Europe instead? What if they'd brought *their* religion to replace Christianity?"

"Now, there's something to think about. Napoleon dressed in buckskin." We chuckle as I reach for my thermos of hot tea for two.

Allison has a surprise, sugar cookies she baked herself, wrapped prettily in a red tin box. She holds out the tin, remarking, "I'd like to know what made you so interested in Indian culture."

"I wondered why the beliefs of the Indians and the Europeans were so different from one another. What had happened in history to cause the differences? Why would two disparate cultures, that came to share the same geographical land mass have extremely opposite attitudes?"

"I see. You think all humans were like cave dwellers, and some changed much more than others. You wanted to know why the pioneers from Europe were anxious to build cities, roads, dams, and farms."

"Yes," I say slowly, "But more than that, why do the Indians call the Earth, Mother," while we say planet, or world?"

"I don't know. We never say mother planet, or mother world."

"The natives respected and revered nature because the prevailing perception was that they needed nature to survive."

"Do Americans now think they don't need nature?"

"Some, heck, most people behave as if they don't."

"Well," Allison proclaims confidently, "I know I do! But, you're right. I'd feel funny saying, Mother Earth, or Father Sky, around my friends. It's just not used, I don't know why."

"There was an attitude change. I used to ask my professors, 'Why?'

"Not one could answer me. Finally one said, 'Why don't you figure it out? Let me know what you find!'"

Allison leans closer, "Did you? Did you figure it out?"

"I do believe I did."

"You did? How? Did Miz tell you?" Allison asks, fascinated.

"Oh, she didn't know, either, but she encouraged me. I had to make many, many journeys away from my center and back, before I became satisfied with my own story. I had to learn the stories of many people I had never met, creating many dots and arrows, many collisions, and happy reunions at intersections."

"Have you gone back to tell the professor?"

"Who?"

"You know. The one who told you to answer your own question."

"Oh, him," I snicker, "I can't remember which one he was anymore."

"Oh. What kind of stories did you find? What did they teach you?" Allison urges me on—those big eyes brimming with curiosity—that most dangerous elixir of all mankind—the will to know, to know at all costs. The Indians thought too much curiosity could bring trouble; that it was better to not know everything; that forces more powerful than them were to be trusted. Nature could not be a fool, but people always behaved foolishly.

"I will tell you about a story that I found after returning from Osnaburgh. I was curious to know if the Ojibwe who resided there, had a creation story like the Christian one, but I didn't find it. Luckily, I found another one from the Sandy Lake Cree up on the Severn River. Like the Ojibwe, the Cree speak an Algonkian language, and many Ontario natives speak Oji-Cree—a mixture of both tongues. They have been acculturated in Canadian schools and society, however they retain many of their traditions like hunting, fishing, trapping and gathering plants. Therefore, they preserve an intimate connection with nature."

"Have you been there?" Allison asks, "Is it near Osnaburgh Lake?"

"No, it's so remote, it's 200 rugged miles further northwest. The Severn River flows 300 wide miles from Sandy Lake up to Hudson Bay."

"This Cree story probably dates back thousands of years, back before any written historic European creation myth, for it was rooted

102

in a time when all people were hunters and gatherers."

"You mean Europeans, too, like the Norwegians?"

"I like to think," I say cautiously, "that the Cree's ancient lifestyle must have been much like my forest-living Germanic predecessors who felt kinship with trees and bears, who believed that women had special, spiritual attributes, and could have as much, or more, power than men. Some could foretell the future by communicating with nature. Some of those females were even worshipped as living goddesses."

"Did the Sandy Lake Cree worship goddesses?"

"No. I do not believe so, however, I was delighted to discover that a female created the first life. Well, let me tell the legend as I learned it in the book *Sacred Legends of the Sandy Lake Cree* by James R. Stevens: Out of the first light came Omamama, the beautiful Mother of the Earth with long black hair who never grew old and was always kind and happy. Out of her womb came the spirits of the earth and sky. Her firstborn was Thunderbird who lives in the West, and who makes the rain, and protects the Cree people from a terrible sea serpent. Her second-born was Frog, who would be the shaman for all the other animals and would have control over the insects of the world. Third from Omamama's womb was Wasakayjack, who was in the form of an Indian, but had supernatural powers so he could take on the form of anything he desired. He is the trickster who always gets in and out of trouble, and causes children to listen and laugh . . ."

"And learn!" adds Allison, smiling.

"Many, many years after Omamama created Wasakayjack, he in turn, created the Cree people."

"*Ahhh*," exclaims Allison, "So a man, or a trickster, created the people. Right?"

"Right. Fourth-born was Wolf who would be companion to Wasakayjack. Fifth-born was Beaver who actually came from a different world where they had human characteristics. Omamama then brought forth from her womb all the birds, fish, insects, and other animals, and also the trees, flowers, and other plants. The spirits, plants, and animals had to learn to live on the earth in harmony before Indians were introduced, and so it took many years while the earth grew more beautiful and bountiful.

"Wasakayjack was living a happy life with plenty of food and the friendship of Wolf, but then he began to have troubling dreams that his friend had been killed by the serpent in the water. When he found it was true, he was very sad at heart, so he went to avenge the death by walking to the river and searching in the water. Kingfisher flew over to console him. Wasakayjack was very impatient with the antics of the bird and warned him, 'Go away,' but Kingfisher said, 'I know who the killer of Wolf is, the mean serpent in the river.' Wasakayjack was so grateful that he gave the bird a patch of gray and red fur from his clothing. He proudly wears this, even today.

"Wasakayjack climbed upon a log and went swirling into the fast waters of the river, fighting off serpents at each whirlpool he encountered until he was exhausted. He drifted upon the shore of an island where the same serpent that had killed Wolf, lived with his two serpent sons. As they slept in the sun, he crept up on them, and shot an arrow into the father. Before the others awoke, he ran back to the shore to the log.

"There he met Frog Shaman, arriving to save the life of the father. Wasakayjack offered to accompany him and be of assistance. When Frog Shaman wasn't looking, the supernatural Indian clubbed him on the head, skinned him, and slipped the skin over his own body. He then proceeded to the wounded father serpent and the two grieving sons who were expecting Frog Shaman. Wasakayjack cleverly explained that his medicine would only work in private. The sons willingly went off into the woods to wait. Meanwhile, Wasakayjack slit open the father, threw away his heart, and covered him with the frog skin. Feeling satisfied, he left.

"Then came a great flood when the lakes and rivers rose so high that the plants and animals began to die in great numbers. People suspected the serpents in the water. Perhaps they were causing the havoc. Wasakayjack stood on the last piece of earth—an island that was disappearing fast. He called the animals together to build a great canoe. The beavers cut down the last trees. The muskrats dove for roots to bind the logs together while the frogs chinked the sides with mud. The birds built a great big nest lined with feather down and while all the animals scrambled aboard, Wasakayjack completed the roof just in time, for the canoe lifted with the water as the island sank from sight and dark descended.

"The animals drifted in the sea and storms for many years, until one day the sun shone again. It was then that Wasakayjack realized he'd forgotten any earth out of which he could make another land. The beaver offered to dive underwater to find some mud, but he floated up dead without any. The otter tried, but he died, too. Wasakayjack tied a vine around the body of the muskrat and he went down, down, and down; but then the vine went limp, and when it was pulled up, the muskrat was dead, but in his tiny paws was a bit of mud. Wasakayjack boiled the mud in a clay pot till it flowed so far, it created a new earth. When the wolverine didn't return anymore, he knew there was enough space for everybody.

"Wasakayjack had a vision that there were many Indians like himself having a powwow, so he thought it would be nice to have people on the earth. He fired up his clay pot again by placing it on the back of the turtle, and with his hands he shaped one figure that was too black so he threw it across the ocean where it grew into a different race of people. He put more clay on the turtles back and began again, but this time the clay was too white, so he threw that to another land.

Finally, he made a nice healthy olive-brown color and decided to keep it right there.

"After Wasakayjack created humankind, he continued to have adventures and influence the behavior of men, women, and all the animals to live in balance and harmony with each other and with Omamama, the Earth Mother."

Allison and I are silent—contemplative, like a mother and daughter in church together after the sermon ends, before the next hymn. The minister tells us, "Turn to page forty for a song." The organist heaves herself into the tune, and we all join in. Well, our bodies do, if the sermon has been effective, and our minds are still absorbing the lesson.

"I love that legend. It sure is different than our creation story, isn't it?" says Allison, looking up at me, then at the pond, where the water around the cattails is beginning to freeze.

"It sure is different," I say, rubbing my hands together for warmth.

"I wonder how many creation stories, or legends, still exist around the world. Just think, all of them different!" she points out.

"There was a time when each culture had their own legend. That's a lot of creation stories. As far as I know, they were all rooted in the land where the people evolved, even specific places, mountains, rivers, valleys, and so on. People had constant reminders of what happened where, or what became of so-and-so by that rock. They took stories with them when they migrated, but they often changed them to fit the new location, to honor the new land. They changed to survive in a different place, rather than changing the place to please themselves.

"I mean, if you lived in Madagascar, and you moved to Alaska, and you were dependent on hunting and fishing, you'd probably want to start a spiritual relationship with polar bears, rather than monkeys. To be living in Alaska, and have a religion that originated in a foreign land seems odd to me."

"Are you referring to the Indians or whites, in Alaska?"

"I'm referring to both. And all. Christian, Buddhist, or Muslim, everyone. Natives believe spirituality originates in place, not people or ideology."

Allison says, "So you think all people should have a religion unique to where they live?"

"Yes. With stories about their natural life-giving land."

"But," argues Allison, "Omamama is a person who made the whole earth!"

"Omamama was born from light, and she made the spirits that live in the sky and on the earth, but she didn't make the sky and earth."

"Well, who did? What do the natives think?"

I chuckle, shake my head, and say, "I don't know what's in the minds of the Sandy Lake Cree, or anybody else. Just like, nobody knows what started the universe. I happen to agree with the Indians. It's a mystery. Sure, lots of Indians are Christians now, and perhaps they believe that God started it all, but that doesn't make it knowable. It just means that some Indians prefer a legend that originated far away, across a continent, across an ocean, in a land where people spoke Arabic, the language of the Muslim Koran, or Hebrew, the tongue of Semitic Jews centered around Israel; a legend about people who wear robes and turbans, eat pork, olives, and wheat bread, who live in hot deserts in stone homes, and who worshipped landmarks where they believed something has happened to somebody— something worth remembering—FOREVER."

"That part sounds like the Cree. They both had holy places, didn't they? The Cree and the Christians?"

"How many Cree Christians ever go to Israel, or know the names of five holy places over there? I'm willing to bet—not many."

Allison listens to me go on. "Think about the kingfisher's role in the Cree legend. He performed a good act, helping Wasakayjack find the serpent, and received a gift in return. Every Cree child who heard that story would think of that every time he or she sees a kingfisher bird. Why? Because they live *with* kingfishers! They are not going to relate to a temple they've never seen, nor ever will. Furthermore, the Cree legend includes *all* kingfishers, whereas *one* building carries importance—speaking metaphorically. Of course there are many historic buildings."

"I think," Allison says carefully, "You're telling me that religion is not very helpful, unless it's somehow tied to the land."

"Helpful for whom?"

"For people everywhere."

"There's more to it than that," I say, with finality that I hope does not sound rude, but I'm tired and hungry.

"Allison, the cold is beginning to chill my bones. My left ankle and foot feel it first. I need to warm my blood. Let's find a cozy, restaurant or coffeehouse for the next time we meet. Would you like that?"

"Oh yes. I'm sure! I'm sure we can think of one. This park bench is sure to be frozen with snow soon. Look at the sky to the west— might be a few inches of white, fluffy stuff by morning."

We head toward our cars, "I almost forgot," I tell Allison before opening the car door of my black Prius, "*Miigwech*, for the maple syrup!"

"I'm glad you like it!" she says in return, waving, as she sprints back toward school.

As I drive away, I'm once again visited by a familiar memory: that eureka moment, when I lay in bed reading the Bible, searching for answers. Why and when did humans begin to disdain anything wild? This occurs in the minds of early Near Eastern and European peoples. The Sandy Lake Cree origin myth was a clue to my answer, but first I had to read my own ancient history, and compare it to the Cree. Why did we change, and they didn't?

The most powerful impression I received from the Omamama legend was the belief that a single woman created all the spirits that made human life possible. She was kind! She was loving! She cared about all of life—not just humans. Oh, how I wish my Lutheran ancestors had discovered *her*, instead of a wrathful, warmongering man-god.

Chapter 13

SAND SOUP TASTES GOOD WHEN WITH FRIENDS

What does the term "Indian" mean?

University of St. Thomas

Thinking about my dear friend Dayshun, I'm surveying the heart of Minneapolis from my third-floor window at the University of St. Thomas, while waiting for students to file in for class. Snowflakes dip and glide, swirl and fly—graceful, yet aggressive, strong, yet weak, separate, yet connected.

Yes, I am like everything, and everything is like me. Feeling as though I'm a part of the cold story unfolding before me, makes me glow with warmth inside.

The city, slowing down under heavy layers of snow, like thick feather quilts, reminds me of Mother's quaint Christmas village that she arranged on the cotton-covered fireplace mantle: tiny Middle Ages' huts with curving rooftops, windows lit with wee candles, dwarfish figures surrounding a manger scene—baby Jesus, Mary, Joseph, a donkey.

Dayshun would never have such a scene in his home, or sweat lodge, up at *Asabekonezagagaiganing* (Nett Lake). I smile, imagining him tucked under the bright, comfortable, cozy quilt I stitched for him, plopped into his fat easy chair by the wood-fired pot-bellied stove, his freezer stuffed with ducks and moose he shot; his poor black lab mutt outdoors in his dog house listening for wolves—their haunting howls rolling across frozen Pelican Lake, rabbits on the move, mice burrowing under the snow, owls perched in branches.

I feel my spirit stirring. I want to jump in my car and head for the woods—any woods. Everywhere in Minnesota today would be a snowy magical kingdom of silence and peace.

I wonder: If no two snowflakes are alike, would no two soap flakes be alike? Would no two grains of sand be alike? *Hmmm*, yes, we're all separate identities, but when we work together, we can make a magnificent whole: a mountain of glaciers from melting snow, a washtub full of billowing soapy suds, a sparkling white beach of silica quartz sand.

"Good morning, Judy! How are you?"

Bob Erickson, the social studies teacher who has hired me for my job, arrives to set up the slide projector. His energy and enthusiasm for teaching reflects his deep love for learning, especially experiential learning, which is why he and his wife Sue have traveled to all corners of the globe, and are continuing into their retirement years, on bicycles, on camels, in rickshaws, and kayaks. I was lucky to be in Florida on an island where our paths crossed. (Remember the path of life that Miz taught to me.) Bob isn't at St. Thomas just to disseminate information. No, he wants everybody to know and appreciate our world, and love learning. He's very connected to each and every student with a concern for their individual interests, and he never ceases moaning about all the financial cuts for education, which he describes as a lack of respect for teachers and their profession. We chat about the paper handouts I will use today, and about the weather forecast, then he scurries back to his office, saying, "I'll pop my head in after class to say goodbye."

During my introduction to the students, I say, "Any teacher who wants to educate children about indigenous people, must understand the vast diversity of their cultures. Therefore, we will have an overview of comparative artistic expressions created by tribes from Alaska to Arizona, and California to New York, with a strong emphasis on our own Midwest region. We'll look for similarities and differences over time.

"Native expressions continue to reflect a closeness to nature. However, after European contact, materials from trading, and ideas about artistic expressions caused an expansion of Indian art. Today, we can find ancient ideas produced next to modern art using the latest technology. Indeed, there really is no such thing as Indian art—only art created by individuals, just like any other artist. The term Indian is not what any of the indigenous people of the Americas call themselves, therefore we should identify them by what they call themselves. Also, many of these people have their own nation, such as Mohawk Nation.

"If you want to be correct, remember that the Dakota live in the Minnesota area, the Lakota in the Dakotas, and the Nakota near the Rocky Mountains. They share a similar language.

"Now that I've said all that, I do still hear natives refer to themselves, or each other as Sioux; or perhaps Chippewa, Ojibwe, or Anishinaabe. Ojibwe is another form of Chippewa, whereas Anishinaabe means, "human-Indian, or Ojibwe speaking person.""

Katherine raises her hand, "Why is it so important that we use one name or another? I mean, I think saying Indian Art is fine."

"This is a very complicated and confusing topic. I asked several native artists what they felt about all this, and wrote a paper about it, which I'll share with you. Read it, and we'll have a short discussion in the future."

It is break time. Students disappear down the hall while I observe the fluffy white stuff accumulating outside the window.

I recall driving through life-threatening storms between Grand Forks and Minneapolis. Today, I'll have a tough drive home. I love my new Prius, but it doesn't love ice. I believe the storm is coming from

North Dakota, a thought that reminds me of my oldest son who played hockey when we lived there. His team won the Grand Forks City Championship. Leonard also had a lead part in a play at school. My daughter, Lisa danced a solo number to the song "I am Woman," in an evening performance. Johnny showed a flair for the unusual when he took his dad's *Playboy* magazine to show-and-tell in first grade. He was the one who kept us laughing. Heath liked his one year in half day nursery school, and we loved attending movie afternoons at the university, especially the comedies. We had to hold onto our folding chairs to keep from falling off when Buster Keaton was featured—we laughed ourselves silly.

After we moved back to the Twin Cities, we had memories of many great going-away parties, and tried to stay connected to our North Dakota friends by traveling to visit them. Jodi and Joe returned to Boston; Tom, to Regina, Saskatchewan, then on to Japan; Clair and Jim moved to North Carolina; Dick and Avis to Wisconsin; George, Brady's good friend, a musician with a brilliant mind, moved to Evergreen, Colorado. All these Doctor of Education students went on to have successful careers in teaching. All, except my husband.

Two true flower-love-children, Ira and Sherry, who had done their student teaching at Fort Totten, decided to get married before they left town, fearing disapproval from at least one parent. Ira was Jewish, and Sherry was not. Ira was from the French Quarter in New Orleans; Sherry from inner-city New York. Cross-cultural marriages were very controversial in those days, especially black-and-white unions; but even religious differences caused disapproval—Catholics shouldn't marry Lutherans. Indians should marry Indians, and so on.

We drove to Fort Totten on the Spirit Lake Indian Reservation, not far from the site of the powwow where my heart had been stolen by the sound of a Lakota drum. There, Ira and Sherry celebrated a genuine hippie wedding with a crowd of friends from far and wide.

Ira had built an oak arbor in a wooded clearing by the lake shore, festooned with colorful wild flowers, pink and blue silk ribbons, and prairie sage. We joined together in a line to follow the giddy couple on a path to the arbor where we stood in a circle while George played his guitar and sang. She wore white cotton. He wore a creamy gauze loose shirt and new blue jeans. Vows were repeated while their wrists were tied together by a red ribbon—Dakota style. (When eagles mate, they lock talons and do a free-fall in the sky—signifying trust).

We took turns sharing kind words to honor the couple, then broke the circle to enjoy a hearty communal feast with food, spirits, and songs, until nightfall when we held hands and pranced around a blazing fire.

Back in Minneapolis, the newlyweds pulled up one day in their pickup truck. They were on their way to Arkansas. In the back of the pickup was a gift—a horse! A Pinto pony for Lisa, our sweet, horse-loving daughter. She named her brown and white pony Thunder for the west direction where he'd been born at Spirit Lake Reservation. We found a stable while Lisa got a paper route, delivering newspapers to help pay for her horse. Her hard work was rewarded when she won a ribbon in barrel racing. We were all so proud of her.

That night the kids slept while we sat around the round oak kitchen table, reminiscing about Ira and Sherry's fun honeymoon, which had been our gift to them, a week in the Boundary Waters Canoe Area Wilderness, in wild Minnesota. Ira and Sherry had never been in a canoe before, nor eaten a fresh wild blueberry pie, nor seen a bear.

We seemed to get along together very well, but the next thing Ira said startled my imagination, "How would you like to join our commune?"

Husband and I shot a look at each other, then back at our friends. A level of excitement rose in their faces as they hurriedly described their dream. My heart sank deeper with each new revelation, however, not so for Husband—he was swallowing the "acid"!

They had purchased rural farmland in Arkansas where they planned to teach, and run a communal chicken farm. Ira had enough savings to buy the chickens, and the profit from their sales would buy more for the next year. We were the first people they had invited, but they had friends from New York and New Orleans who were interested. We would all have to live in one building until we built another one.

When I pressed them for more information, I learned they had bought the place "sight-unseen," and were on their way there. Undaunted, my husband gushed, "This sounds wonderful! Judy, let's go see it!"

I quietly replied, "How far is it from town?"

"Well," Sherry replied, in her soft sweet voice, "I don't know, but we wouldn't want to hang out with *them* anyway, would we?"

I wasn't sure what she meant, but another red flag had been raised. It was my duty to put a stop to this nonsense. Therefore I, who was older, and questionably wiser; and who loved Indians, but would not live in a teepee, spoke up, "I lived a hippie lifestyle before the term existed," I cautioned, "And it's a lot of hard work!"

I told the story of how we had moved to a dairy, hog, and mink farm right out of high school and lived in a trailer in near-poverty while Husband got a teaching degree and I raised two babies. I went on to describe how we'd managed to build a nice two-story house on a wooded lot in a suburban neighborhood with dock rights on Lake Minnetonka. I assured them that farm living had been a valuable experience, but I disliked being poor, and far away from family.

But Husband insisted that we go see Arkansas some day. Little did I know how soon some day would be.

During that summer, I returned to UND to earn physical geology credits, which meant I'd do a field trip to the Black Hills. Husband took the station wagon and four kids to a friend's cabin, and I was allowed to drive his newly purchased red Corvette, an antique with dubious distinction. So dubious, that I drove it to a garage to see if it was safe enough to make the long solo journey to Grand Forks.

Driving over to Lou's on Long Lake, I was still furious that my mate had bought such an extravagant toy, when I had to scrimp and save to make ends meet. He always found cash to go hunting, fishing, and boating with the guys, but I had to paint house exteriors for tuition.

I loved Lou—kind, fat mechanic in greasy bib overalls who always had a joke for me. We stood over the Corvette, which had a pretty good body, while Lou removed his cap, scratched his head, spat on the floor, and gave me his diagnosis. Looking more at the car, than at me, he wearily said, "Let me put it this way, honey," spitting again, like he had something bad to say, "If you were my wife, I wouldn't even let you ride in it. Do you know what's holding this thing together? Coat hangers! Underneath, its full of coat hangers. Lot of money to fix it up. Can't do it fast enough for you to use it. Sorry, honey."

He was embarrassed for me. I felt angry and desperate.

"Can't you just fix the worst parts? I mean, it does run," I pleaded.

"Well, if you drive real slowly, and stop for fresh air often enough, and don't take it any further than you have to . . . ."

"Oh, I can do all that! Thank you, Lou!"

He shook his head, "Well, don't blame me if . . . ."

"Don't worry. I won't."

I made it—crawling along for 300 miles to Grand Forks, choking on exhaust fumes that sought to kill me. It was pouring rain, yet I had to keep a window open.

On a perfect summer day, I joined other geology students as we traveled in a van toward the western part of North Dakota, stopping for the evening to camp near Mandan. I felt so free. It may have been the first time in my life that I traveled anywhere by myself—that is, without children or family.

Beyond the clearing where we'd pitch our tents, the tall grass prairie beckoned, luring us to explore, so we followed a leader, single file, off into the waving reeds, higher than my head. The scent was alluring, like the earth itself was rising up to meet me, as I plodded on, keeping track of the person in front of me, who abruptly yelled out, "Watch out for the barbed wire fence!"

Too late! I felt a sharp slice on my shin like a knife cutting my leg down to the bone. I dropped to the ground. A nasty gash, five inches long, began gathering blood. A silent panic began to spread among the surrounding students who had heard my cry. Keeping my cool, (four kids teaches you that), I held my leg as high as I could and asked for a dry T-shirt and a belt. As the intrusion grew bloodier, I wrapped the shirt around it, then held it tightly as someone secured it with the belt.

Two guys offered to drive me to the Mandan Hospital in the van. Speeding down the freeway, one of them said, "Too bad we don't have any whiskey to sterilize her wound or dull her pain."

I lay in the back on the floor with my leg raised. "I have a pint of brandy in my backpack. Help yourself. I brought it to share with coffee around the campfire," I offered. But they said they were driving, so I drank a few swallows and left the bottle in the van.

The doctor who stitched me up was interested in fossilized ginkgo leaves or trees, so we had a stimulating conversation about geology, and soon I was on my way.

The guys were full of jokes and kept me laughing all the way back to camp, where I discovered they'd drunk all the brandy while I was on the operating table!

The hair-like scar on my leg is a reminder of that summer of '73. While the Native Americans were staging protests around the country, and going on extended walks seeking support, the nation was riveted on the Watergate Hearings. (This was back in the days when congressmen and women still had a sense of legal morality and constitutional intent, and demanded standards of themselves—as high as those forced on the public—values that "went missing" after the year 2000.) President Nixon told lie after lie, digging a deeper and deeper hole, until on August 8, 1974, he became the first president to resign in office. Gerald Ford became the next leader of the nation.

In the fall of 73, I entered the University of Minnesota with a goal of being accepted into the College of Education a year later. I studied very intensely to receive good grades, and I took extension division classes so I could be at home with children, while Husband continued teaching high school.

We planned a family winter vacation to see the Arkansas farm, and also the sunny Florida Keys to visit Nick, who had gone to Outward Bound Classes with Dad, and who had since moved away with a new wife, leaving Pam with two infants to raise alone. I felt angry with Nick, but Pam wasn't. She said the world needed more love—that anger was not the answer—although she was devastated and hurt. I thought the world needed a whole lot more common sense.

Several people we knew were getting divorced, yet I seemed to be the only one with a truly good reason to do so. Others simply said they couldn't relate to each other anymore! They weren't being punched around occasionally. They weren't from a divorced family like me who suffered the pain. I didn't want that for my kids.

The snowfall over Minneapolis is becoming a blizzard. My students return. They stand before me with hopeful faces, asking me if they can leave early. Slipping out of my reverie to make a decision, I say, "Wouldn't it be nice to be in Florida today?"

They grin at me. Some say, "Yes!" while others say, "NO! This is great for skiing."

I add, "And for Mother Earth. Minnesota's summers are becoming too hot and too dry. Okay, Go. Drive carefully. We'll discuss the meaning of Indian art next time."

Bob Erickson thrusts his head inside the room, "I see you let them go home early. Good idea. You better go, too. You'll need more than an hour to drive home today! Bye!"

Chapter 14
TALK TO THE TREES
Why can't people create new stories that work better in today's world?

Signature Café, Saint Paul, Minnesota

The heavenly scent of brewing coffee and baking bread greets me, as I stop to brush the snow off my thick-soled boots in the doorway of the Signature Cafe, an intimate, reliable eatery I love to share with friends. I settle into a quiet corner table with a view of the Prospect Park neighborhood to await the arrival of Allison.

No mansions in sight. No other businesses, either. Rather, stately homes aging gracefully under fresh paint, all huddled close together in the snow, lining short hillside streets. Quite unlike most of the Twin Cities grid system laid down on the gently rolling prairie. Close by is the Mississippi River and the University of Minnesota, my alma mater.

Shall I order the salmon salad, or the crab cakes? Wine or tea? Gone are the days of beef tips in rich Béarnaise sauce—I must watch my cholesterol.

Allison breezes through the door, her infectious smile and positive energy fill the room, reminding me of my youth when there was always the future in which to start anew.

She cautions, "Can't stay long, but I have a day off next week."

We chat about weather and radio shows. I tell her the cafe is advertised on the radio, 950 KTNF-AM, a station for progressive politics with Thom Hartmann's show. I met him at a Signature Cafe party and recommend his book to Allison: *The Last Hours of Ancient Sunlight.*

After we order lunch, Allison says, "I've been thinking about the Cree story you told me about Omamama, the Mother of the Earth, and

Wasakayjack, the supernatural male Indian who eventually created the Cree people." She throws up her hands, saying, "Gee, that story is sooo different than the Bible. I mean, we think the earth was made in seven days! The Cree don't say that, do they? Do they even know about the Bible? If they did, wouldn't they think their story must be wrong?"

"What do *you* think, Allison?"

"I've been raised a Lutheran, but science proves that the earth, and the universe are millions and billions of years old! The Bible must be wrong. I suppose the Cree aren't right or wrong, because they don't claim to know."

"I know for sure," I begin, "that the Cree, and every native in the world, learned about Christianity, eventually. I used to sit on the floor of the Wilson Library at the 'U' in the anthropology section, reading original texts written by missionaries, like Jesuit priests writing to superiors in France with counts of numbers of souls saved and numbers of native deaths; battle reports carefully recorded that proved the success of making areas safe for settlement, things you'll never hear in grade school Thanksgiving curriculum."

Allison shakes her head, "I hope to learn more of this. I bought some books at the bookstore about Indian history."

"Please also search for the original text. It's always more exciting to read unedited history, however, beware—not all of it is accurate. The male ego tends to inflate heroic deeds. Ha! There's no better example than the Bible."

We laugh vigorously, and loudly, Allison adding, "You're right!"

Our server takes our lunch order and refills our cups with tea and coffee.

"The first explorers claimed the Indian's land for European kings. Traveling with them were the priests who stayed to build the missions and 'tame the savages' through conversion to Christ. Next came the traders who robbed them of all their natural wealth in exchange for rum; and the cavalry that murdered, or herded them onto reservations with the worst land; and then the government officials who signed treaties they never intended to honor. Those who survived disease and starvation left the reservations to hunt for food, but were caught, then shipped in shackles to faraway prisons. Surviving children were removed from parents and shipped to Christian boarding schools where molestation was common, where they were punished for speaking their own language, where they 'became like white people.' Many Indian parents gave up their own children 'for a better life.' After all this, the reservations were often divided into family land plots, which was another government ploy, because individual families, desperate for money, sold off acres to whites who then built summer lake homes. Indians moved into the cities amongst the poor people, and having lost faith in their own customs, they became ashamed of any of their own members who practiced the old ways."

"Whoa!" Allison says, stopping me, "I've never learned this in my schools—well, perhaps I didn't want to know. I feel guilty."

"Me, too. I don't know which was worse—slavery of Africans, or the genocide of Indians, who, by the way, could not be enslaved, which is why blacks were brought over from Africa."

We eat in silence. I have never learned to control my passion on this subject, and I don't intend to, so I don't apologize for saying what needs to be said. I'm thankful that so many natives now have a much better life, and I'm grateful for the efforts and sacrifices of those who fought to create those changes—brave men and women.

Allison speaks up again, "I think of my parents as practicing Catholics, yet they view the Bible as religious poetry. They say it has lots of wisdom and is a worthwhile guide for morals, although Mother practiced birth control. However, they've never even read most of the Bible. I guess they pick the parts they like."

"Very, very few Christians have ever read the Bible, so I don't know how they can base any kind of truth, or reality upon it."

"If it's mostly myths, isn't it just like the Ojibwa story? I mean, do the Cree really believe in supernatural Indians and frogs that can talk? Do they?" asks Allison.

"I don't know, but is it any different than Christians believing in angels—humans that fly in the sky, or a man who can walk on water, or all of creation appearing in seven short days?"

I let her think on it, then ask, "Don't you think the Cree story really happened?"

"No! Do you? I mean, we have science now. Why would the Cree believe?"

"I don't know, and I don't know what the Ojibwe think. I can only guess that they, just like us, created a perception, or a worldview, that reflected their experience with nature at that time—whenever that was. I know that traditionalists don't agree that their people originated in Asia. Rather, they began on the land they now inhabit. So, you see, science has challenged all cultural beliefs—not just Christian ones."

"Why," Allison says thoughtfully, "Why can't people just create new stories that work better in today's world?"

"Traditions give people identity and security in a group. Shared ideas give us strength and comfort, and we need meaning in our lives, guidance in some form or other. A lot of folks are willing to suspend scientific evidence to retain all that."

"I suppose," Allison says slowly, "That's why so many people are searching for a religion they like, kind of like finding the story that suits them, or the people they feel at home with."

"After Miz taught me about the map with dots and arrows, I've always thought of me as on a journey within the entire cosmos, and my purpose is to create relationships. It's not a religion, rather a simple way to think. I'm a story within a story, and so are you. We research

123

the tales of those who came before us to understand their worldview."

"And," adds Allison, "some of us change those stories to suit new, and often selfish, needs—like reinterpretations of the Bible."

"When I became interested in native cultures," I begin, "I wondered if a story existed in Euro-Western, or Near Asian lands, that predated the Bible. I wondered if tree and animal worship lasted right up to Biblical times." I hesitate, "You see, Miz told me to talk to the trees when I couldn't solve a personal problem. I began to sit with the same maple tree until I got my answer, but I also learned that the tree didn't need me as much as I needed that tree, and that trees can teach us about life in many ways. And they never do stupid things."

Allison leans back, delighted, "I have a favorite tree, too—and a favorite rock. They have known me all my life." She giggles.

"Do you like the salmon salad?" I ask, trying to lighten up.

"*Nummy*. Yes, it's real tasty," Allison says brightly, and then, "May I ask, what happened to Miz, and the group that went to that powwow?"

"Oh! We went to another powwow the next summer, outside of Thunder Bay, Canada, on Mount McKay, 1,000 feet above Lake Superior on a ledge, where we pitched our tents with a breathtaking view of the horizon.

"That's where I met Eddy Cobiness, an artist seated before his tent, creating professional sketches with black ink on artist's paper. I told him about the show I'd attended at the Walker Art Center in Minneapolis, titled 'American Indian Art—Form and Tradition.' The show was huge, covering all mediums of traditional expression north of Mexico: baskets, masks, blankets, weapons, even sand painting and a tipi.

"Eddy said he was an Ojibwa from Manitoba, a member of a prestigious group of seven contemporary Canadian Indian painters who were then achieving national acclaim for their abstract art.

"Eddy said he'd like to have a show in the States." I advised him about our architecturally fabulous new Native American Center in Minneapolis, and offered to send him information."

Allison motions for the server, reminding me we have to finish our cake and leave. She says politely, "Excuse me, but I have to get the kids. Let's have a long leisurely afternoon next week. Okay? Was Cobiness the beginning of your Indian art interest?"

"I suppose so. That fall, Roger, another "Miz groupie," and I arranged a show of fifty-five works of art with Eddy in attendance. We had great press coverage, thanks to Roger, so the show continued at General Mills Headquarters, followed by another that winter at the First National Bank of Minneapolis Public Gallery. That show included all seven Canadian artists.

"People wanted to buy the work, but Eddy lived way up on Buffalo Point Reserve, so Roger and I became temporary representatives."

"Sounds like work, and fun!" Allison notes, pulling on her jacket.

"It sure was, but I met so many interesting, influential people. By the way, although you're class with me has ended, would you like to continue our meetings?"

"Yes, I sure would. Thanks a lot," gushed Allison, "See you soon!"

Chapter 15
PAPAGOS, MORMONS, AND HYPOCRITES
Why did the Papagos need to become Mormons?

Signature Cafe

The Signature Cafe bustles with diners, the early luncheon crowd chatters as Allison and I slip into our corner table, ordering coffee and tea. (I sip copious amounts all day long at home.) Her car is being repaired—the mechanic says it won't be fixed until morning—thus we settle in for a leisurely afternoon.

My lovely, smart student-mother acquaintance is becoming a friend whom I appreciate because I'm growing old and have many stories to pass on to someone who wants to hear them.

"I'm sure curious about your pendant," Allison says shyly, "It looks like a circular maze."

"Yes, it's not the loon from Osnaburgh. Oh my! So many things happened to me after Roger—my university friend and member of Miz's Indian 'wannabe' group, after he traded this neckpiece with me during my last year in school. I gave him a painting I made. It was like a chain reaction, like the connections didn't stop coming."

We sip our drinks as I caution Allison, "Are you up for a long story? Or, should I make it brief? Of course, that's impossible for me."

"Oh no! I want to hear it all, if you have time," she says eagerly.

"*Hmmm.* Well, let's see. I wore my maze pendant to a reception where I met a Hopi man who was studying at Macalaster College to become the tribal treasurer for the Hopi Nation in Arizona. Perhaps because I was wearing the maze; or for whatever reason, he invited me to go to his village and attend corn dances that very spring. I made a plan to travel, meet his family, study Indian Art, and interview artists

126

for my senior thesis. Another woman I hardly knew, fluent in several languages, had a family friend in Southern Arizona, and after finishing her Dakota class, which is where we met, she was going down there to visit them on the Papago Indian Reservation, where her friend was a Mormon missionary who was currently superintendent of schools.

"Well, Allison, *that* certainly got my attention, so I invited her to ride along with me and share expenses. Little did I know how badly that plan would work out," I exclaim, rolling my eyes and shaking my head.

"She didn't ruin my trip at all, but things did not go well between us, unfortunately. Katrina was slightly shorter than my five-foot-five inches, had long hair, almost black, whereas mine is auburn; had a milky-white, freckled complexion, compared to my easily tanned olive skin; and mischievous brown eyes, unlike my hazel-green ones. She said she was from Europe; related to the Rothschild's in France; raised in Lapland where her father was a journalist and writer; that she was part Eskimo (her word), and hoped to meet a nice Eskimo boy on the trip to the Southwest. I had told her I'd be visiting the Institute for American Indian Arts, which had students from all over the United States, including Alaska. She hardly appeared more Indian than I, with zero Indian blood, but talked as though she was proud to be an Indian. Katrina was studying Lakota, adding it to the other nine languages she knew."

"Sounds like an interesting person," Allison says.

"She wasn't dull company, and I figured that as long as her imagination didn't get us into trouble, it would be nice to have some companionship. Also, we were both living 'on a shoe string' and didn't mind sleeping in dorms or with friends along the way—like on the Hopi and the Papago rez."

"I had warned Katrina that I had a long list of artists to meet, and an intensive itinerary to complete within a limited amount of time because I had to get back to my children who were being watched by a husband from whom I was separated, and who didn't plan to stick around longer than we had agreed."

"The first artist we met was R.C. Gorman in his studio in Taos, New Mexico, a famous painter of Navajo women and landscapes. The next day, at the Institute for American Indian Arts, we met several more artists, including an Eskimo that Katrina became fond of as we remained in Santa Fe for four days, learning a wealth of information. Then we were off to visit Pueblo villages, including Santo Domingo where I met a jewelry artist and her mother, Judy and Rose Rosetta, (women I would see again in thirty-two years). At Zuni, we slept in the car on the edge of the Pueblo village by a modern school."

"Geese! I've slept in a car before, " says Allison, "That's no fun."

"It was okay. I had a small sleek, dark-green Chevy Vega with seats that folded down for sleeping, but I lay awake for hours mesmerized by the moonlight radiating down on a majestic plateau rising out of the flat desert. Shadows on the cliff face changed continuously. I followed moonbeams till I fell fast asleep, my tired head on my arm, the left arm with the wrist that always wore my most precious possession, a silver-and-turquoise needlepoint bracelet that my husband gave me after his trip to Zuni years before. I slept with earth, air, water and fire out of which my bracelet was formed."

"Wow," cooed Allison, "I'd like to see it sometime."

I lowered my head, and sighed, "It's gone, and I still miss it. I don't want to talk about it. The memory makes me sad."

"I'm sorry you lost it," she said with sympathy from her heart.

"Actually, it was stolen, but that's another story." I hesitate, "I have always hoped to have another one; but I'd like it made by the same person, because I believe that the creator of an object puts his or her mind into their work, and it remains with it forever, like a kind of energy, or power. Most things made today have no power like that. Only a few people understand what I'm talking about. It's all part of the connecting, giving-away system of the universe."

"Have you ever been to the Southwest?" I ask Allison, as we order lunch, "I fell in love with it."

"Nope. Sure would like to go some day."

"I think it's such a sacred land, full of beauty and people who still try to live the old values, against increasing odds. They have such courage and perseverance."

"So far, you seem to be having a pretty good time with Katrina."

"Ah, Katrina! The trouble started when we arrived at Sells, Arizona, but on the way there we visited Fort Apache and McNary where most of the residents worked in a lumber mill, the Fort Apache Timber Company. At White River, tribal headquarters, we passed the Theodore Roosevelt Apache Boarding School built out of dull red adobe bricks, with bars on all the windows. One mile later, we stopped at the Seven Mile Elementary School where Apache children ran up from the playground to greet us. Next, we drove by the East Fork Mission, a Lutheran founded organization."

"Lutheran? Gee, hard for me to imagine Geronimo's family as Lutheran!"

"Oh, Allison, everywhere we went was stunningly beautiful, rich red mountains, ancient gnarled cedars, stately towering pines, black volcanic sands, and endless sky. A paradoxical paradise, truly a land of vibrant contrasts, rushing wide rivers or arid arroyos, vast blue horizons with golden-red sunsets or cold gray skies.

"Vegetation seemed to grow sparely, yet considering the scarcity of water, the desert was relatively lush with amazing diversity. The Sonoran region reaches far down into Mexico. The land of Minnesota with 20,000 lakes has few exposed rocks compared to the Southwest where the earth's crust lies open to interpretation, as though the bare essentials of existence are all that support any life. This makes each plant more deserving of our attention and reminds us how fragile and strong life is, for so much of the beauty has not changed for millions of years. The people know this and are fiercely proud of their unchanging, yet changing, land."

"What about the people?" Allison asks me, "How are they different than Minnesota Indians?"

"I hadn't gotten to know them yet, but I soon would! Leaving Tucson, it was 84 degrees outside. The sun blinded my eyes as I steered my sporty, compact Vega along Highway 86, crossing the second-largest reservation in the USA, then named Papago (now known as Tohono O'odham) where 9,000 Tohono O'odham lived in small scattered settlements, mostly at the ends of dirt roads. The farms and green irrigated fields of Tucson fell far behind, while the desert rolled away in all directions toward lavender-blue mountains.

"Katrina had agreed to drive half the time, saying she could operate my stick shift, but this turned out to be not true, and she wasn't willing to learn, so after driving all the way from Zuni in one day, I was extremely tired when I stopped the car on the narrow asphalt road on the edge of Sells. The place felt deserted. It was so still; then a lone bird greeted us from somewhere, perhaps from the cottonwoods that grew sporadically among adobe homes ahead of us.

"Across the highway was a small police station with a telephone on an outside wall. Katrina crossed the street to phone the McLaughlin's, her friends who were expecting us for the night or longer.

"The night air chilled me, and I felt lonely for my children. Prickly pear cactus along the ditch discouraged me from getting out to stretch my legs. I yawned and closed my eyes, chuckling as I recalled how Katrina had flirted with an old Apache guy that morning, telling him that she was looking for an Apache boyfriend, and that she herself was

Indian. He was politely amused, joining us in some good-hearted laughter. I reminded her later that she was looking for an Eskimo (someone closer to her own kind). She replied that there may not be enough of them in Arizona to choose from.

"Katrina got back in the car saying that no one had answered the phone. We decided to try to locate the house.

"A glorious sunset splashed the bland adobe buildings in pinks and purples, but no one was outside to see it—no action on the unpaved, dusty streets of Sells. We drove up and down, back and forth, seeing no street lights or lights within homes in darkening Sells. Slowly, we again passed by the police station, which had one bare bulb lit over the front door, then turned a corner, easing our car over the bumps down another street. Katrina cried 'Stop!' as she compared the numbers on her scrap of paper to the ones on a stone pillar by the curb. 'That must be it,' she said. A sign proclaimed: The Official Home of the Superintendent of Schools for the Papago Indian Reservation.

"I stared at it in great wonder, for it was quite different than the neighboring homes on the streets: A tall chain-link fence with barbed wire on top protected a perfectly flat, flawless, green lawn and a neat house with polished glass windows. Inside the metal gate a surly, growling, hungry German shepherd dog snarled warnings at us. Silently, I watched him salivate, until a neighbor, a man with white skin and red hair, opened his screen door to yell that he knew the McLaughlin's had gone to Tucson, but would return in a couple of hours.

"We thanked him, I felt glad to drive away, and if Sells had a motel, I'd have headed straight for it. Instead, we drove back to our friendly public phone and waited, feeling safe by the police station. My legs felt stiff and cramped, forcing me onto the street for a hike.

"In the glow of a few street lamps, I wandered past homes huddled together, or scattered about—no main street in evidence. The houses were either constructed of pinkish-brown adobe bricks, or if they were made of wood, they were caked with years of earth blown against their sides. I'd seen photographs of desert dwellers squatting by stick and mud tips, or living in caves, and these homes appeared substantial in comparison.

"Discarded automobiles, assorted scrap heaps, old plastic toys, and clumps of sage, grass or flowers sprinkled the townscape. The place didn't feel threatening or sad. It was like a poor, but unapologetic, village that had always been that way. How could anything feel run down when it had survived so long? Yes, I was among survivors.

"The newest buildings I saw were the school and police station. We were only about thirty miles from the Mexican border, and I wondered if the duties of the police officers had more to do with that fact than with the town itself. There was no bar or restaurant. Perhaps that's why it was so quiet. Then, why did the McLaughlin's need a fierce guard dog?

"Returning to my car, it occurred to me that a Minnesota license plate could be an object of suspicion. Katrina was dozing with her seat adjusted back. The car clock read ten o'clock p.m. I studied the stars and watched a pickup truck cruise by whose occupants were 'checking us out.'

"Flipping on my miniature flashlight, I read information from a pamphlet. Nearby, there were Catholic, Protestant, and Mormon missionaries serving mixed-bloods, full bloods, converts, and pagan Papago and Pima natives. The Pimas are close cousins to the Papago. They both speak a tongue related to the Aztecs, and have occupied that area for over nine thousand years. The Pimas, who live in the semi-arid river valleys, are the oldest, continuous human inhabitants north of Mexico. The Papago, living in the arid deserts undisturbed for most of their past, remained, even during the Ice Age along lakes and streams under cottonwoods and hickory trees, hunting mammoths and wolves that long ago disappeared. By the middle of the sixteenth century most tribes of the Southwest lived right where the Spanish found them—some in permanent villages with elaborate irrigation systems for growing corn, beans, and squash which they brought up from Mexico.

"Evolving from the desert archaic cultures of Mexico were three related traditions: the Magellan or Western Pueblo, the descendent and more widespread Anasazi Pueblo of the northern Southwest, and the Hohokam who were restricted to the Salt and Gila River drainages of southern Arizona. The Zuni of today may be descended from the Mogollon, and the Papago from the Hohokam. The Papago were called the Bean people for all the beans they grew, and they are famous for making baskets and pottery. Katrina's next phone call produced good luck. We drove back to the McLaughlins', relieved when we saw that the nasty dog was safely in the house.

"As I parked the car, my headlights framed a scene right out of my first grade reading book, *Dick and Jane*. Mr. and Mrs. McLaughlin, waiting under a bright yard light by the gate, waved cheerfully at us— their darling angelic daughter by their side, wearing a pretty white dress under a crispy cotton pink print pinafore, a satin ribbon in her curly hair. Father wore a suit and tie, Mother, a frilly summer dress. Puff, the kitten was probably asleep in a silk basket. Dick, the son, was perhaps at Wakalaga Lodge summer camp learning Indian crafts. (Spot, the dog, was the necessary scapegoat, protecting the surreal perceptions of his owners.)

"Little Sally" silently watched while Katrina exchanged hugs, compliments and news, during which I learned that my hosts were missionaries whom she'd never met before! They had mutual friends who were missionaries back East, who they discussed with enthusiastic pleasantries before they turned to me, making me feel welcome.

"We carried our bags into the house, after which the guard dog was returned to his post by the gate. I felt like I'd entered a spotless furniture display in a Sears Roebuck store in Lincoln, Nebraska: deep orange, shaggy carpet, new "colonial" furniture, a TV set with a large screen, a framed print of Jesus over the couch, a modern kitchen with wood cabinets, and an air conditioning unit set into a window, running full blast, although it wasn't too hot outside. Mrs. McLaughlin led me to 'Sally's' room, left me alone, then led Katrina down the hall to her own room. Mother had showed me where to find extra blankets if I got cold because they never opened windows!

"I plopped down on the bed, desperate for sleep, knowing I had to return to the living room to become acquainted. The soft mattress felt so good, unlike the hard bed in the car. The pink-and-white room was sugar and spice and everything nice. Sally's bed reminded me of my childhood friend, Diane. We were not allowed to sit on her bed. It was like a picture for viewing only.

"My bedroom, when I was Sally's age, had displays of bones, bird's nests, bugs in jars, stacks of comics, Nancy Drew books, crayons, paints, paper, a chalk board, an old sewing machine, a basket full of fabric scraps next to a doll for whom I sewed new dresses. The hardwood floor had woven rugs, and the walls were papered with pale blue. Two large windows overlooked a typical post-World War II suburban backyard with a separate garage, a clothesline, swing set, sand box, and small garden. My dad and Uncle Bud had built our Cape Cod-style house on former farm land that became a subdivision, with access to a streetcar line to downtown Minneapolis.

"I rose from the bed, crossed the fuzzy white carpet, thinking how different this was from my life and from the Papago's lives, too.

"Entering the living room again; seeing all the windows closed with heavy drapes, I realized nothing inside was a reminder of outside. I felt that the McLaughlins found the desert unpleasant; that perhaps they'd rather be somewhere else. I bet they wished they lived in Tucson."

Allison, patiently listening to my long story, cocks her head, saying, "Well, what were they like? I don't know anything about Mormon missionaries except they like to collect birth records."

"They were polite to me, as we sat around a wooden coffee table with coffee, ice cold Kool-Aid, and peanut butter bars. The McLaughlins were just over middle age, lively conversationalists, and except for their choice of living location—they were like mainstream, middle class, conservative Americans. Having the attention of the school superintendent seemed like a great source of information, because I desired to ask questions about the local natives."

Allison stops me, "Did you ask him about the Mormons?"

"I was curious about their personal perceptions as Christians, but I decided to keep my feelings about proselytizing to myself. I was, after all, a guest in their home, which I appreciated. Anyway their talk focused upon Katrina, and the works of the mission at other Indian reservations, which I listened to, then let my thoughts wander until I grew very tired, and decided to excuse myself and go to bed. However, Mr. McLaughlin suddenly asked me who I was.

"I explained that I was a student at the University of Minnesota, studying art created by living artists who were indigenous Americans who worked in a contemporary style. I didn't tell him that my other goal was to learn how they think about their world. Nor did I mention my leather maze pendant that lay safely in my purse.

"He rose from the couch, went into another room, and returned with a book. He was a big man with a pink face and jet-black hair combed back. I saw that his hands were smooth and unflawed when he placed the book on my lap with a flourish, saying, 'This is the finest book ever written about American Indians, a Time-Life publication, part of a series on the Old West. This one is titled, *The Great Chiefs.*

"While he carried on about its virtues, I glanced inside the front and back and found no indication of Indian authorship. I then asked him about a few books I had read, and he'd never heard of any of them, *Black Elk Speaks, Lame Deer Seeker of Visions, Bury My Heart at Wounded Knee.*

"After he didn't rise to fetch more publications, I had the impression that the Time-Life was the only one in the house. He didn't ask me any more questions, thus I listened to him extol about his book as he referred to the Papago as the savages over and over again in a heavy Southern drawl. Leaning close to me to make his points, his strong mouth and intense dark eyes, his straight hair slicked back close to his scalp, I could easily imagine him serving a sermon to save the souls of the lost heathens in his flock. With each point he moved closer until I could smell his peanut-butter breath; yet I let him explain his fervent mission to reform the evil Papago.

"He was terribly enthused about teaching me things—well, his own views on things, 'that I couldn't possibly know.' Either he assumed that my white skin made me an automatic sympathizer to his big cause, or he 'smelled a rat' and knew my heart.

"I asked him how long the Christians had been converting the Papago. He said since the Catholics arrived with the Spaniards a few hundred years earlier; and although the priests met much resistance, they persevered and prevailed, opening the way for the Presbyterians and Mormons.

"Allison, I must say, I lost my cool and suggested to him that the Papago's own spirituality may have served them quite well."

"Oh, oh," Allison said, her big eyes shining, "What happened?"

"He bristled at that. He quickly claimed that all of the advantages they now had, white civilization had brought to them. His voice began to rise: 'The savages were saved by Christ! If they hadn't been enlightened, they'd still be lost in darkness! Before the whites, they hardly knew the difference between good and evil! Could I possibly imagine how difficult it must have been when they didn't know Christ and had to live in blindness?'

"Then, he slapped his knee hard, sputtering that the only possible hope for the survival of Indians was the anglicizing of their heathen ways!"

"Oh my god!" Allison stammers, "What arrogance!"

"I sat there in silence—stunned, angry, feeling trapped—torn between good Lutheran manners and healthy German-American shouting! McLaughlin's wife and Katrina had stopped conversing. They sat watching me as if I had caused something terrible. All I did was ask a couple questions. I stood up, excused myself, feigning weariness, and left my domineering host clutching his Time-Life book, red-faced and flush with victorious energy.

"The front door was a fleeting option. I didn't relish the thought of finding myself outside being gnawed upon by a mongrel, which may still be an unconverted heathen, therefore I slipped into my dark bedroom, grateful to be alone. Through the drawn blinds, slits of light crossed the carpet, the walls and me—black and white stripes—like a prisoner's uniform. I opened the slats and peered out the closed window. A yard light gave the grass an artificial hue. It was the only street lamp as far as I could see, except for the bare bulb at the police station. The barbed wire fence surrounding the backyard was much taller than I. Beyond it lay the little village, uniformly earth-colored, shabby, but peaceful.

"An eeriness engulfed me, a sensation that I was a prisoner that couldn't escape without the help of the McLaughlin's. Who were they trying to keep out? Trespassers on their grass? They didn't need any barbed wire for that—a fence would do. Certainly, the pacifist Papago wouldn't disturb them. Why were they so fearful? Because some drug smugglers might show up? Mexican intruders? Perhaps they simply owned more possessions than anyone else and they were the only ones who had to fear robbers. Psychologically, they may have been trying to protect against the mysterious, foreign perceptions of the people and the land. After all, they saw life in such narrow terms that intrusions were inevitable."

Allison said, "Oh stop! You'll make me feel sorry for them. I think that they knew, underneath all that façade, that they weren't perfect, and they didn't want anyone else to know it."

"Perhaps, but I've never witnessed such a display of self-righteousness and disrespect for the people he was responsible for. Amazing!"

"What did you *do*?" Allison asks, appearing agitated.

"What *could* I do? I put on my cotton nightshirt, sat on the bed, and surveyed the room, trying to soothe my frustration. That bedroom reminded me of a Pillsbury cereal news ad I saw, where the entire child's room was wallpapered with dolls, and the actual same doll lay on a doll-printed bed spread, and I wondered if a child could go mad in such a setting, and become like the doll. Somebody at Pillsbury was eating too many sugar-coated cereals!"

Allison and I laugh.

"Sally's room wasn't that bad. It just seemed that gold-and-white French provincial white lace and ruffles, and countless stuffed animals and dolls, smelling of perfume seemed foreign in the desert.

"There was a knock on the door. I opened it. Katrina was standing there in her nightgown, saying, '*Psst*. Can I come in?'

"'Sure,' I said, 'Can't you sleep?' She was acting so nice.

"'I just need to talk to you for a minute,' she said, not looking at me.

"'Oh, you're telling me to keep my views to myself?' I replied.

"'Oh no! Not that,' she whispered.

"'Well, what then?' I wondered, curious.

"'Don't you think the McLaughlin's are nice—even if you disagree with their religious ideas? I mean—look at this lovely home! Aren't you glad they'll let us stay here for two nights?'

"'Well, I'm glad to have a clean bed. But, what do you want to talk about?'

"'*Hmmm*. You know how I told you I'm an Indian?'

"'Yes?'

"'Well, I'm really only a tiny bit Eskimo, and so it really wouldn't be lying if I told them I'm not Indian,' she said, looking at the floor.

"'What do you mean? Did you tell them you're not Indian?'

"'Well, not yet. But, I'll have to.'

"'Why? Why do you have to tell them anything?' I was confused.

"'Because I think I could get a job here, but I'm sure they wouldn't hire me if they thought I was an Indian. He thinks he can get me a teaching position here,' she said, excitedly.'"

Allison hit the table, "Oh! That little hypocrite!"

"I said, 'So what! Just tell them you're part Indian. For gosh sakes—this IS an Indian reservation.'

"'She got tears in her eyes, and cried, 'But you don't understand! I'm asking you not to tell them!'

"'Oh yes, I do understand,' I hissed, 'And I think it stinks. You want to be an Indian when you're around them and a white when around whites. And you know that the McLaughlins don't like Indians,' I cried.

"'*Shhh!*' she warned me, 'Lower your voice.'

"She began to leave, looking hurt and indignant. Before she opened the door, she turned on me with narrow eyes, and in a mean, threatening tone, said, 'If I don't get a job here—it could be YOUR fault!' She shut the door.

"I fell onto the bed, dumbfounded."

Allison stopped me, "Excuse me, I'm going to call my mom and check on my kids. We have lots of time before the garage closes. I need to hear the rest of this story! Then, we'll get my car."

While Allison was on the telephone I thought about Katrina. She wasn't in the McLaughlins' kitchen the next morning, nor was the superintendent, who had left for the school; so I had coffee with his wife, listening to her say she never got lonely because she often left to go to visit her family in another state and she loved to dine out in Tucson or have dinners in the homes of the other (white) teachers. She said she knew several Papago people, but when I asked her if she found it exciting living among them, she exclaimed, "Exciting? Exciting? My, my, no. We avoid socializing with them as much as possible. Of course, we *have to* at church and my husband has to at work. I mean—that *is* his job." When asked if her daughter liked it there, she said, "She doesn't trust them either."

She said she had to leave, but Katrina would be back later, after I was done looking at student art. She told me that their neighbor was the art instructor at the high school, and he offered to take me there to see some pictures that the students did, and that I was invited to a dinner party that night to meet "some of the nice people that live here"—all teachers.

140

Chapter 16
EVERY DAY IS A NEW GIFT
Why must it take 300 years to convert your savages?

Sells, Arizona, Tohono O'odham—The People of the Desert

The neighbor and art teacher was the same redheaded man who had hailed us from his screen door the previous night. Bill, recently appointed to his job by McLaughlin, jokingly admitted that he knew nothing about art, however he needed a job, and the art teacher had been fired—something he didn't explain. Bill was a single, affable guy who had no class that morning, so he showed me his school—a large, new modern brick facility that appeared well equipped, although Bill complained that they had few supplies.

In a classroom with shades drawn to shut out the morning sun, he opened a file cabinet, removed a stack of student's drawings and handed them to me, "Help yourself. Take what you want."

Surprised, I said, "I wouldn't consider taking someone else's work without their permission." I felt like I was prying.

Shrugging his shoulders, he said, "Suit yourself. What do you think of the work?"

"There's nothing unusual or extraordinary about it. Thanks for showing it to me," I replied, returning it, just as a student appeared in the doorway to tell Bill that the principal had sent him to guide me to view the basket collection at the Catholic mission. Thanking Bill for the short tour, he winked, and reminded me that I'd see him at dinner that night at his house.

Jerry Antone, a Papago high school senior, very bright and serious, was optimistic about his future. At the historic Spanish St. Catherine's Mission, we admired fragile treasures in a chilly dim, stone-walled

141

room filled with baskets, mostly coiled in curved shapes, created from willow, bear grass and yucca. Some had held cactus wine. They had designs of animal effigies, human figures, and other geometric formations.

Jerry said that the Papago made more baskets than any other tribe. They made pottery, too, often red designs on an unclipped buff, or a smooth red ware with black decorations and figures. They also made mysterious little statues—fetish figures, and some textiles. It felt strange to be in the cool adobe room, examining baskets that were utilitarian necessities to the creators, but had magically become collectible art, only to be locked away in the dark and enjoyed only by special eyes. I thought it peculiar that some objects, given enough time could grow in value, while others became buried trash. I supposed that humans have always, everywhere created ideas about such choices, and that perceptions about value and quality are unique to human-animals. I also thought how ideas about beauty have changed with evolving cultures, and I tried to imagine a Papago basket next to Constantin Brancusi's 1917 "Male Torso" a minimalist steel sculpture. How was it that primitive utilitarian objects didn't change for thousands of years in the Sonoran Desert, yet Europeans invented art like Brancusi's?

Jerry replaced the simple padlock on the door and led me into a garden courtyard as pristine as a medieval fairytale, Here was undisturbed beauty created by one simple motive—orderly beauty. In the center of the quaint earthen mission, my eyes gazed upon rectangular sunburned plaster walls, verandas, and mysterious wooden doors leading into rooms. Narrow stone paths neatly crossed a flat courtyard, an emerald-green velvet lawn dotted with flowering fruit trees bearing pink blossoms, permeating the air with fragrant perfumes. Vines dripping with lavender pea shapes clung to veranda beams and dripped down in glorious clusters, a carefree contrast to the walls and lawn.

That quiet, sunny sanctuary, privately safe from changing time and ideas, did make the world feel orderly and peaceful—even perfect, according to the laws of man. I looked up at the sky and imagined the surrounding desert made by Mother Earth. It had lived in beauty for thousands of years without the help of humankind by being connected to all the plants and animals. It remained free.

Jerry, my attractive, polite guide chose a bench in the sun where we could speak about his dream to become a photographer. That struck me as paradoxical, because his culture had once believed that to capture the image of another was to have stolen their soul.

We spoke about change. Despite the lack of conveniences in Sells, most had electricity, television, and indoor plumbing. He was delighted when I confessed that I was really more interested in abstract expressionism and conceptual art in general, than in ancient baskets. Avant-garde ideas interested him, too.

We talked about photographers. I asked him if he was familiar with Ansel Adams, Diane Arbus, Dorthea Lange, and others. We discussed artistic or commercial possibilities and I promised to send him some information about possible schools where he might apply for college.

"Why don't you talk to Bill, your art teacher. Perhaps he'll help?"

"He's an idiot! He knows nothing about art! He isn't even an art teacher!"

His sudden outburst startled me. Frustration bubbled deep in my heart while he related a sad story of how the former art teacher had been fired because he grew too friendly with the students and had been accused of smoking "pot." Jerry said he was a good art teacher; that the students learned a lot; and he remained in town still friendly with the students. Jerry, obviously dismayed by the situation, was eager to leave the reservation and seek enlightenment elsewhere, even though he loved his people and the land.

"I need to run back to school for a class, but I can show you around some more afterwards," he offered cheerfully, "You can remain in the courtyard. I'll return in an hour."

"Great! Come back, but you'll find me by my car under the grandfather tree in front of the mission. I'll be reading about desert dwellers—like you!"

He grinned and ran off down the street.

The Signature Cafe oozes with friendliness and fabulous food. I'm glad it's located on my way home from teaching at St. Thomas and happy, too, that Allison likes to meet me here. But where is she? She left our table to call her mother who cares for her two children. She has to phone the garage where her old Ford is being repaired. I hope that everything is okay.

While waiting for Allison's return, I notice a magazine cover sitting on a table, a black-and-white photograph, and I wonder what became of Jerry Antone after I left Sells. After he returned to class, I read that the Pueblo and Papago were late in coming into the reservation system. Most tribes had been reduced to small allotments by 1887 when the Allotment Act was passed by congress to divide traditional land held in common by a tribe, into individual plots of land for families. That resulted in the reduction of Indian land holdings by two-thirds, and the increase of reservations to over two hundred and fifty. Immigrants poured into the West for "free land," while fleeing despotic, intolerable conditions in the old country. Then, they in turn suppressed and denied the freedom and political justice of the natives in the West.

In 1917 the Papago reservation system began, and the loss of their land resulted in the need for more rationing of food, while Indian superintendents leased the reservation lands to American cattlemen.

144

The money collected from the leases was to be held in trust, like the land, by the secretary of the Interior, as it is today. (Jerry said later that Phoenix and Tucson carelessly waste water faster than Mother Nature could ever replenish it, while the wise Papago watch in amazement—knowing the value of fresh water.)

Another change happened in 1917—sharp hostility between the Catholics and the Protestants. By the early 1900s they were gaining converts in Papago villages, although most Indians were called Catholics. In fact, many actually were not, and instead were still believers of traditional spirituality.

The Christian church, all across the Americas prohibited all native religions. The Bureau of Indian Affairs led the way. Children were torn away from families by eager social workers doing "good," or boys and girls were given away by desperate, impoverished, starving parents. Thousands of youngsters were shipped miles away to boarding schools where all family influence would disappear. The Indians were effectively stripped of any avenues of self-determination. Everything about them was to be reformed: land would be held individually; economic achievement would come as a result of farming; education would be in the school or church system; extended families would be broken up; spirituality would become religion, or seeking salvation through the white man's god. This is called forced assimilation.

The BIA paid superintendents and government employees to have jurisdiction over all Indian affairs. The superintendent was to maintain law and order; manage tribally owned resources with his own choice of employees, and all of this without a system of checks and balances for there was no real local government. Indians were to be trespassers on their own land. Water from their own irrigation systems was diverted to white-owned cattle ranchers or Mormon farmers, while the natives were expected to farm on the worst dry scrublands. The ranchers hired few Indians.

There were no avenues for Indian leadership. Societies broke down, making them dependent upon the superintendent system. (People often ask me why Indians have an alcohol problem. Anyone subjected to all this mistreatment would have a problem. I'd get drunk, too!)

Yet, the Papago suffered less than many tribes, because they were farther away from high-density, white-populated areas; and also due to the nature of their lands, the allotment system simply couldn't work. Consequently, they still have some of their political and spiritual system. The Papago and Pima are unique for they were never uprooted, transplanted, or forced into migration to the lands of another Indian tribe. Their land seemed so undesirable that even the whites didn't want it at first, so they have enjoyed a greater sense of continuity while other tribes suffered more under conquering foreigners.

Sitting under the shade of a tough old cottonwood tree, I thought back in time—before the whites arrived: For over 9,000 years, while Assyrians were being slaughtered, Jews were slaves in Egypt, Zoroastrianism spread, the Persians under Cyrus conquered the "world," Jesus Christ was crucified, Protestants murdered Catholics and Catholics murdered Protestants, and Cortez defeated the Aztecs. During all of this, the peace-loving "bean eaters" of the Gila and Salt River country sang songs while they ground corn, gathered mesquite for their fires, drank saguaro wine on the beginning of the Papago new year, weathered dust storms and drought, prayed for rain, fended off attacks by invading Apache and Comanche warriors, and lived in harmony with the earth and sky.

While some European nations circled the earth, reforming, improving, and defeating nature and its inhabitants, the Papago refused to attack, violate, or encroach upon other life. Indeed, they regarded

146

war, or warlike thoughts as a form of insanity. They had cleansing rituals for warriors to return them to normal—unlike their enemies who glorified in raids and deeds of prowess, and who were a constant threat from the East, forcing the Papago into defensive positions, which they successfully deployed.

The Papago built without forced slave labor and without a class system of laborers. There were four principal leaders, and they chose one who was best suited to be the main one. They were chosen for characteristics that had nothing to do with their warrior status. Maybe they were the ones who took four hairs from the head of an enemy, for they never took scalps, but rather—four hairs!

Wastefulness was abhorred, and everything was used sparingly. Modesty and austerity were the greatest virtues. If the Apache dancers were aggressive and extremely emotional in their ceremonies, the Papago were just the opposite.

The desert dwellers are rightly proud of their skills that make survival in arid places possible—and they should be! They became great engineers when they constructed miles of irrigation canals in the area where the city of Phoenix now stands. It was a gigantic feat that put hundreds of acres into cultivation for thousands of years and was comparable to the systems found in Mexico built by the more famous Aztecs. The Pima to the north, with more water, were sedentary people, while the Papago were semi nomadic.

Jerry returned, as promised, to the mission, to find me lying on the grass, soaking up sunbeams like a turtle, storing vitamin D for the remainder of Minnesota's winter. I put my reading aside. We jumped in my car, and drove to the BIA craft shop called The Papago Arts and Craft Guild, where two native women proudly displayed several baskets for sale. We then went to a privately run shop where I was shown more creations. Suddenly, my heart leaped! There was the man in the maze—on a circular, slightly curved, coiled basket, ready to re-enter the maze.

"Oh, there he is!" I exclaimed.

"There is who?" Jerry said, looking around.

I reached in my purse, removed the pendant and placed it around my neck. The woman's eyes widened. Jerry smiled in amusement. They exchanged looks, nodding their heads knowingly, saying nothing.

A warm glow in my heart told me that I was a part of something. Still, they didn't offer to explain the design, which was just fine; because I believe in allowing mysteries time to unfold, which they always do, if I'm patient. Therefore, I didn't blurt out, "Tell me the story!" I would know it—if I deserve to know it—when I've earned the gift of knowing about the maze. Life is a wonderful transformative circular, never-ending puzzle.

I was thrilled with my basket purchase, thanked the shopkeeper, and stepped outdoors in the fresh, dry desert air with Jerry. He stopped me and pointed toward the Southeast, "There is a mountain over there named Mount Baboquivari. There are stories that go back hundreds of years about a figure some call the Earthmaker who may still be on that mountain." His eyes met mine. He glanced down at my pendant and said nothing more.

I drove Jerry back to school and have never seen him again.

Allison reappeared after a long phone call she had made in the back hall of the Signature Cafe, "My mother contacted my dad, and he's going to take care of my car today, so I don't have to worry about it. She had trouble locating him; and meanwhile the kids wanted to talk to me about the powwow I'm taking them to next weekend."

"*Ahhh*, good. You're lucky to have such good parents, and they're fortunate to have you, too."

"Thank you, but it will be better when I have my own place after I graduate. Hopefully, I can live near my parents."

"I'll take you home after we finish the story about Katrina and the McLaughlins."

"Yes! Katrina had come to your bedroom to ask that you not tell the McLaughlins that she might be a tiny bit Eskimo, because Mr. McLaughlin was the superintendent with power to give her a job, but he would never hire her if he knew she was an Indian. How crazy is that?"

"Well, things got even more crazy that night. However, that afternoon, we had a great time together. The sun was still high in the sky when Katrina and I rode west out of Sells to locate Hikiwan where an elderly basket maker lived. We had to be back in Sells for dinner.

"We didn't talk about the previous night, nor our morning apart. I thought about freedom, connections, patterns, and directions in the desert. My heart felt full. My body felt strong—my hair blowing out the car window as we sped along the highway. Warm, dry winds from the west. Arms tingling after being trapped in wool all winter. Passing by the most barren land I'd ever seen—strangely beautiful, exotic pink and gray sand; wide plains interspersed by dry washes, scents of sage, cactus rising up in weird, distorted shapes. The intensity of sunbeams shimmering on sand like waves reminding me of summer days on Lake Superior. The sun knows how to make any surface dance.

"At a dot on the map named Hikiwan, we met a quaint, wrinkled grandmother who had seen many seasons come and go, probably many tourists, too, as she sat in the shade of her modest mud hut, weaving a basket. She said her name was Juanita Lewis, but she spoke no English. Her fingers flicked this way and that as we tried our best to communicate. Her gnarled, strong hands never stopped weaving between gestures. Her stout fingers knew what to do without her full attention. She was warm and gentle, her face crimped into deep crevices that marked her years like a sun calendar. We remained awhile for she appreciated our company, but the day grew hot, and conversing was difficult.

"Juanita rose to enter her hut. She wore a navy-blue dress with a small white print on the fabric, a red kerchief on her black long hair, and white socks under her sandals. We waited while she slipped into the dark interior behind a blanket. *How could anyone survive here with no electricity or running water?* I wondered.

"Her large, stooped frame reemerged from the door. In her hands, she carried two grass baskets, each about seven inches tall and wide, with little lids that had a loop in the top. She handed the precious coiled gifts to Katrina and me. Surprised and overwhelmed, I tried to refuse; but she was very persistent, forcing me to accept her generosity. I was able to force some money on her, but not nearly enough.

"I felt like crying. I didn't even know her, yet she gave me something that required great toil to produce. That gift became my measuring stick for giving. Juanita was the most impoverished elderly person I could ever imagine meeting, yet she had so much to give.

"Her niece, Clemencia, joined us for a while. She was able to translate for us because she spoke English. We talked about the noisy Ryan Field airport, an Air Force base we'd passed before Hikiwan.

"Then Katrina and I went to another settlement named Charco 27 before returning to Sells. We passed a sign advertising the Papago Indian Rodeo in November. I wished I could be there. Near Sells, we passed a new housing project with clean white frame houses—all with green lawns, paved streets, and tall fences. It was new housing for the teachers on the reservation. I thought, *Those must be the homes of my dinner partners tonight.*"

"Oh, Allison, I had a bad feeling about going to that dinner."

She replies jokingly, "McLaughlin doesn't sound like your cup of tea. I hope the food was good, even if the company wasn't."

"The guard dog was tied up in the house when Katrina and I arrived back at the McLaughlins'. They said we were going next door to Bill's, the art teacher, for dinner. I could already hear guests laughing, and smell cooking. Mrs. McLaughlin removed a cellophane-wrapped dish from the refrigerator, suggesting that we clean ourselves up, then meet at Bill's house. She swept through the door, swinging her full circle skirt against the doorframe, allowing the screen to clatter behind her. I heard her heels click on the pavement as she crossed the sidewalk, then I glanced at Katrina. Her eyes were ripe with merriment. She seemed to love to see me miserable, and she knew I was. My stomach had a sick pit in the center.

"I steadied myself, went into my bedroom, flopped on the bed and thought *Damn their dinner!* I got up to dress, thinking, *Oh, why didn't I bring my AIM T-shirt?* I'd wear it!

"After a shower, I cooled down, reminding myself to be centered, stable, and dignified. I would keep my mouth shut and be a good listener."

Allison says, "Well, what did you wear? Did you wear your pendant?"

"I wore a colorful long cotton skirt, a simple white blouse and the Papago pendant with the little man figure and the maze of life. I entered Bill's door with a good attitude, trying to forget the things Jerry had confided to me at the Catholic mission. I thought I could overlook the racist remarks I expected to hear from the Mormon teachers, and ignore Katrina's two-faced behavior.

"Bill greeted me with a dish towel apron over his baby pot belly, a spoon in his hand, and exuberance on his red face. He bounced about the kitchen, lifting lids on pans and checking the oven. The smells were enticing. My appetite jumped at the sight of a big beef pot roast and browned potatoes.

"After introductions, eight of us gathered around the dinner table, which was set nicely with china dishes and flowers. Bill asked me to sit on the end opposite of him, with superintendent McLaughlin on my right side. Bill brought forth endless amounts of food from the kitchen, while making corn meal pancakes at the last minute—my favorites.

"McLaughlin said a prayer. Everybody closed their eyes and bowed their heads while I peeked around the table: the preacher on my right, then Katrina, then the preacher's wife, then Bill on the end— watching me—then, a couple from Maryland who had moved there with a family months before because his father got a job in maintenance at the Indian Oasis High School, District Number 40, and he hoped to get a job with his father. There was one more teacher there, also.

"I filled up my plate, thinking how nice a glass of wine might be, but there wasn't any, and it didn't matter. The beef was delicious. I complimented the chef and Mrs. McLaughlin for her Jell-O mold salad, and caught bits of conversations as they all talked about things at the school in southern accents—using 'you all' and 'is that right' quite often.

"About halfway through my meal, after being blissfully ignored, McLaughlin said, 'How are you girls enjoying your trip?' I let Katrina answer, and she said, 'Oh, I love it here. I think the desert is quite beautiful. Judy and I had a nice ride today out to the west of Sells where we met Jaunita Lewis, an elderly woman who gave us each a basket. We couldn't believe it.'

"Mr. McLaughlin then turned to me and asked if I saw any artwork. I said I'd seen amazing baskets at the Catholic mission and in two shops, and that I'd bought one to take home, similar to my pendant. I added that, 'It's quite amazing that people with so little can still find a way to make money out of such a difficult environment. I think the Papago are extremely clever.'

"After a moment of quiet, Bill interjected, while passing a platter

152

of corn cakes. He said, 'She saw artwork at the high school, but she was not impressed with it, so she handed it back. I guess there's no great talent around here. Never has been and never will be. I don't know how these people ever got along before we came.'"

Allison tightens her face in a painful expression, then groans, "Oh my god! How condescending."

"It gets worse! McLaughlin stopped pushing a slice of beef around in its juice, then looked sternly at me. He said in a low tone, 'Do you realize that these savages had nothing before? There were no schools, churches, or services of any kind! They lived like animals, with silly superstitions and crazy beliefs. They did absolutely nothing. It was really sad.'

"Bill jumped in, 'Yeah, these savages would be so primitive without us, they'd just up and die! Or, go out and get drunk!'

"Everybody laughed so hard, including Katrina. McLaughlin continued to insult his own flock, saying, 'Yes, young lady, (I was actually thirty-five years old), if you want to see art made by artists, you'd better go look for your civilized folks. You're not going to find that here. Maybe you could make your trip worthwhile if you sell baskets. You could buy them real cheap and sell them for lots in the cities. Hey, I've heard some people will pay hundreds for old baskets from around here. That's why they're locked up in the mission, to guard them.'

"Bill raised his fork and declared, 'Yeah! The savages would probably steal them and sell them to buy some booze!'

"Everybody laughed hard again. Katrina also, but she was avoiding looking at me, like she was getting nervous. She had ceased eating her dinner.

"McLaughlin would not stop, like he was trying to draw me into an argument. All the others at the table obviously supported his views. He said, 'You know, you seem to have some romantic notions about these

Indians, judging from your question last night; and I have to say that you can't really know about people unless you live among them, like me. I understand these people, and they need the discipline of religion to put some order in their lives. Jesus Christ is their only hope. By gosh, if I have to spend the rest of my life getting God in them, I will!!!'

"The room fell silent. His face was the color of beet pickles and his hands shook. Katrina's face looked white—and sick, yet she stared at me with wide eyes—waiting. I had stopped eating. They were all waiting.

"So, I let 'em have it!

"I said, 'The Papago have survived on this land for thousands of years. They lived through an Ice Age, surviving giant mammoths that went extinct. They lived through arid conditions when drought emptied their irrigation ditches. They survived servitude to the Catholic missions who practically enslaved them and from whom they caught the white man's diseases like smallpox. They survived attacks from the Apaches and Comanches. They survived starvation when promises made by the United States government were broken, and the rations didn't arrive. And they did all this without YOUR God—or YOU!

"I paused, then raised my voice, 'How can you possibly think that the Papago can't survive WITHOUT YOU? It is YOU who could not survive without all your conveniences. You'd expire without your refrigerator, your air conditioner, your supermarkets, your cars, and trucks. It is THEY who could teach us all about survival!

"Allison starts cheering, "*Yeaaaaaaa!* Good for you!" The diners at the next table look at her with disapproval, so we settle down a little.

"McLaughlin and Bill appeared livid. Katrina looked worried. Bill stood up and pointed his finger at me like I was the devil himself in his dining room. He said, 'I can't believe what you're saying! Do you really believe we should all go back to living in stick and mud huts like them? Do you think we should call a medicine doctor, a dirty old man with rotten animal skins hanging from his head? Maybe that's just what you need!'

"No one disagreed with Bill, so I continued to defend the Papago, and myself, pointing out, 'What I told you, Bill, is true, and you react by giving me extreme examples, instead of acknowledging their admirable survival abilities. No, we shouldn't all go back to living in mud huts or tipis, although they're perhaps preferable to high-rise tenement buildings with cockroaches, rats, and greedy landlords. Adobe homes don't pollute the earth or waste precious trees, and with land to grow a garden, people can control their food source. I think most cities are awful places around the world. I'd feel safer in a tent on the prairie or in the woods any day.

"I paused before continuing to expound my humble opinion upon my very captive audience, sitting there like thunderstruck stones. 'Look, we don't NEED all the things we THINK we need. It's just plain nuts to be watering a green lawn of Kentucky grass in a desert! The Indians know this. They have wisdom and common sense. I'm sure they appreciate indoor toilets, but do they need the gospel, too?

"Katrina gasped! I thought she was going to faint. In fact, I learned later, she did go to the toilet and vomit!"

I break into laughter with Allison almost falling off her chair.

"I continued to respond, I said, 'That medicine man you mentioned may know some things that you don't—some things about strength in adversity, modesty in consumption, harmony with nature and mankind. Above all, they could teach the Christians how to wage peace in the world. How many wars have been waged over the meaning of the Bible? The Papago never had the good book and they are called peacemakers!

"I leaned closer to McLaughlin and asked, as politely as I could muster, 'Why must it take 300 years to try to convert your 'savages'? Maybe there's something in their own religion that they still find valuable. Maybe it has integrity, or honesty!

"I looked at Bill, thinking about Jerry and his accusations about the 'art teacher.' Then, I rose slowly from my chair, pushed it back, and addressed Katrina, 'I don't feel very well. I'm going outside.' Then, I turned to Bill and said, 'Thank you for the dinner. I'm sorry if I allowed my opinions to interfere with your good time.'

"Nobody said anything. I moved slowly, weak-kneed toward the door. As I let myself out into the chilly night air, I heard the conversation rise again behind me. Where to go? I felt too wobbly to walk; so I went to my car, got in, and sat down with my seat back, trying to relax. Would Katrina come out?

"No, she didn't. I sat there wishing to flee, and I would have if all my things were not in the McLaughlins' house, behind the barbed wire fence and the guard dog. Should I drive around and cool off? I had my car keys in my purse, but I was so tired, and mad.

"A big wet tear ran down my cheek. It felt good to cry a little bit. I didn't feel so lonely any more after the stars came out. I crawled into the back, unfurled my sleeping bag, and curled up, clutching my Papago pendant, wearing my Zuni needlepoint turquoise-and-silver bracelet.

"It must have been about four o'clock in the morning when I suddenly woke up in the black of night. My car was surrounded by police cars with their lights whirling. My eyes were blinded by flashlights from all directions. More angry than frightened, I held my hand over my eyes and scowled, 'What the hell are you doing?'

"The officer close to my open window grinned, 'What are *you* doing here? That's what we want to know.'

"I replied, 'I'm sleeping, or trying to.'

"He asked, 'Why are you sleeping here? Please get out of the car.

We need to see your driver's license.'

Allison says, "This is preposterous!"

"Allison, I wasn't scared—just puzzled. After all, they must have noticed my car earlier by the police station. I figured that, because of my Minnesota plates, I was a suspicious character or something."

Allison chides me, "It didn't occur to you that you were a lone female—an attractive one at that—and they could have raped you?"

"Oh no. They were Papago Indians. I trusted them!"

Rolling her eyes, Allison says, "Well, continue . . ."

"Maybe they thought I was a drug dealer. Good grief. I glanced at the house to see if anyone was peeking outside, but with all the lights, I couldn't see. I didn't expect to be rescued, but I wondered if *they* had called the police on me. How could I explain to the cops that I wasn't in the house of the superintendent of schools because I had been self-righteously defending all tribal peoples? Sally's silly bedroom looked pretty good at that moment!

"The officers checked my license, then handed it back to me. They opened all the car doors and half-heartedly poked around, looking bored, but curious. One said, 'So, why are you here? Out of gas?'

"No, no. I'm not out of gas. I'm the guest of the people who live here, but I got into a little argument with the woman I'm traveling with, so I came outside to sleep. I know that sounds silly, but that's kind of what happened.'

"'Ho, ho, ho! Women troubles, eh? There must be a man involved! Yes, a pretty girl like you? She must have been jealous. Did you take her boyfriend? Ho, ho, ho! Get back in the car. I hope you can clear up your little disagreement tomorrow. It's a long ride back to Minnesota. Good night. Sorry to have bothered you. Have a safe trip back.'

"Off they drove—laughing, leaving me standing by the car with all the doors open. I looked at the vicious attack dog who hadn't even barked, and said, 'Some guard dog you are!' Then, I saw a curtain move in the front window of the McLaughlin house. Damn!! Back in my car, I couldn't sleep. The sun would be coming up soon, for I saw a faint slit of light in the sky toward the east. Suddenly, I fell into sort of a daze, started the car engine and drove toward an opening on the horizon, toward Baboquivari Mountains.

I had escaped. I knew I had to return; but, meanwhile, I was free. Not knowing, nor caring where I was going, I just knew the sunrise was calling me down that road."

Allison laid her hand on my shoulder, "You must have felt exhausted. What an awful night! I hope the next day went better for you. I'd like to stay for more, but I promised Mom I'd make dinner for her, so I'll be going now."

"Thanks for listening. Cook them a good meal. *Gigawabamin*."

Chapter 17
MOTHER NATURE CREATES ONLY
HEALTH AND BEAUTY
Why would anybody want to kill I'itoi?

Boboquivari Mountains, Arizona

Allison left me alone. I slumped back in my chair with one more cup of tea, reminiscing about that last day in Sells.

There I was in my little Vega driving down a narrow asphalt road into the desert. Strangely, my exhaustion soon turned to intense relief and even joy. The sun on my face felt like a beautiful song—a melody without words. A hazy pink glow washed the desert in a serene light, as though I was wearing rose-tinted glasses, casting a magic spell over all of Mother Earth's creations.

A shiver, like a jolt of energy, crept up my spine. I knew I was right where I was supposed to be at that moment. When this happens to me, I'm suspended from all timely constraints or fears. I'm so aware of my smallness from birth to death. Every day is a new gift. My attitude reflects gratefulness, or it doesn't. It's my choice. Each day in my life is also a teaching, and part of that teaching is about death and wisdom. I had an overwhelming urge to walk.

Eventually I pulled the car over to park in a wide spot in the road. Rolling down my windows, gazing at the nearby plants, I caught a movement in the bushes, probably some critter startled by the car, a bird? Perhaps a coyote? The distraction alerted me to my surroundings, pulled me out of any negative thoughts, pulling me into a vast sea of silent sage. Soothing dawn air moved freely through the car—moving me to get out and greet the dawn. If I was going to go for a walk in the desert with chill-raising goose bumps on my arms, I needed my shawl. Gathering my white cotton skirt around me, tying back my loose dark hair with a red bandana, slinging a small orange backpack over my shoulder, I began by hiking along the road, thinking of Dayshun, my Ojibwe friend up North. He told me, "Whenever I feel troubled, I go for a walk." He wouldn't tell me to do it. He'd suggest an example to follow. I thought about Miz, my mentor, and life as a map.

Life is like a road map. How did that connect to the Papago maze? I was trying to learn who I was, and that depended upon where I was. In one sense I was place-dependent in Minnesota-prairie-forest; yet, in another sense I was connected to the universe, to the maze, to something that didn't speak English, Papago, or Ojibwe; something that wasn't Lutheran, Mormon, Lakota, but rather that which couldn't be spoken of in any language or religion. Something that existed before plants or animals. Something that created me would be the same thing that would force me to yield in old age, and turn me back into a tree, stone, or anything beautiful—for everything Mother Nature creates bears health and beauty.

Those thoughts comforted me. If I wasn't responsible for my destiny, I could just BE, instead of trying to control my future. I could invite life to find me—just give myself up to it, for a while anyway, and see what happens—right there in the solitude of saguaro heaven.

A red stone lying in the ditch caught my eye. After passing the stone, it called out to me. I turned around to see a face looking up at me, a red face. I picked it up and turned it around, examining its three-inch height and one-inch girth, its solid soft color, noting that its texture was smoother on one side than the other with angular features. Turning it this way and that, I decided it could only see me from one perspective. What was it trying to tell me? I looked around for more stones, but found none other like it.

My hand received the little head nicely, so I gently closed my fist about it and looked into the desert. Tall, thick-ribbed saguaro sentinels; squat prickly pear plants; red-tipped ocotillo, like sprays of fireworks; spikes of yucca; grass short and green grass waving and gold, and a rock outcropping, gray and red; all begged me to come hither. So, I did.

The pink hue in the sky had turned to a sharp, clear blue, the shadow of Boboquivari, now deep green and lavender. I thought I'd walk toward the outcrop at the foot of the mountain, just to soak up the rhythms of the desert, restore my energy, and talk to my friend, the small red man in the stone. I felt as if I were seeing the desert for the first time. Actually, I was. Because, the day before, I saw it, but didn't connect to it—big difference.

A covey of quails chased each other, ignoring me. A scurrying roadrunner ducked away, off in search of insects and lizards. Then, I remembered snakes, scorpions, ants, and bees, and wished I'd worn my shoes with tall sides. No matter, in confidence I walked like a welcome intruder. I was among friends!

I hiked through yellow, pink, and red spring blossoms, stepping around boulders, dirt mounds, and scary cactus. A tiny gold-and-black warbler darted by, lit on a branch, chirped "hello" and moved on. The roadrunner skittered by boldly, causing me to giggle at his comical behavior. I thanked it for my laughter, remembering that everything is a gift, even a smile, or a laugh, remembering that I have good friends and family to smile or laugh with me.

Checking the sky above, I realized that the sun had gone behind a cloud; but within minutes the cloud was gone, and the sun kept moving over the belly of Mother Earth rounding her ever-pregnant curvature.

Surprise! A coyote leaped around a big rock! I jumped, startled. He was startled, too! He looked at me, backed up, furled his tail, and took off like a dart. Perhaps he'd been chasing a mouse and found me instead. Perhaps he was the critter I saw by my car. I yelled, "*Yiiieee!* Come back, silly critter. Are you afraid of a strong woman who comes from the North, the land of the snow and the loon?" I laughed again—like a loon.

I ambled on. The sun grew hotter, my shawl dropped lower, until I stopped to tie it around my waist, over my blouse. I started off again, my sandals gathering dirt between my feet and soles. The fine clay of Mother Earth filtered into the folds of my white skirt, in the fringe on my shawl and lay sprinkled in my long brown hair like red stardust.

The smell of the earth was intoxicating. However, I became thirsty and thought of water. But I wasn't going far. The mountain would surely be not too distant. I turned to look for my car again, my marker, but it was gone. No mind? I'd just climb an escarpment and find it, I began watching for a rock. Soon, a nice high flat one came forth. I asked rock if rock and I could sit upon him, only to learn that I still wasn't high enough to see the road; however there appeared to be a rise ahead, so I hiked toward it, thinking about the crazy dinner party. Katrina—did she make apologies for me?

Did she get a job? What a hypocrite!

Climbing up an outcrop of sharp rocks, I slipped a few times, then reached a ledge with a view of the road about one mile away. I lay and sat in the sun, allowing my legs to dangle, watching my shadow on the right side. A lizard snuck across my toes. I pulled my body up straight, and peered around for snakes. Feeling safe, I raised my face and said a prayer.

Then, I picked my way down the rocky gray, crumbling stones—much trickier than climbing up—until I rounded a flat boulder, almost black on one side. Stopping to adjust my sandal strap, I spotted a strange shape etched into the surface, a small carved, or drawn spiral, seemingly part of the stone. Yet, only a human could have created such an image. Wow! An ancient petroglyph. A deep shiver ran up my spine! Maybe the Hohokam who came before the Papago had made it!

Joyful about my discovery, a spiral in my mind, a red stone in my hand, I pranced on thinking, "Ah, I only have a few blocks to walk. Ha! City dwellers measure space not in moons or days, but in blocks, lines, and squares." My little green Chevy Vega waited faithfully. I was Roy Rogers, or his wife Dale, or little Sugar, the daughter, returning to Trigger. I reached the car, feeling mighty thirsty.

Shortly, I heard a car coming, one with a loud rattle. Standing by my car, I watched the noisy contraption draw closer. It was a vintage Ford pickup truck of an nondescript color that had faded into a dull green or blue rust, plodding along at forty miles an hour, clunking as though it had a loose part, or several.

Frankly, I wasn't sure if I should hide or drive away, thinking that some weird character might harm a lone woman in the desert. But I knew I had power within me just then, and that nothing would hurt me, so I stood watching the jalopy grind to a halt. Ohhh my. Such a sight. I saw that the figure in the cab of the truck was so old, he made Juanita Lewis look like his daughter. Maybe she was. He peered at me with black squinty eyes, moved his jaw back and forth, opened his thin mouth, exposing copper-colored teeth. Maybe he was chewing on something. I immediately liked his brown, leathery weather—beaten face, his scruffy short black hair. I'm a real sucker for cowboy hats. His low yellow stained straw hat still contained a measure of dignity. A rusted antique rodeo button pinned to the band looked like a collectible item. His eyes told me he was curious why I was there. I spoke to him first.

"You're Indian, aren't you, Grandpa?"

"My English ain't so good, lady, but I git by. I've lived in the desert here my whole life, seen that mountain every day of my life," he said slowly in a surprisingly strong voice.

"Baboquivari?" I asked.

"Yep," he replied.

"I see you've got a load of hay. You're a cowboy? Maybe a rodeo rider?" I suggested, half-teasing.

"Did my part in the rodeo more than onest or twiced. Yes siree!" he said, nodding his head.

I was extremely thirsty, so I asked him to excuse me while I went in my car in search of water. He said he was sorry he didn't carry any, but that he should, because his old Ford often got thirsty. The only liquid in the cooler was one warm, last bottle of Schell beer from Minnesota. I pried off the cap and was about to drink when the old fellow with amazing sprightliness jumped out of his truck and came over, saying, "Hey, don't forgit yer ol' buddy here!"

I apologized, "It's all I've got. Sorry, I'm out of water."

He laughed, "Oh, that's okay. I'll be glad to share it with you. I don't mind beer."

I found a cup and gave him half the beer, much to his delight. We sat together in the shade of his truck on the edge of the road and said nothing.

What should I say?

He didn't smell too fresh, but by then neither did I. I said to him, "Aren't you going to ask me why I'm way out here at this hour of the morning? The police would. I know that for a fact."

But he just chuckled, "*Tee, hee, hee!*"

I asked him what was so funny, and he said, "I was just thinkin'—I wonder if my wife would believe me if I told her I was a-sittin on the road drinkin' beer with a nice lady from Minnesota!"

We both giggled. Warm beer never tasted so good, but then I guess I'd never tried it before. We sat quietly for a while, listening to birds singing.

Then, the Indian startled me. He said, "I *knowed* why yer here."

"You do?" I said, glancing at his face as he gazed upon the

164

mountain. "You do? Why? Why am I here?"

"Cause of that mountain there."

I slowly said, "A student named Jerry told me it's sacred."

"What do you think?" he said to me.

We studied the mountain for a long time, till I remembered the red stone, so I showed it to him, pointing out the face. He remarked that he didn't see so good anymore, saying, "What cha got there? *Hmmm*. It might bring you good luck. Take care of it."

Then I said, "It talks." And he said, "It what?"

And I repeated, "It talks to me."

He didn't laugh when he asked me, "Wha'd it say?"

"I don't know," I said, "It only speaks Papago!"

"*Oh, ho, ho! Tee, hee, hee!*" He slapped his knees. We both laughed.

He then said, "I see you got I'itoi on that neck piece yer wearin'. That's how come I knowed why yer here."

"I'itoi? What is that? Who is that?" I wondered.

He faced me. I felt like I was being drawn into a deep cave through the openings in his eyes. I held my breath. Would he tell me anything? I didn't ask. He stared back at Baboquivari as I sat in anticipation. With his boney, brown hand, he reached into the pocket of his worn blue jeans, pulled out a crumpled handkerchief, tipped his hat back, and wiped his forehead. He calmly stuffed it back in his pants, then tugged at his dusty cowboy boots, movements suggesting he was adjusting himself for something. But what?

He spoke softly, mysteriously, "I knowed you was out there. And when I come down the road, sure 'nuff, I seed you commin' across the way there, the sun on your hair. I knowed what you was there for. Surprised you didn't git eat up by ants—those snakes, too."

"I saw a snake, and a coyote. I sure surprised that coyote!"

"Ha! I doubt that. Are you sure it was a coyote?" he uttered, those dark eyes again—latent pools of hidden secrets, fierce warrior eyes. Then, they grew warm again, instantly. He said, "How can you be sure of anything? How can you be sure I'm a man?" He laughed again, and I wondered if the beer, which was gone by now, had touched his brain; wondered, as I adjusted my shawl close to my shoulders, what he was thinking, as he set down his empty cup and folded his hands on his lap.

I couldn't stand it anymore, so I finally said, "Maybe someday, somebody will tell me the story about that mountain."

His gaze set upon the mountain. He began, "I see you mean good. I'll tell you 'bout I'itoi. He was the man who was made by Earthmaker out of the sky and the earth. He was made to help coyote and buzzard to put things right, 'cause when the earth was first made there was nothin' but darkness and restlessness. All there was, was Earthmaker and buzzard. Then came the greasewood plant, the mountains, and the clouds. Earthmaker had to flatten everything out so that it reached the horizons in all directions, and then he made I'itoi. Coyote is the messenger between the earth here, and the heaven there. Spider, she come along, too, to help sew things up. Maybe you saw spider out there? Maybe you saw buzzard? Buzzard made the rivers flow in all directions by diving into the valleys with his big, wide wings."

At that point, the old man spread his arms out and dipped one way and then another, demonstrating the movement of the great buzzard. While he spoke, his hands motioned all the happenings in the air, slowly, gently. It was difficult to understand him, for he intermingled Indian and English.

"Earthmaker made the four directions. He made the north, the south, the east, and the west. He made the sun, the moon, and the stars. He made the people from his own body. But he forgot to make them die, so there came big fights between them, when there were too many. So a great big flood came to get rid of all the people, and so he started all over. Only those who had special powers were saved. Earthmaker,

166

of course. And I'itoi, coyote, and buzzard. They could do things to hide, get away, and escape. After the flood, I'itoi made new people, and so everyone called him Elder Brother."

I wondered out loud, "Did I'itoi just make the Papago people, or did he make all the people on the earth?"

"He made all the people," he replied.

"Even the Apache?" I said.

"Even them. He can do anything. He taught the people to do everything. How to grow food, build homes, find water, everything."

"Where is I'itoi now?" I asked.

He was quiet. Kept looking at the mountain, rubbing his hands together.

Then he said, "I'itoi was around here, up there, over there. He was killed four times. But he came back four times, back to life."

"Why would anybody want to kill I'itoi?"

"Like you people might say, he got too big for his britches."

"What do you mean? Was he conceited? Did he turn mean?"

"No, not exactly. He lost his way, you see. He forgot who the boss was. He forgot that Earthmaker had made him. He only had the power to do what Earthmaker let him do, but he thought he had so much power that he didn't need Earthmaker no more. He told the people that he himself would be the big power, and run the show himself. Coyote tried to warn him not to git so high an' mighty, thinkin' he knew everything, and such, but he told coyote to git lost. I'itoi, some folks say, had a big, fancy house built. Treated the people like slaves. It was so high, it reached into the sky. That's where he went to live."

"What happened then? Did Earthmaker kill him?"

"Yep. But, first, all people began to do bad things. Fighting, and shooting the animals. Things like that. Earthmaker moved the sun further and further away till snow and ice came on the earth. Still, nobody would listen. Finally, Earthmaker sent a great rumbling over

167

the earth, like an earthquake that just made that tall house crumble to dust, with all its jewels and gold and stuff like that."

"Did that cure I'itoi of his bad ways?"

"Sort of. Finally, he did learn his lessons, but Earthmaker put him out of sight. He's the little man in the maze."

"Where is he?" I asked the storyteller as he pulled out his kerchief. But, he said nothing. Just kept looking at the mountain.

"Is he on top of that mountain?" I asked, as he wiped his wet brow.

"Some say he's underground someplace," he said, sounding tired.

"Has anybody ever seen him?"

But, no answer. A truck came speeding down the road, blowing dust on us, snapping me back to the present. The old man didn't seem to notice. He was lost in thought. I worried that I'd overtaxed his strength. So I shut my mouth. We sat for a long time like that. Me, trying to remember all he said. Him, just thinkin'.

"I thank you," I offered, "from the bottom of my heart for your sharing."

"My wife's the storyteller, not me," he replied quietly.

"But, it's not just a story, is it? It's really much more!"

"What do you think?" he said, like a reply—not a question.

I said nothing. We sat awhile more. Then he rose to his feet, opened his squeaky truck door and climbed in.

"Got to git goin'. The ol' lady might be wonderin'. Say, Where you headed, anyways?"

"I'm going back to Sells, if I can find my way," I said, laughing.

He explained directions, and then started up the engine of his antique truck.

"Just a minute! I have something to give you.!" I yelled, running to retrieve a big tin of chocolate chip cookies I'd baked at home for the trip. I couldn't think of anything else I had that would be appropriate to give a man, so I set the tin on the seat beside him, hiding a twenty dollar bill underneath.

"What's this? You don' need to give me nothin'," he said.

"It's only cookies, but I made them myself with real fresh butter."

He fumbled with the lid; but it was stuck, so I reached in, "Here, let me do it. They stay fresh longer with a tight lid."

"*Oh ho ho. Teee heee!* Cookies! Cookies! What a morning! Cookies, beer, and a pretty girl. Yes, yes, what a morning!"

With a full heart, I watched him pop a whole cookie in his mouth, shift the floor stick into gear and rattle slowly onto the road. He waved, heading south. He disappeared out of sight, and I got in the car, heading north, wondering how he'd explain the cookies to his wife, if that was where he was really headed. His last words echoed in my mind, "Ya should come to the rodeo sometime."

I parked the Vega in front of the McLaughlins'. Unwilling to knock on any gate door, I sat there and waited, wishing I could take a nap. Bill, the art teacher came out of his house, presumably on his way to work. But, oh no! He walked right over to my car. I rolled the window up most of the way, leaving a crack open. He put his fat face close to the glass and sneered at me.

"Mah goodness ! Ya all sho' does look like a wretched mess this mohnin! I'll bet you didn't sleep a wink last night! *Ah, ha ha!*"

I could see down his throat as he pulled his big, pig face away and laughed all the way back to his house. I was so mad, I laid my hand on the horn till Katrina came running out of McLaughlin's house.

"Stop. Stop it! I'm all packed and ready to go," she insisted.

Mr. McLaughlin came out of the house, carrying my bags and set them down on the street. Katrina carried them across to the car, while I hastily loaded them into the back. I then returned to my driver's seat and watched as Katrina kissed and hugged everybody. She sprinted over to the car and jumped in, all fresh and giddy. I drove off without saying "thank you"—glad to be leaving them.

Later that morning, while driving along, Katrina turned to search for something in the back seat. I said, "Is something lost, or what are you looking for?"

"The cookies. I can't find the cookies. I'm hungry for one. Where did you put them?"

"I ate them," I lied.

"What? ALL of them? This morning?" she said, incredulously.

"Well, we ate them." I said.

"You ate them all? You must feel sick?" she mumbled, sounding wishful.

I whispered to myself, *Oh, coyotes don't get sick from eating cookies.*

"What? What are you saying?" She sounded annoyed.

"Nothing. Nothing at all."

Chapter 18

THE TIMES THEY ARE A-CHANGIN'

Are these all your kids?

Minneapolis

Before my marriage deteriorated into its final death throes, when a measure of respect and friendship still lingered, my teacher husband announced that he planned to spend his future summers as an instructor at Outward Bound, an organization that began in England with the philosophy that physical, sporting challenges create healthy, strong men and women. One of their worldwide camps was in Ely, Minnesota, in the north woods.

I was dubious that outdoor skills could convert my man's strength into something healthier than wife-beating, or mental cruelty. My life was shrouded in secrecy and shame, my bruises hidden under long-sleeved blouses, my tears wiped away for the sake of the children. (I could only laugh later, when he told how scared he was when his kayak tipped over, and he hit his head hard on a boulder—alas, nothing changed.)

His teacher friend, Nick, also signed up for the month-long program. Nick's wife, with two babies, I with four, dropped the two adventurers off at the Duluth bus station, waving goodbye as the bus pulled away; me, feigning sadness and sorrow.

My friend turned to me, "Well, I suppose you'll be busy studying or canning?"

"Hell no!" I confessed, "I have a plan. We're going Out West!"

Appearing shocked, she blurted, "Does HE know your plan?"

"Of course not. He'd never let me go, if he knew."

She shot me a quizzical expression, and studied the three-year-old in my arms, and the other kids lined up beside me. Oldest son, terribly excited, exclaimed, "Mom, are we really going OUT WEST, where the cowboys are?"

"Yes! We have to hurry back to Minneapolis and pack. We leave in two days!"

"Whoopie!" they cheered.

Lisa said, "Can Big Red go, too?"

The Irish setter cocked his head, met my eyes—those soft, pleading brown eyes, his chest heaving up and down in the July heat, his long tongue drooling like a dripping faucet on the pavement. I sighed, "If Red wants to go, he can."

The kids yelled in unison, "He wants to go, too!"

Red barked, "*Woof!*"

"Watch out, Wyoming!" I cheered.

I had sold an antique chair HE never liked anyway, for enough money to cover gas and food for one month—no motels or restaurants. I don't think we'd ever stayed in a motel yet. We always visited friends or family, sleeping in their homes.

We pulled away from our house in the maroon Ford station wagon, with a tightly packed car-top carrier I'd built out of pine boards and canvas, stopping only at the post office to mail Mother an itinerary of our expected route, urging her not to worry, and saying we'd call from Jackson Hole just to check in.

Each day of the trip, we sent Daddy a postcard from wherever we were, so he wouldn't be lonely for us. Cards stamped like: Black Hills, SD, Glacier Park, MT, Jackson Hole, WY, and Yellowstone Park, WY. When I phoned Dad and Mom, they surprised us by making arrangements for us to stay at the Rogers Guest Ranch for a weekend of riding horses and hiking. We also went to the annual Jackson Hole Rodeo.

We ended our circle trip in Ely to pick up Dad/Husband. Before he said, "Hi," he asked, "Where did you get the money?" He wasn't angry. He was so full of himself, there wasn't room for anger. He wanted to have a party and invite our friends to see a slide show of him at Outward Bound.

Which we did. There he was on the screen: running down a dirt road to lose weight; climbing ropes to get in shape; clunking his helmeted head on the bottom of a stream as he failed to upright the kayak fast enough; standing on a rock having defeated the stream, and the kayak; with his group eating granola; with the group around a campfire. He gave many details about his biggest challenge, the dreaded "solo"—a three-day ordeal in which the participant is left alone with no boat, few provisions or tools. The weak soloists, who fail, get weeded out. He fought to survive by tolerating mosquitoes, scrounging for berries, rolling up in a sleeping bag under a tarp, and getting by with only three wooden matches. But he lived to tell the tale!

After the show, which I'd watched from a quiet corner of our living-room, determined to not talk about *my* adventure, lest I deflate his fragile ego by drawing attention to myself, I rose to go to the kitchen to check on my pot of chili, when he said, "If anyone has any questions, feel free to ask."

My friend Marilyn had one, "What did Judy do while you were gone?"

He grew red-faced. He hesitated, "Oh, she stayed busy."

I heard Nick laugh. I stopped in the doorway when my neighbor blurted out, "I'll say she did! She built a pine car-top carrier and sewed a canvas cover for it; packed a cook stove, sleeping bags, tent, clothing, food, including dog food, for a month for five people. She took the kids and dog on a camping trip out West, on an adventure."

"You went Out West?" another woman asked, "For how long? Where did you go? With *all* the kids?"

I actually felt bad for him—having to share the spotlight with me.

"Yes, I took the kids, one in diapers, and Big Red, camping and cooking in parks for thirty days. We drove 2,500 miles through six states, saw twenty parks and historic sites, stayed at a dude ranch, attended a rodeo, and ate in three restaurants. I changed diapers over one hundred times (disposable ones didn't exist back then), made meals over a campfire sixty times, set up a tent fifteen times, all with the great help of the children. I was often so tired, we slept in the car. Red was our watchdog.

"Did anything go wrong?" asked Pete, our Navy veteran friend.

"Lenny blew his thumb open playing with firecrackers right before we left, so we had to keep a clean dressing on his finger until it healed. He was in charge of keeping the baby out of trouble. Fearless little Heath ran off all the time, so we put a belt around him with a rope on it when we visited the canyons. Lisa had the chore of feeding and watering Red. Johnny helped, too. Everyone gathered wood, cleaned their dishes, played games—I'm so proud of them."

"Oh my God! Marilyn exclaimed, "What HE did was NOTHING!"

I couldn't look at his face. "Well, I lost ten pounds without any solo, jogging, or ropes courses."

Twenty years later, I did something I didn't know existed—my own "solo." A vision quest with Ojibwe Indians—not so far from Outward Bound, Minnesota.

On a windy autumn day, we were awakened by tree branches scratching the house outside the bedroom window. The children all still fast asleep in their rooms, those beautiful babies that had bound our marriage together through thick and thin, those blessed gifts for whom I would do anything, those reflections of ourselves that we hope will grow up to be happy and healthy. But when is there no longer a nurturing environment? When is fear and insecurity so debilitating that one can tolerate it no more? Oh, I could for myself, and I had for many years, but when I watched it harming my children, my grief was so deep, I had to find my way on a new path and take them with me.

I had been horrified to find Husband, in a rage, kicking my son while he lay on the floor, trying to shield himself from his dad's cruel blows, as the others watched helplessly. I was sick enough myself to think, "Hit me, but not my children!" How could I even have accepted *any* abuse? How could I have believed it would not happen again when that promise was always broken? How can a person so nice, and seemingly a good teacher and church deacon, be so opposite to his family in private?

I had to get him out of the house before someone wound up in the hospital.

I lay still in the dimly lit bedroom, trying to summon the right words that I'd imagined saying one million times before, however, in a strange twist of events, he spoke first.

"I have some news," he began while dressing for work. In a jubilant tone he added, "I've decided to accept the college teaching job in Superior, Wisconsin. You'll love it up there, Rick and Mavis (friends from Grand Forks) found a real nice house way back in the woods, far away from town—real good deer hunting! They're so excited that we're moving up!"

Stunned to the bone, I quickly woke up, thinking, "Superior? That awful industrial wasteland full of bars and girlie shows? Rick and Mavis? The two sweetest home-bodies you'd ever want to meet?"

But that's not what I said, "When are you going?" I was calculating—weighing my options, trying to ward off fear. Although I was glad this time had finally come, I worried about an uncharted future. I needed to graduate and find a job before any separation.

He sounded enthused, "As soon as you finish your pre-ed classes. You can finish your last two years in Superior at the University. We can ride to work together," he said, chuckling confidently.

He was so cocky. He had my whole future planned to suit his. He was so self-centered and conceited, he hadn't even considered that he should consult me about such decisions, or that I could possibly have a plan of my own. But then, I really didn't. Why should he think I'd not welcome a change in his status and income? I had no career beyond housekeeping, no reliable income of my own, and no family that I could convince that I was worth assisting.

I couldn't speak. My heart beat fast. The house was deathly quiet except for the wind outside the window, knocking oak branches against the house—*tap,tap,tap.*

The clock in the corner went *tic,tic,tic.*

He stood at the foot of the bed, watching me, that cynical grin on his face, that gleam in his eyes, that bullying stance in his body; all those features that told me he knew I was agitated or indecisive and that he had me under his control.

What should I say? I felt defiance growing in my veins, but out of fear for his temper, I had to appease him somehow.

Dawn broke. A ray of sun filtered through the oak tree, crossing the quilt in an undulating pattern. I drew that energy into my body, forming a mental shield until I felt my womanly power.

"I'm not going with you," I heard myself say bluntly.

"What? Why not? What will you do? What about the kids?"

"You have chosen the schools you wanted to attend, and I will do the same. I will graduate from the University of Minnesota."

"You can't stay here without me, and I'm going," he insisted, more in disbelief than in anger, "It's a good advancement for me and a good school for you."

"It is a good school and a good opportunity for you, however a move now would be impossibly difficult for me, and I'm happy here."

He hung his head and stood like a boy who has just lost his mother, in the only moment of humility I ever saw in him, he pleaded, "I feel as though something is being cut out of me, and life will never be as good as this again."

I thought, "This is good? For who?"

He moved to Superior. I began my junior year in Minneapolis. I had to take all day classes for the next two years. We commuted back and forth with the children, but never talked about divorce, although a separation was inevitable. I wasn't ready to throw in the towel just yet. I had to graduate and find work.

Also, I had another decision to make. I'd become enamored with the world of art. Friends were urging me to become an artist, because they knew me as a creative person. They didn't know that I might become the sole breadwinner for four children in my near future. I saw a teaching job as a guarantee to care for them. My College of Education prerequisites had been completed, including child psychology.

But, well, *the times—they are a-changin'*" and dreamers were "*a-blowin' in the wind*," "*movin' on*," and "*goin' with the flow*."

I changed my major to Liberal Arts with a double degree in Studio Art and American Indian Studies.

The kids and I managed on the money that came from Superior. They were marvelous helpers with chores and baby-sitting, or I could not have survived those two years. I rose before dawn to shuffle the children into readiness for school, then drove one hour in heavy city traffic to my first eight o'clock class, with flash cards taped all over the dashboard with twenty-letter words in Ojibwe, like: *Miskwagamiwizagaiganing*, or water that appears red—Red Lake; and *mizizak*, or horse fly; and, *Anin wa ezhayan owisini nagaj ina?*, or Are you going over to eat later?" (I should have been studying Chinese to become a foreign diplomat, but my mind didn't work like that.)

My school friends supported me emotionally, while I immersed myself in motherhood at home—cooking, cleaning, sewing, homework, PTA. I managed to keep up with my annual canning and jelly-making in the fall.

Husband and I went on a trip alone to salvage whatever threads of love remained, a last ditch attempt to revive an eighteen-year legal union. But the paint wouldn't stick to the canvas.

We traveled to see Jim and Clair in: Chapel Hill, North Carolina, where they both taught in alternative schools. They built themselves a cedar, dome-shaped home in the forest. It was full of wholeness and love—everything happening in one large circular room. Clair didn't miss curling on the ice in North Dakota.

Jodi and Joe had settled into Lexington, Massachusetts, working with special education children. We all cross-country skied around Walden Pond on a magical snowy day with no one else in sight. I vowed to read the writings of Henry Thoreau. I could not have known then that I would be back in Boston in eighteen months, from a return flight to Switzerland. Nor, could I have known that I'd return fourteen years later, to honor Henry and David Thoreau's one hundred and fiftieth anniversary of canoeing the Concord and Merrimack rivers, by retracing their celebrated expedition in my own canoe.

Like everything in life, my graduation was marked by mixed emotions, a balance of joy and bitterness, and beginnings and endings. Husband and I knew we would part ways, but we hadn't made it final, nor public, so all friends and family were invited to the party at our home after the ceremony at the University of Minnesota.

My budget was tight. I sewed a dress instead of renting a graduation gown. Alone in this regard, I felt more odd than proud.

My dubious parents attended the ceremony, but never showed up for my party. They explained, "We thought the ceremony was enough. Sorry."

I later learned they were angry with me for trading my marriage for an education, because if I'd only stayed at home, things would still be okay.

Oh well, they had been mad at me when I got married, too. They didn't approve of my choice. Mother insisted that I wear a short pink dress, and nobody was invited to the wedding. They could come to the house, eat cake, and leave a gift! Oh well, again. When I told Mother why I was getting a divorce, she was quick to disagree. She furrowed her brow and replied, "Oh Judy! Don't you know that all men knock their wives around from time to time?" (Thank God, my generation was fighting for higher expectations!) I forgave her such things, because she had been a wonderful mother in all other respects, providing me a healthy, happy childhood.

As things turned out, there was a party the night before the graduation party.

Rose Barstow, an Ojibwe elder from Mille Lacs Lake, was my Ojibwe language teacher for the past year. For an unknown reason, she made my life miserable in class, even though I tried so hard and ended up with an "A" in my third quarter.

She had a tiny bird-like body and a big attitude. She had long stringy gray hair, peering owl eyes, a puckered, prune face, and a manner that could put fear in me; except that I knew some things she wouldn't want me to know: she had a reputation for enjoying nightclubs and fancying herself as a woman deserving of a man's attention.

When she shook her finger at me and demanded that I sit in the front row, all the other students protectively stood up and also moved to the front with me. She didn't like that. Another day, she called me into the hall to say that I must have spring fever because I misinterpreted a sentence.

I spoke to Miz about this, and Miz said that my personal power must be strong, or perceived as such, or Rose wouldn't need to challenge me like that. "Don't allow her to get to you!" Miz said. And I didn't. I created a story for myself, that the aging woman was probably a bit jealous of a much younger one. Most people just shrugged off her quirkiness.

Because I was on a personal quest to learn how Ojibwe people think, and because Miz was teaching me about giving away and power, I decided to include Rose when I mailed invitations for my graduation celebration in June. I never expected her to attend.

On the evening before the big event, way out on the west side of Lake Minnetonka at my home, we were all in a whirlwind, cleaning and cooking for the next night's festivities.

Glancing out the window, while vacuuming the carpet, I spotted a long, rusty, low-slung Buick slowly pulling up out front. We all squinted through the glass and waited.

"It's Rose! Rose Barstow!" I yelled, alerting the kids, pulling curlers out of my hair, yanking my apron off.

"Isn't she the mean teacher?" Heath asked, pushing against the window, "What's she doing here?"

"I don't know—she's one day early."

The boney, brown-faced bird began to walk up to the door, while one by one, three brawny, barrel-shaped Indian men squeezed out of the car and ambled along behind her. I opened the door, "Hello!"

"Where is everybody?" she chirped, "Are we too early?"

"Yes you are! One whole day too early!"

"Oh, *geeze,* and it's such a long drive out here, too. You really live in the sticks, don't you?"

By now, all the children were gawking around me, at the unusual foursome on our front steps. "Get back to work," I ordered, "We still have a lot to do."

"Oh, oh," Rose uttered in a worried tone, "Maybe we should go, but I am kind of thirsty."

"You better come in then, and I'll find some refreshments. Sit down and make yourself at home."

"This is my family," she offered, stating names, as each brown giant found a chair, "Don't worry about us. We'll just stay a few minutes."

The curious children filtered back in the room—to do chores.

Rose seemed baffled, "Are these *all* your kids?"

"Yes. Please meet Lenny, Lisa, John, and Heath. Thanks to their good behavior and cooperation, I've been able to attend college."

"I never knew you had any kids!" Rose said, her mouth hanging open. "Where is your husband?" she inquired when I returned from the kitchen with the beverage of their choice—red wine.

"He lives in Superior, Wisconsin, where he teaches education classes."

"I didn't know you were married," she mumbled, sipping the wine.

"Oh yes—eighteen long years!" I bragged, like I had earned another Girl Scout badge.

Rose seemed visibly shaken, as she exclaimed, "You mean, you drove all that way, getting up early every day . . ."

"Five-thirty a.m.," I interjected, "Five-thirty a.m.? To attend my class, and take care of four children and a big house . . . ?"

"With a garden," I added.

"And no husband at home to help?"

Lisa piped up, "I take care of my horse and do my paper route."

The boys said together, "We take care of Red, shovel snow, and do dishes."

Rose actually had tears in her eyes. I offered them cheese and more wine, making them all so happy they stayed for three hours.

The next night I was amazed when they all returned and remained for the whole evening—Rose telling anyone who would listen what a wonderful student I had been and she was so proud of me.

Within a few years, she phoned me from her hospital bed to order a special vest because she knew I was sewing to make money. I delivered it to her bedside and offered it freely but she insisted she pay me. She passed away not long after that, leaving a little hole in my heart.

At my party, I felt a spirit—Brady Barber—my Fort Totten Dakota friend who died. Thinking about his love, and absence, made me cry.

The morning after the party, I awoke to a brilliant sunrise streaming through the windowpanes like a message saying, "Get up! Come out and honor me with your presence!"

I scurried into my clothes and ran through the budding spring woods to my "talking tree"; my fully leafed sugar maple mama, who held my back while I leaned against her sun-warmed trunk, sharing a sacred moment, sharing my thoughts about Brady—how he'd chased me around the trees on campus and become my confidant in times of trouble—urging me to go to school.

I thought about Miz, too, telling me to talk to trees.

My tree had lost a large limb. It lay across the wee stream that flowed into the channel entering the lake. Despite her loss, Ms. Maple kept right on living, sprouting new shoots.

The sun rose like a regal yellow orb, spreading radiant beams across the still lake, like lines of fairy wands shimmering over a glassy surface. Shielding my eyes, the sun rose higher until my whole face glowed.

My wise tree often kept my body dry in a rainstorm. She offered me energy and vitality in snow storms , for she held fast when winds ripped through her branches. And on quiet days, she gave me peace.

182

Her maple sap was appreciated by birds which repaid her with songs. One day, my steady friend would die and become earth, and her seeds would sprout and flourish in her soil, and so her cycle of renewable living would never cease. I could not have a better role model than she.

I ran my hand across the smooth roots that held the dirt firm on the wet clay bank, turned my head up to smile, and told her, "Most of all, I love you for creating only beauty."

I walked back to the house feeling taller, lighter, and stronger. After all my efforts, I was finally a college graduate.

Chapter 19
THE INDIANS HAD NO CONCEPT OF
PERFECTING NATURE
How can you be more important than what you eat?

University of St. Thomas

The slide projector is ready for my presentation about traditional and contemporary Indian art and artists, most of whom I've personally met and interviewed from Coast to Coast, in schools, galleries, and studios. They work in many mediums, vary from elderly to youthful, may have white skin or dark, have lived in a city or on a reserve, can have angry political opinions or none at all; but like all artists, they share a passion for self expression and discovery.

I begin addressing the class, "American Indians traditionally did not think of art as a separate entity, but as a part of the unified whole of existence. Objects were created for functional usage. They were meant to be used—not just looked at, whether for spiritual or utilitarian purposes. There was no elitism concerning art—it fostered no separate individuals or groups of artisans and patrons, although some were more adept at creativity than others. Also, some Northwest Coast tribes, did have artists who specialized in one form more than others. It was often true that art was the result of dreams by individuals who taught songs or patterns. Some art wasn't shared, due to the manner in which it was conceived.

"Indians developed no art standards based on money and no competitions for judging objects. There were no museums, either. There were no distinctions between artifact, craft, and fine art, and no collectors who bought art in galleries. Art schools didn't exist; and I doubt there were arguments over such things as form, composition, line, color and originality, although this may have occurred occasionally since some tribes were far more strict about individual expressions than others. Dozens of taboos influenced native activities in many ways."

Steven dims the lights while I start the slide projector and begin the presentation: face masks woven out of corn husks by the Iroquois in New York, kachina figures dressed like spirits from the Hopi in Arizona, buffalo hide parfleche bags that held pemmican all winter in underground caches for Dakota families, totem poles carved by Haida people on the Queen Charlotte Islands, pottery from the Pueblo artists at San Ildefonso near Santa Fe, Ojibwe moccasins with floral beadwork, speckled red pipes from Minnesota, abstract oil paintings from Santa Fe art galleries, modern stone sculpture from New York.

The show ends. The lights come on.

"Any questions or comments?"

Sara speaks up, "I'm just amazed at all the diversity!"

Tom adds, "Yeah, I guess I always thought Indians were, well, kind of, all alike."

"Oh no! They were quite different in many respects. Some were very successful agriculturalists who grew beans, corn, squash, and tobacco; raised turkeys and dogs; and created villages with hundreds of residents, and sophisticated art. Then there were others who were hunter-gatherers and lived more off the land. Tribes traded meat for corn, stones for shells, and so forth. They knew about the oceans, lakes, and rivers far and wide through the moccasin telegraph. Many, such as the Anasazi in western desert country, lived on the edge of starvation searching for berries, rabbits, acorns, or whatever, while living in stick shelters or caves," I pause briefly.

"But they, too, probably made pictographs, wove mats and shoes, tanned hides, and made crude pottery.

"Just like people the world over, some lived better than others."

Roberta comments, "Geography must have been an important determiner for the kind of culture each tribe developed. Some had good rich farm soil, but others didn't. Some had bison, and others didn't."

"Yes! The Calusa Indians lived along the Gulf Coast of Florida, and they ate so much shellfish and ingested so much calcium, they grew very tall with their healthy bones; they built tall mounds out of the shells. In Ohio, during the Adena-Hopewell period, earthen mounds were made—some shaped like giant animals."

Terry notices, "Everything seemed to be decorated—some things very simply and others very lavishly."

"Most objects were created for utilitarian use, like pottery, baskets, sleeping mats, and clothing. But many items were used for ceremonies—costumes, drums, and pipes—things like that. Each tribe had its own rules or taboos about the creation of sacred objects."

"Can you tell us what you mean by 'taboo'?" Sara inquires.

"All natives had or still have, social religious customs that banned or prohibited certain behaviors. There were taboos about sacred places such as the pipestone quarries and Lake Minnetonka—two places of such importance that no disagreements among tribes could occur on those lands. There were places to avoid like burial grounds. Personal relationships had taboos—such as: don't stare into the eyes of your in-laws, or those of a wolf.

"My friend Dayshun Goodsky, an Ojibwe elder from Nett Lake, told me to never throw eggshells into a fire. He didn't know why. The reason had been lost, like most taboos."

Roberta says, "I would think they'd be happy that those old customs have died out, wouldn't you?"

"Conformity to customs can have negative and positive effects upon a group-oriented society. Not all beliefs were prohibitions, but rather customs to perform certain duties, such as giving thanks to the deer you just killed, or placing tobacco in dangerous rapids, or singing a certain song, or doing a dance to achieve some ends.

"Remember, natives didn't have lawyers, courtrooms, or judges. They governed themselves through personal ethical behavior prescribed by a system of beliefs and taboos. Sure, a lot of superstition, and silly stuff went on; but then, they thought we did crazy, things, too."

Steven raises his hand to speak, "Like what? What did they think we did that was crazy?"

"Like locking people into cold stone boxes, sometimes for years. They thought jails were utterly inhumane and cruel. Indians would banish a trouble-making nonconformist from the tribe, and that person would have a difficult time surviving without group support. America now has far more prisoners than anywhere in the world. Perhaps this is because our for profit system doesn't work as well as the 'taboo and belief' system of primitive societies!"

Oh dear! There I go again, expressing personal opinions in class. Where is the line between personal opinion and sharing knowledge? I don't know, because I think in connections rather than divisions.

The room is so quiet, I hear the heat system click on. The students stare at me, but I know they're only thinking hard. Good! On the other hand, perhaps students should be included in the Ojibwe taboo about looking into the eyes of your elders, or in-laws.

"Let's return to Roberta's comment about the geographical influence upon art creation. Domesticated sheep came from Europe with the Spanish who conquered the Southwest where the Pueblo, Hopi, Zuni, and Navajos live. Before that, the finest weaving was being produced in the Central Andes Mountains—in South America, from vicuna and llama wool."

"Did the Indians copy designs from each other?" Steven asks.

"They did copy each other in many respects, such as the use of horses, metals, plants, and so on. Perhaps they'd learn how to make paint, but then apply it in new ways that created cultural identity and traditions. Only plains Indians had eagle feather headdresses that fell to the legs. Other tribes had their own designs, songs, and dances. Adaptation and conformity created balance.

"American Indians were far more interested in preservation of order as they understood it, than they were in change for competition. They didn't think changes they could make would improve what the Great Mystery had already provided."

John asks, with doubt in his voice, "They didn't turn down guns when they could get them to fight their enemy, did they?"

"True," I say, "They needed guns when aggressive Europeans began exterminating the natives and forcing them onto their neighbor's territory. Indians knew the consequences of accepting new technology, but were fighting against extinction of their race."

"But," John argues, "Women must have been glad to have metal pots to cook in and needles to sew with, and cloth fabric,"

Terry says, hopefully, "They did want those things, but not at such a high price, like the smallpox disease that wiped out more people than guns."

"They used art to try to make the Europeans go away. The Paiute natives who lived on the plains had a leader named Wovoka who had a dream that he taught to his people; and if they performed this dream, life would return to the old ways. They designed special shirts with symbols and a dance with a song; and belief in this endeavor brought temporary relief to the hearts of weary, starving plains dwellers.

"Back in the 1970s, a Minneapolis museum had a show of these haunting, spiritual clothes—some with a bullet hole in them. They were attacked while dancing, by US Calvary soldiers who accused them of plotting against the government or planning an attack on new settlers. They weren't armed.

"Let's take a break and return to have some fun. Let's learn how to make a dream catcher."

"May I ask one more question?" Roberta says eagerly, "Was there a spiritual dimension to the art of Indians?"

"Most art made today is created for the same purpose as that made by nonIndians—personal expressions of feelings and experiences that may or may not offer a message to a viewer. After all, almost all natives today are as likely as you or I to shop in stores, watch TV, buy a car, eat at McDonald's and serve in the military.

"However, traditional work continues to be produced in the old ways—like designs, songs, and stories that carry cultural identity from one generation to the next in repetitive activities performed carefully, and mindfully, to please spirits; to induce spirits to be mindful of the people as a whole. Artistic expressions could have serious consequences, good or bad, depending on the intent of the artist who could affect things—like a medicine man or woman.

"Generally, it was more fortuitous to be in harmony with the spirits in all of Mother Earth's creation than to be an individual at odds with the rhythms of the world. Some tribes allowed more individualistic expressions than others.

"Thoughts and acts were insurance that the rain would fall, the corn would grow, the people would prosper. If things happened in a predictable manner, people would be rewarded.

"Do you see this pendant that I'm wearing? It represents the circle of life and much more, for this tiny person at the top will spend his life on a quest in a maze. And like art—it is personal and universal all at once. It is about change and continuity. It is about infinity and limitations," I explain, stepping in front of my desk, holding the pendant forward, and removing it from my neck.

Tenderly, I run my fingertips across the three-inch circular embossed design. My piece is solidly crafted from leather with a black

189

pattern of a maze that has four parts with an opening at the center top where a tiny man with a feather on his head, begins or ends his journey, having traveled to the black dot in the middle. Carefully tracing the curving pattern always brings me to the center. I've never seen anything like it among the Dakota or Ojibwe people.

"It's quite handsome with a braided leather chain that goes about my neck and silver tips at the two ends."

"Where is it from?" John asks, peering closely—touching it.

"My friend, Roger got it from a Southern Arizona tribe called the Tohono O'odham or Desert People. They use this image on baskets, pottery, and even silver," I say, writing on the blackboard. "Please say after me: *Taw-haw-no Aw-otahm*."

"*Taw-haw-no Aw-otahm!*" the students repeat in chorus.

"They were called the Papago when I received this as a gift, way back in 1977. The 'bean eaters' live near the Mexican border in the Tucson area."

"Is that where you bought it?" Steve asks.

"No, a friend gave it to me in Minneapolis. I knew nothing about the Tohono O'odham, but the gift inspired me to go to the Southwest where I'd never been. I was about to graduate with a degree in Art and Indian Studies; and, for my senior thesis, I decided to photograph and interview as many living Indian artists creating contemporary expressions as I could. I was just as interested in traditional art, but it had already been well documented, and I'd learned that few people knew that Native Americans were producing art similar to the styles of Picasso, Seurat, Braque, and Klee, or in abstract expressionism, cubism, pointillism, and so on—paintings that usually depicted Indian subjectivity in Euro-Western styles.

"Of course, in art classes I learned that Picasso got his ideas from ancient African designs—work that didn't try to portray nature in perfect representational forms (which photography purportedly

190

achieved), and I theorized that Picasso wasn't doing anything new at all because our native ancestors had always been abstractionists. They just didn't have framed canvas to paint upon.

"I wondered why humans had evolved from creating 'meaning' within the essence of a feeling or event, to striving for perfection and order as we see in the works of painters like Albert Bierstadt.

"The 'civilized' world's argument over what is abstract or natural in painting became a discussion about realism, and Paul Klee stated that, 'The relativity of the visible has become evident.' This was quite different than thinking of painting as a window showing life itself as natural, or real, when in fact, painting was merely reinterpreting perceptions of individual artists.

"The American Indians had no concept of perfecting nature, nor any idealistic vision of what it should be other than what it was in a wild state—or as the Great Mystery had given it to the people. They created no images of a god or gods personified because humankind was a humble creature equal to bears, bison, deer, and so on.

"Think of it this way," I say cautiously, slowly, so it will sink in to their brains, "How can you be more important than what you eat?" I ask, stepping closer, "How can you even exist without animals and plants?

"You see, natives didn't glorify themselves nor their great deeds in works of art by inventing a human god with a personality that they made images of.

"Why? Because to them, god was a mystery—an abstract mystery, a force that inexplicably gave life."

Steve raises his hand and asks, "The Indians on the plains made hide paintings with battle scenes. Didn't that glorify themselves?"

"Yes! They were very proud people, yet frowned upon boasting. But they celebrated most victories over their enemies and some artists recorded them like we record history. Indians made pictures of animals

191

more than of humans. They received strength and power from animals which is probably why they formed clans named after them, and even thought of themselves as physically connected to them. This system worked to protect the health of the tribe. Clans were groups related by blood through the father's or mother's line. The Ojibwe once had about eighteen totems or clans, and marriage was prohibited between them. All the tribes had a static Neolithic lifestyle similar to that of Europeans who lived by the Mediterranean between 4000 and 3000BC."

Roberta has a question, "The figure on your leather pendant—well, is that a god?"

"NO! And now is not the proper time to talk about it. Certain things should be spoken of in prescribed ways," I reply, teasing them a bit.

"Let's make dream catchers, now."

Chapter 20

BY FULFILLING OUR ROLE,
BALANCE WILL BE SUSTAINED

How can we think in circles and connections?

University of St. Thomas

Three perky women arrive early for their Indian Art class, students who will begin teaching grade school next year. Their blue jeans fit so tight, they look glued to their legs; low-cut fitted T-shirts in pink, yellow, and blue accentuate their youthful figures. Chattering with animated hand gestures, they acknowledge my presence with polite radiant smiles, then move into desks in the back corner.

Like giant Barbie Dolls: straight, smooth blonde hair; pink and pearly flawless skin; small, narrow noses; full glossy lips; long eye lashes; and yes—thin bodies. The effect is a combination of seductive innocence and beauty without subtlety, modesty, or originality.

Some of them do have interesting jackets, sweaters, or purses that look used or worn—*out* of fashion along with the *in* fashion jeans. The scruffy look was *in* when I became a mama hippie. God, what fun! I don't wish to return to that era of extremes, yet I would prefer it to the placid, dull, commercialism of computers, TVs, and cell phones.

I felt sure my women students wouldn't want to be me at their age, before my hippie era. Back then, I was unhappy about certain things, like my old electric washing machine. I'm positive none of these women ever had her arm sucked into a roller on a ringer-washer machine. Heck, they've never even seen one. A white round steel tub on four legs, a motor attached on the underside, a contraption sticking up on top with two ivory white rubber rollers the size of fat rolling pins that parted open and shut by pushing a lever back and forth. The soaked, soapy diapers rocked in the noisy drum, then they were squeezed through the rollers, one by one, by hand, into a second tub of rinse water, then run back through the rollers into a woven reed basket on the floor. This, I carried up the basement steps—outside to the clothesline; or, in the winter, hung on a line in the basement. Everything was cotton and retained wrinkles. Therefore everything needed to be ironed, except diapers. (Can you imagine washday *before* electricity?)

One night after canning sweet watermelon pickles, tucking four children into bed after story time and washing the dinner dishes, I descended into the dim, damp basement with a heavy pail of soaking, poop-stained diapers, thinking of my friends and relatives with their new automatic top-loading square machines that did everything.

I plopped the mess into the tub, added soap, and hot water from the hose, put the lid on tight and sat down to wait. Six deep shelves of canned goods stood on the opposite wall, quarts or pints of cherries, pears, peaches, apples for pies, apple sauce, apple-green tomato mincemeat, apricots, stewed tomatoes, tomato juice, watermelon pickles, sweet sliced pickles, dill pickle spears, blueberry-rhubarb jam, tomato-orange-walnut conserve, and corn relish.

My weary shoulders drooped while focusing proudly on all the shiny, gold-lidded jars full of bounty, a display similar to the one Mom created every fall in the basement. Counting each one, I arrived at a number exceeding two hundred. My labor had saved a lot of money for my family, and we would eat better than we would have if I had to pay retail store prices. Someday I hoped to have a freezer.

I almost fell asleep, I was so exhausted; but I returned to the clunky washing machine to force the diapers through the rollers.

I stopped the swish-swish of the agitator, switched on the hum of rollers, and began the monotonous job of feeding diapers through one

194

side and listening to them fall on the other. Such a tedious task wore me down. I felt like I was a thing—a cog in the machine. My mind wandered: nature's repetitive, cyclical ways were good, but did the diapers have to keep coming? Did the cleaning have to go on and on? Did the cooking? The sewing? On and on?

Plop, plop went the diapers.

Ouch! My fingers were grabbed by the rollers! Then my arm entered the machine! I screamed! It hurt like heck! Pushing the release button gave me some relief, but I was still stuck, so I had to push the reverse button to roll it back out—my poor red arm.

My scream woke the family. They came running down the basement steps in their pajamas—their faces horrified when they saw me holding my swollen, throbbing limb, my body jerking from heavy sobs, a gush of tears landing on the clean diapers below. Feeling stupid and angry with myself for being careless, I welcomed the sympathy and hugs of the children. Everybody could see what had happened.

My husband stood back, grinning. He chuckled, "Why did you do a dumb thing like that?" he laughed.

A volcano erupted within me!

"I'm not using that stupid machine again!" I warned him, "YOU just bought yourself a new deer hunting rifle. You can also buy me a new washer—one without a roller!" I demanded, running for the door before he could hit me—or stop me.

After driving across the city, crying, I woke his parents at midnight, pouring out my heart, telling them what a jerk their son was.

The next week, a new automatic washer arrived on our doorstep.

The women students at the University of St. Thomas have so many new luxuries. Yet, I want to warn them, "Don't get married or have children until you're well educated, because half of you will end up raising a family alone, and with explosive population growth, and shrinking natural resources, you will have a harder time surviving in a competitive, capitalistic-modeled society. Millions of men will be unemployed and have no land of their own to support families, thus women will be on their own as frustrated men join wars fought over resources. This is already true in much of the world."

I knew that hungry women will do things they don't want to, like stay in abusive relationships. I wavered because I believed that marriage isn't only a union of two people, but a sacred bond uniting the blood of two families. I struggled with questions: Would my kids be better off without a dad in the home, or was my suffering something to tolerate for the sake of the family? How would I feed children unless I had a good job? I knew I could never count on child support. I loved my family of in-laws, and didn't want to leave them. Grandparents, uncles, and aunts—all play important roles in families. Can friends take their place? I don't think so. Family history—good or bad—becomes personal identity and provides meaning and understanding of our world.

My mentor, Mizinokamigok, an Ojibwa teacher from Nett Lake, Minnesota, had told me about traditional Indian divorce, "You just put his things outside the wigwam or tipi!"

Anthropology classes taught me about extended families in native cultures and how children were raised by a group, and never dependent upon one or two caretakers. The Ojibwe had two ways to identify themselves: by blood or by their clan.

My relatives were scattered all over the country. My tribe was small.

St. Thomas students are the children of the Iraq War period in history. Actually, it's an occupation by an invading nation that is spreading to neighboring countries. The water-boarding and the killing is sickening- thousands of soldier and civilian deaths, billions of dollars. Progressive grandparents, like me, believe the nation has "gone to hell." George W. Bush, elected president by illegal means, and his secretive staff, is purposefully bankrupting America's middle class while conducting a thirty-year war (begun by President Ronald Reagan) against Franklin Roosevelt's New Deal legacy of social democracy. The nation's debt to foreign creditors, such as China and Japan, will be inherited by generations to come; inherited by my students and their children who will first suffer a recession and then a world of depression.

All of this was preventable!

Back in the sizzling 1960s, when John Kennedy and Lyndon Johnson were presidents, the Republicans and Libertarians thought America had "gone to hell," because young people like me were in the streets, protesting unconstitutional treatment of women, Indians, Blacks, and blue collar workers. We were the Vietnam War generation, angry about the draft for soldiers who were being shipped to Asia to die in another war concocted by leaders "fighting Communism." (World War I also began out of dubious origins, and lack of diplomacy.)

Both wars enriched defense contractors with billions of dollars, shifting money away from social needs, but the Iraq War was also bleeding the spirit and soul out of the people, filling us with remorse and shame. However, news about protests was rarely reported and indeed, the occupation itself was no longer news! What would Benjamin Franklin think about our brand of freedom of the press?! He could not have imagined that it would cease to exist from lack of news coverage.

Many years ago, like so many fairness and justice-minded young parents, I harbored an idealistic ambition. I planned to get my degree in education and teach American Indian children in ways that would encourage them to be better educated. However, in the 1970s, the American Indian Movement began schools to develop materials about Indian culture and provide an alternative to public education. I decided to change my focus to the study of Indian Art, and pursue my own interest in sculpture and painting.

There was one big problem with my goals. I was moving toward a messy divorce with four children; and I had no idea how to get a job, since my only employment outside of my home had been working in a Dairy Queen one summer in high school. I didn't know what I should do. My feelings shifted from a pit-sucking fear in my stomach, to an excitement verging on euphoria, at the thought of being free, and creating an opportunity to grow and explore the world. Most of all, I wanted to meet more people doing meaningful things, people curious about the ways we think as humans. (I now know that homemakers have the most meaningful work in the world.)

Here I am forty years later. Nothing ever gave me more satisfaction than teaching Indian Art, and I love the enthusiastic, respectful St. Thomas students, some who are student teaching in the AIM school in St. Paul. My life's journey traveled many directions, just like Miz had said, "Life is like a road map. We go in many directions, but we always come to intersections, or connections; and we end up where we began, hopefully with more wisdom than when we started." Over the past years, my staunch belief that humans have much of value to learn from native peoples, has intensified. My passion for understanding the differences between Euro-Western and American Indian thinking has led me on adventures that I never could have imagined.

St. Thomas students use square seats, square tables, and square notebooks. The room is square, as is the school building, and the property lot on which it sits. The city only follows the contours of the land where building on a square is impossible. Every inch of America might be a square if planners could have their way.

My desire is to teach students to think "in circles" and

"connections." I must explain why the Indians thought like this. I don't explain why we don't, because I don't have time to explain 10,000 years of world history in this class.

I hope that teaching through stories, and showing Indian art, the class will develop methods they can pass on to their pupils—concepts that are more conceptual than rational.

I have found clarity and common sense in such thinking patterns, qualities that have "gone missing" in today's society. In America, and elsewhere, particularly in an urgent crisis like climate change we seem to be brain dead.

I now think in patterns, stories, and pictures. If we thought in patterns, rather than logic, we would possibly not be threatened with our own extinction—a looming catastrophe that could create an imbalance so extreme that mammals could not breathe or eat. All of this is preventable!

Some people are causing these problems at the expense of the rest of life. Some believe their god wants us to die, so he can create a justifiable end to sinful humans. Some think there's inevitability inherent in creation, so that humans have no power over their own destiny. Others, like myself, live with hope. We believe that our relationship with Mother Earth and Father Sky is based upon an attitude of duty and reciprocity; and that, by fulfilling our part, balance will be sustained, and we will live in beauty and good health *right here on earth.*

And even if I'm wrong, I choose to live in hope and happiness with a sense of responsibility, instead of gloomy fear and despair with a sense of self-denial.

This is not only the best of all possible worlds—it is the *only* possible world provided for mammals—that we know about. I would rather die on earth than live on Mars or anyplace else.

PART 2

Chapter 21
HOPI DANCING—SINGING FOR CORN
AND MOTHER EARTH

How did the meaning of art differ between the Hopi
and modern contemporary artists?

Hopi Indian Reservation, Shungopavi, Second Mesa, Arizona

Shivering in melting snow in front of the Signature Cafe, I wave goodbye to Allison, as her dad pulls away from the curb. She waves back, her fine hair shimmering like corn tassels in the breeze. The Ford van disappears around the corner.

I slip into my sleek, aerodynamic black, electric hybrid Prius, thinking how my dad, a savvy car salesman, helped me buy or maintain my cars after I was divorced. I had no idea how I'd earn money after the deadbeat dad left for Colorado. My parents blamed me for splitting up the marriage by going to college. Never mind that he was a selfish wife-beater! I tossed myself at the mercy of the world, desperate for something better. I was truly on my own.

Prior to the split, I'd traveled with Katrina in 1977, doing research for my senior thesis on American Indian contemporary art. During the time that I visited Santa Fe, Sells, and Second Mesa, I still hoped to pursue my interest in becoming a sculptress following the encouragement of my teachers. I was fascinated by modern conceptual artists like Joseph Beuys, a German. I was beginning to realize that the differences between Indian and European artistic expressions represented not only work, or objects that I could see, but an entirely new way of understanding the world. Modern art appealed to a side of me that loved anything unusual—fun, free expression, funky materials, or multiple meanings. Creation could be or mean anything the artist desired with no restrictions imposed by societal norms. The last thing an artist wanted was to be a conformist.

When I was a teenager, I fell in love with Dixieland jazz while babysitting at the neighbors. Jelly Roll Morton and Louis Armstrong filled the Gisvold house with New Orleans music while the kids and I danced till we dropped. Now I have my own collection.

In college I read Jack Kerouac's *On the Road*. I adored Flannery O'Connor's quirky style. I loved Bob Dylan's poetic lyrics. Thus, I learned that change, the more—the better, was a highly desirable American value imbued in all aspects of our culture; and those who created it were rewarded with praise, and often money.

However, deep within me were conflicting instincts. Synthetic fabrics and plastics grew up with me, and I hated them from the beginning. The worst invaders were ugly plastic flowers and drinking "glasses." They weren't even necessary—we had real flowers and glasses made out of glass. I had nightmares about the earth becoming covered with things we didn't need, that never disintegrated, that were ugly.

My journal writing in 1976 during art school, included: "I hate plastic dishes and flowers for what they symbolize, yet I work in fiberglass in art now. Fiberglass is manipulated naturalism. Must I justify the things I dislike, if I'm to make peace with myself during my time on earth?

"In conceptual art one can no longer discriminate between object and image, natural and synthetic, reality and counterfeit.

"My artwork (and sometimes me) is tucked away into corners of this house like some crazy cousin that one is (sad to say) ashamed of. It disheartens me because I'm excited about what I've created and would like to display it, but our house has few guests anymore. My mother asked me which of the children made the fiberglass shirt! She

203

thinks I should paint pretty scenes. That would justify my artistic existence to those around me, but then I'd be silly to change just so they can pat me on the back and say, 'You're an artist!' I do long for a bit of praise and understanding, but I'm afraid to display it, lest Husband, in a temperamental rage, smashes another piece like he did my wood one. I hide it from him. He knows it. It's my way of letting him think that he's more important than my art. He wants to maintain power over me, and he's jealous of my new life. Also, perhaps I'm afraid of criticism—afraid it may discourage me."

Additional journal entries: "There is no absolute—only an unknown universe. The infinite and the will are the basis for all existence. These, we can only sense with feelings while searching for the mysterious. Living as a universal being should be our greatest concern, for if we care about *all* life, we nurture a relationship of (wo)man *with* earth (a circle), not, man *on* earth (a line).

"I believe there's no right and wrong, no yes and no—only likenesses and differences. The Chinese and Indians seem to know this. The Christians don't admit it, and the old scientific absolutism didn't permit it. Einstein feels that by respecting life, we find spiritual relationships with the world. (How did he show that feeling by helping to invent a bomb to blow up the earth?)

"There's good change and bad change. Women's liberation and enlightenment have helped women to not have to use beauty to further their own social and professional progress. Perhaps this is our greatest gain.

"They say tomorrow is the first day of your life. Ha! My laundry basket says it's wash day again!"

One last journal entry: "April 1977. I have just traveled to Charco 27, Arizona, and back, and the miles of comprehension and discovery are much greater than the miles registered on my car's odometer. My trip through the minds of others was a reflection from them onto me and back. Desert people have so much to teach me.

Driving toward home, away from the warmth and coziness of the Signature Cafe, tiny raindrops sprinkle my windshield. I remember the rainbow at Hopi village. Deeply etched memories of my 1977 trip with Katrina continue. I recall what happened after we left the two-faced McLaughlins, the Mormon missionaries for the Papago Indians.

Katrina and I were civil to each other as we drove from the Papago Reservation to Flagstaff, encountering a roaring snowstorm on the freeway, causing me to pull off the road. Visibility was almost zero; however, with fear mounting as fast as the snow, I was soon anxious to leave, before we were buried or smashed into by a giant truck.

Alas! The tires became stuck. A sickening feeling in my gut eroded my confidence. Katrina was blessedly silent. Traffic seemed to have ceased. We sat uneasily in a silent white tomb unable to see out. I wasn't worried about freezing to death—that sort of thing happened in Minnesota and the Dakotas. But this was Arizona for God's sake.

A police officer pulled up, got out, knocked on our window and ordered us to "move on." "I would if I could !" I replied, trying not to sound sarcastic. He sounded an order, "You must, or you'll be buried here! I'll stay behind you after you get going to be sure you make it to the top of the mountain pass. It's not far."

Like a miracle, we got back on the road and crawled along until safely out of the storm without the escort of the officer who quickly abandoned us. The little green Vega had performed well.

After a late morning tire change at a Standard gas station, we drove to Cameron to the Navajo Arts and Crafts Tribal Enterprise, then on to Tuba City passing the Painted Desert—red and green shades of soft and harsh textures—a paradoxical mix of magical mesas; an exotic landscape for the eyes of a Minnesota girl who's been raised among bucolic pastures with grazing milk cows and dense dark, moist forests full of big, fat beasts like moose and bears.

At Margaret's Indian Store I photographed pottery and blankets, carefully recording the origin and style of each for my slide collection.

Nearing the Hopi villages around 6:00 p.m. we enjoyed a sweet-scented desert rain followed by a glorious full rainbow—an arch of many hues and hopes—a good omen, I believed.

At Hotevilla on Third Mesa I asked for the Tribal chairman, but he was at a Tribal Council meeting so we left for Shungopavi at Second Mesa to locate Yvonne Smith, the wife of Hiram Randolph Smith, the Hopi man I'd met at a reception in St. Paul, Minnesota, who had invited me to the Corn Dance. He remained at Macalaster College, studying for his degree in accounting, to become the tribal financial officer, but he'd written to Yvonne to say we would be arriving on this day.

A feeling of awe swept over me as I slowly drove up the steep, dusty incline toward an adobe village perched high upon a broad mesa. An intense awareness of myself in time gripped me like a moment of epiphany, like stepping outside of my skin and watching myself enter a special happening in my short life on earth, like knowing that what was about to unfold was predestined, like feeling completely comfortable that you are where you belong at that moment for a purpose yet to be determined.

Easing the Vega to the edge of the narrow, quiet road, I set my car brake and turned to marvel at the pink and purple misty sky: the rain shower continuing eastward; the brilliant sun, low in the west, filtering through fast moving billowing clouds. Never in Minnesota had I seen such a spectacle. Far below: miles and miles of vanilla-colored, flat, arid sagebrush land; vertical cliffs of ivory and golden rock topped by flat surfaces. I could not imagine living in a place so difficult to cultivate with precious little rainfall and moisture often arriving only in floods. Yet, the Hopi, meaning 'The Peaceful Ones,' have inhabited the Southwest longer than any other people, for they migrated in successive groups beginning thousands of years ago settling Pueblo villages from the Grand Canyon to the Pacific Ocean and from Utah to Southern Arizona increasing in population from 2,000 to 10,000 since the Spanish arrived in 1528.

Shifting the gears, the car droned forward, upward to the mesa top where we stopped, hesitating about our next move since we only had a name to search for. Low-roofed adobe homes, handmade of clay and stone foundations, clay bricks and mud plaster, rose out of Mother Earth like giant square mushrooms. Fine dust that would normally cling to bushes, cars, pickups, and people, had been washed away by the rain, yet no puddles remained. The earth drank every drop.

Katrina wondered out loud, "I wonder which home is Yvonne's?"

A cluster of curious, jovial barefoot Hopi kids ran toward us to ask us who we were. Thus we solicited their help, while treating them to expensive maple sugar candy from the Ojibwe in Minnesota. They examined it, popped it in their mouths, and promptly spit it out!

I apologized and offered them money. They hesitated, then refused, perhaps because Mother was close behind and had instructed them not to accept money from strangers. (I'd been told that it was a fine gift for adults.) The beautiful young woman was Yvonne, and two of the girls were her daughters, Jessica and Gladys, ages eight and six.

Once inside the house, we met several more family members, mostly female or elderly. Everybody listened to Yvonne, Katrina, and myself speak about Minnesota, school classes, families, and our trip. We sat in a small, plain adobe room with one door facing the road; another that led to more rooms. Yvonne led me alone to a strange enclave. The back of the house opened into a vast natural stone cave, unfurnished, except for one lone bed and mattress, the sort one would find in an army barracks. A clean sheet and wool blanket lay on top. A simple chair would hold my clothes, and an ordinary galvanized bucket with a handle would hold my bodily waste. Yvonne chuckled and asked me if I could get by with the sparse arrangement.

"It's more than I have when I'm camping. And, I'm sure the roof won't leak. I bet it's quiet, too."

She laughed, pleased that I was happy. Katrina slept in the girl's bedroom that night. We returned to the front room where the lights were on and the night was upon us.

Yvonne shocked me with her next move, an announcement, "I'm now inviting you both to join us tonight in the *kiva* for a ceremony. I must tell you some things first."

My anticipation and excitement could not have been greater. This was a total surprise. I could hardly believe my ears.

"First, we must wait for an invitation, a knock on the door. We may wait a long time, and we may not get to bed till very late. Also, it will be quite cold, so dress warmly; and if you have a shawl, wear that, too. All the Hopi women will have one on. We will walk to the *kiva* when called. It will become very dark and the path is rough, so stick close to me. When we get to the *kiva*, remain very silent, but when we're allowed in move quickly and push to the left. Let's see now— oh, no cameras are allowed anywhere on the mesa. You can leave your things here, and they'll be perfectly safe."

I thanked the people for allowing us to participate, especially Yvonne who controlled everything. She was a slender, attractive person with long hair, small features—full of energy and grace.

I liked her very much. And all the Hopi elders who sat in wait with us. Yvonne kept warning the children to stay away from the window, but I didn't know why. Nor did I know where the young men were.

We seemed to run out of conversation eventually, and the young ones became rambunctious. I asked them, "Would you like to hear a story? I've created some that my children like to hear, and I can share them with you."

"Oh yes! Tell us a story!" they all cried.

So I began, "Once upon a time . . ." Immediately, all the oldsters moved in with the children and bent their ears down toward me. My story about a haunted house paled, I'm sure, next to their rich tales that taught moral lessons. My awareness of this fact caused me some embarrassment. However, I couldn't just quit, so I went on, much to their amusement and rapt attention. I thought to myself, "This is crazy! I want to be listening to *their* stories." (I would learn in coming weeks that stories told in Indian country are done in the winter when the spirit characters are quiet. I had broken a taboo.)

Soon we sat in the room, listening to nothing but footsteps outside and the crackle of coals in a hearth in the wall.

"*Knock, knock!*" sounded a hard fist against the solid pine door.

"*Woosh!*" The door flew open. A weird, unearthly figure, weighty and forceful, wildly burst upon us.

The startled children screamed, "*Eeek!*" They jumped up while the adults recoiled on their seats. The spiritman was all black-and-white stripes from head to toe, with two matching conical horns protruding from a skullcap. His face was chalk-white with black rings around mouth and eyes. Leaping about on his mismatched shoes, he was more scary than funny. His white hands grabbed Yvonne who resisted in a struggle as he carried her out the door, while the pleas of the children grew more desperate. They tried to follow and save her, but it was useless as the door slammed shut in their faces.

While all attention had been on Yvonne, I boldly peeked out the window away from the body-snatching theatrics and saw a parade of Hopi women and children wearing dark shawls, all with heads bowed, moving in the same direction. Then, I saw Yvonne being hauled away . . . and the crowd lifting their heads to laugh at her! They thought it was hilarious! And it was. All in good Hopi fun. The jokester returned Yvonne unharmed and chuckling as she breathlessly remarked, "Hurry up! We have to go now!"

The kachina pranced off in search of a new victim.

We became one with the scurrying group in the street, heading for the *kiva* for the night Corn Dance, stopping to huddle together in the shadow of the moon against the adobe wall of the *kiva*—like a flock of quiet black crows waiting just below the roof line, waiting to repeat rituals that were hundreds of years old, shrouded in utmost secrecy, and of utmost necessity to assure the survival of all the corn crops, and even, some say, Mother Earth.

In that mysterious atmosphere, I truly felt the weight of my personal responsibility and was honored to be a guest rather than a tourist. I looked skyward into the midnight heavens speckled with glittering stars—no evidence of electricity anywhere. I listened for familiar night sounds, but heard only the chilling breeze, and the breathing of one hundred Hopi packed tightly for warmth. And then I detected faint footsteps on the *kiva* roof.

"Don't look up!" Yvonne warned everyone in a hushed tone.

I didn't mean to, however, out of the corner of my eye, atop the mud roof I saw a kachina hustle downward while grasping two poles, which I presumed was a ladder in a hole descending into the sacred chamber.

Yvonne whispered in my ear, "Here we go! Go to the left at the bottom of the staircase, and choose a seat." I had to steady myself or be upset by the crush on the stairs. Excited and astonished by the competitive vigor to enter, I soon found myself separated from my group, entering the womb of Mother Earth without them upon a stone staircase no wider than myself, stepping into an open space with a very low ceiling, an oval- or square-shaped room with curving corners with seating for the men to the right, women and children to the left.

The women's rows of wood benches faced the center while the men sat upon an adobe ledge built into the wall facing the dance area. Our side had a ledge, too and that is where I sat, in the back row leaning against the cold wall. The stone was hard under my bottom, so I tucked my shawl under me as tightly as I could. Katrina, Yvonne, and the kids sat further up on hand-carved benches. I didn't care. My tiny discomfort was a bit of a sacrifice, a totally appropriate attitude under the circumstances. I understood the Hopi paradigm of sacrificial relationships enough to know how sincere the people were compared to my Christian rituals that were nothing but symbolic. The only sacrifice toward a more godly world in my neighborhood was avoidance of fish on Fridays. If it had been steak, it would really hurt.

Feelings of high energy permeated our end of the room. The grandfathers against the other wall appeared calm and relaxed. They wore clean beige or white pants, white blouses, colorful red sashes, and headbands over hair cut bluntly under the ears. Most women wore full skirts and knit sweaters under their shawls, with sturdy shoes and thick stockings. Since Katrina was probably "being an Indian again," I was the only Anglo in the *kiva*.

The center of the sanctuary held a fire, which was tended by an impressive elderman whose deeply etched face revealed his antiquity. He dressed like the others, however he carried a bag of cornmeal, which he often sprinkled about the floor while speaking prayers in his soft, melodious Hopi language. A small man, somewhat bent at the shoulders, he had silver hair and gnarled hands, and he wore owlish eyeglasses.

The crowd settled down just as the first line of kachina dancers entered the room and formed a pattern on the dirt floor by assuming identical positions in rows, waiting for a signal to begin. The elder who had sprinkled the maize uttered more prayers. The drum began to beat in a slow, steady rhythm, followed by the dancers who moved their bodies in a gentle unison, first this way, then that way, over and over again. The effect was peaceful and hypnotizing compared to the "war-whooping, partridge-strutting" powwow dancing of Ojibwe men of the northern forests. The sound effects of the small drum, (Perhaps *their* god was closer and didn't need a big, booming drum?) and the clacking of deer-hoof ankle bracelets, turtle or gourd rattles filled with pebbles or seeds, the chanting of deep voices, all these devices were so pleasing to my ears. They were also a big contrast to the astonishing display before my eyes.

I saw incredible hand-carved masks festooned with feathers, faces painted in yellows and reds, leather deer-hide skirts as white as new fallen snow, leggings and boots with tassels, and wool woven into geometric designs with colors made from natural dyes of red, white, yellow, and black, and more. If the music was constrained, the costumes were fantastical.

If art is mastering the forms of contrast and paradox, the Hopi had Robert Rauschenberg and Bob Dylan beat by a mile.

But I didn't think I was participating in an artful experience.

No, that evening had roots in human thoughts that preceded the formal intellectualizing of human expressions. The purpose for the Hopis' actions, and the purpose for modern art could not be further apart. I began to understand that if I could identify and explain those two opposing philosophies, I could understand why my German immigrant ancestors thought of the land so differently than the Indians they replaced on the Minnesota prairie.

Several waves of different kachinas came and went until about 1:30 a.m. or later. I didn't know what each represented, but I tried to remember so I could identify them in pictures, or as dolls, later on. I couldn't believe there were enough men to do all those dances. After awhile, I noticed the same World War tattoos on the arms of veterans, confirming that they were changing outfits somewhere in secret, perhaps at the foot of the mesa in the moonlight. I was amazed how they could keep everything so clean and new looking. Everybody laughed when the dancers turned and danced together once.

At the end, a clown kachina reached into a gunnysack and gave fresh fruit, cooked corn, and candy to all the women and children who enthusiastically reached out for it.

I slept soundly in my modest accommodations in the cave room. I didn't have to fall asleep to have a dream. I was living one.

In the morning, around 9:30 a.m., I went to a breakfast at Yvonne's uncle's house where many relatives gathered for an array of delectable choices. Before eating, Uncle Carl directed me to a separate table where I was taught to dip my finger in a small bowl of reddish-brown sweet corn meal and place it in my mouth. I didn't ask for the story of the ritual—my instincts told me I would be prying, or asking the Hopi to share knowledge not meant to be shared, or forcing a Hopi into denying me something when he only wanted to make me comfortable.

How many times have I suppressed my impulses in Indian country? Yet, in due time I have had my patience rewarded. One simply has to let some things come naturally, when they are ready. This un-German way to gather knowledge can be very gentle and peaceful, even graceful.

The next item on the ritual menu was blue corn meal pancakes that were extremely thin and crispy and had been prepared over a hot stone grill with incredible skill. This delicious paper wafer bread was called *piki*. All my pancakes have had corn meal in them since that day, with maple syrup on top.

Gathered around the room, chattering in Hopi, were Yvonne and the girls, Uncle Carl, Uncle Henry, Redford, Sharon, and several grandchildren and aunties—all enjoying tortillas, fried eggs, potatoes cooked with sliced onions, and corn pudding heaped in a bowl. I think it was yellow corn.

Surprise! More dancing commenced outdoors in the stone square with costumes I hadn't seen the night before, although the songs

213

seemed similar. Surrounding the square were rooftops that we sat or stood upon to watch the ceremony below. This time, women danced also, in white linen dresses and trimmings of green, black, and red. Their exotic short black hair locks shuddered with each motion as they delicately moved up and down, shaking a gourd rattle that sounded like pebbles rushing down a stream bed.

I really wished I could join them. My heart, my spirit was with all of them. I didn't need to read a book to know the importance of their gestures. The symbolism inherent in all their behaviors may appear rigid and daunting, bizarre and unintelligent to some folks; but to me, the people were living life to the fullest because they imbued every tiny motion with meaning. Every person had a role to perform that was necessary for the success of each other. This interconnectedness expressed a measure of respect for their system that I found heartening. What is wrong with interdependency? Nothing. We would not exist without it. The Hopi were emulating their experience with nature through their ceremonies, through all of life. Every day was a ritual. Not just Sunday morning.

I asked someone how long the dancing would continue, and they said, "We don't know how many days, but we will know when to stop when certain things happen."

The obvious purpose for the event was to assure the growth of crops, mainly corn. The Hopi believe the kachinas are not gods, but messengers from other worlds and solar systems who were formerly humans who lived their lives according to the rules apparent in the ways of Nature. They appeared to bring rain. Two to three hundred kachinas have been identified. The only other tribe to have kachinas is the Zuni.

Yvonne didn't invite us for a second night, so I wished to leave before she felt she had to ask us. Thus, I lingered alone on the edge of the mesa, peering over a silver-green sagebrush heaven, creating a

214

memory moment, thinking as hard as I could, repeating to myself: I will never forget this moment. My hair, clothes, and feet were coated with fine, powdery reddish-yellow dust, like the stratified rocks lining the road below, like the cars and pickups that seemed like toys winding downward, like the mud brick adobe homes plastered with more mud, like the cottonwoods and sagebrush clinging to life wherever they chose to live. Ashes to ashes and dust to dust. That's what everything is—in the beginning and in the end—a reminder that gave me peace and awe for all the vibrant beauty in between.

I didn't want to leave Shungopavi. I couldn't imagine anything like that happening in my future. (Little did I know it was just the beginning of a life of adventure.) We had to go. There were more artists to interview and photos to take for my thesis. (I wrote about thirty-seven artists, visited numerous galleries, museums, and schools, and received an "A" for my grade.) I was feeling lonely for my children who were finishing another year of school and were excited about summer vacation.

That night I stopped the Vega at a highway convenience store to buy gas and use the outdoor pay telephone to call home. My son said that his father had just taken my daughter to a police station for safekeeping, because he was about to beat her up. Shocked and sickened, I collapsed on the floor, sobbing. Three days later, I was home.

By the way, Katrina met her Eskimo man who loaned her money to fly home. I saw her once again to collect the money she owed me for gas. I wished her well and never saw her thereafter. I trust she repaid her generous benefactor.

Chapter 22

WHY DID PEOPLE STOP PRAYING TO NATURE?

Why were Europeans more technologically advanced
compared to the Indians in 1492?

University of St. Thomas

"Why is it that the Europeans were more technologically advanced compared to the Indians in 1492?" asks Roberta, while the class settles down for a question-and-answer period. Her inquiry excites me. I think to myself how this is my BIG question, the one that spiraled me on a path of unpredictable adventure, that led me to fascinating people, that gave me a fresh attitude about humans and nature. How to reply to Roberta? She breaks my thought with a comment, "Well, it wasn't only in America. The Africans, Asians . . ."

"Yes," I say, "Most people were still in the Stone Age, yet there were vast differences. The Chinese were ahead of Europeans in several areas. One can think of human advances in many ways: colonization of geographical areas, domestication of plants and animals, art and culture, writing, weaving, and so on. However, the use of tools has defined the rise of technology." I hesitate before I venture on, aware that I'm about to broaden the question and we have little time left in class today.

"I have decided that another determiner of human advancement is attitude," I declare with a tinge of pride, like Nancy Drew, girl detective, sharing a clue.

Roberta sounds doubtful, saying, "Attitude?"

"Think about it," I begin with enthusiasm. "All of the ways of advancement that I've mentioned are evidence found by archeologists, but they only tell part of the story. They can't tell us how prehistoric

216

humans thought, or why they made the choices they made.

"Remember, history proves there's no such thing as an unbiased perspective, thus we must consider the source of information we use, and new information is always being discovered that changes how we think about things." I have their attention, but some appear puzzled.

"I see from your faces that I'm getting off track here."

Chuckles erupt from the students, inviting me to smile back, but I'm on a roll and anxious to teach them something. "Have you ever seen a domesticated butterfly? No, why not? Nothing wild can become tame, or useful to human animals until an idea or thought first enters the brain of the human. I don't know of any animals or plants that willingly become slaves to humans. The baboon or chimpanzee that uses a stick, to catch and eat ants in holes, first had an idea that came from his need to eat. Maybe those sticks were our first tools. Maybe stones were, too. Chimps use stones to crack seeds open. If you tie a stone to a stick, you have a club. If you shape the stone and tie it to a stick, you have a spear. If you create a small spear with a sharp, pointed stone made of a particular rock, you have an arrow; and if you use sticks and twine to make a bow with tension, you have a bow and arrow. If you take a forked stick and add a leather thong, you have a slingshot. Choose a long straight limb, and add a sharp stone, to make an axe; or use a bone and make a hoe, or a scraper to clean animal hides for clothing.

"Modern European man began 30,000 years ago. The Bronze Age began in 4000BC in the Near East where we found evidence of the first plough. Later it began in 1600BC in Greece and China. It began in 2000BC in Peru, in South America, where we found the earliest metal-working in the Americas.

"The experts like to ask themselves, 'Was this invention brought with the people from someplace else, or was it developed without outside influence?' American Indians usually claim they originated as humans in the Americas, but anthropologists trace them back to Asia. Perhaps the Indians would have advanced much more without the influence of Europeans, but we will never know." I stop and wait.

Tom says, "That's about ideas, but what about attitudes? You said that you think attitude determines change, too."

"I believe that attitude is how we think or feel about ideas. What do you think attitude means?"

"It's how you look at things. Some days I have a happy attitude, and other days I feel grumpy," replies Tom.

"Yeah," adds Steve, "I act differently sometimes, depending on how I feel that day."

"I don't think it's that simple," says Roberta, "Because people have attitudes about things that they stick to throughout their lives."

I say, "Sometimes for generations. Attitudes held in common are culture and form traditions, rituals, and social roles. Ideas and attitudes create diversity, too, because people the world over think about things differently. Can anybody give me an example of this?"

Mark raises his hand, "The Indians revered nature while the whites wished to subdue it."

"*Ahhh!*" I exclaim, thinking of my old mentor Mizinokamigok, the Ojibwe elder from Nett Lake whom I hadn't heard from in years. She would be smiling at Steve's comment, "*Ahhh!*" I repeat.

"Now use your imaginations," I ask, "And think of all the earth's people 20,000 years ago, wandering the globe, rarely bumping into each other because the population remains relatively small. They carry and use old ideas, but they adopt and adjust with new ones. They all develop language, tools, drawing, weaving, clothing, and shelter. Eventually some domesticate plants and animals. With the advance in tools, they eat better; and, having more time, they develop creative thoughts, or rituals that reflect their feelings. All these bind families together with strong ties, giving frightened, weak, and threatened

218

people an advantage over their animal brothers who have always been far more powerful than people. Humans hunt with groups for protection, and over time they come in contact with other strange groups who have a different set of ideas and attitudes, but also some that are held in common.

"Oceans separated continents which slowed the exchange of ideas. Life changed faster in some places than in others. I like to assume that these ancestors of ours all developed in much the same sequence wherever they were, but they were doing so in a diversity of geographical conditions. Thus, they all prayed to the sun, but in a different language. They all prayed to the rain, but with a different dance.

"Now, class, what interests me most, is not what the dances or songs were, but why did some stop praying to the sun? Why did some stop praying to the rain? What changed?"

The room is still. The clock shows 2:00 p.m. Everyone's in motion, saying nothing. I didn't have enough time.

"You better run!" I caution, adding, "Drive carefully. See you next time."

"See ya!" says Caroline. She suddenly stops and turns to me, "Oh, I almost forgot to tell you. Allison is sick—the flu or something."

I phone my student-friend and learn that she is now recovering from the flu. We set a time to meet the following week. She has monarda flowers in her yard, so I tell her how to make a hot tea that will soothe her chest, as I have done for a long time with wild bergamot, which I save in a tin in my cupboard.

On my way home I pass through Stillwater to eat at Phil's Club Tara Hideaway, barely visible off the highway, tucked into a low ravine. In the Roaring Twenties it sat by a country road. The historic log structure has a neat flower garden by the door, and a dirt parking lot. Inside I relax at a log table with a view of the little room and a cozy fireplace whose blackened boulders wear a shiny patina. I order a glass of fume blanc wine, and a Greek specialty: Chicken stuffed with spinach baked in phyllo dough, and a small salad, all guaranteed to promote a happy attitude. I savor such moments of true freedom, for I have never forgotten how I discovered the joys of good wine, cheese, and chocolate, before Husband left the house forever.

For a time, he moved in and out, but my increasingly more-creative cooking irritated him. He called me pretentious, snobbish, and wasteful. I'd cook a lovely dinner. We always sat together as a family to talk. I may have one glass of wine. He'd tell the kids I'd become an alcoholic and hung out with artsy-fartsy friends. Still, I had the guts to buy real cheese, not the wimpy tasteless Velveeta staple of the 1970s, rather aged sharp cheddar and Roquefort blue. When I put that on the table, he flung it at the wall, yelling, "It stinks!"

Another day he threw his fried eggs at the wall, complaining about the plate they were served on. Once I arrived home late after grocery shopping with all the kids. Obviously angry, he demanded his dinner and accused me of taking too long. I explained how it wasn't easy to shop at several stores for the best buys with kids; and if he'd ever baby-sit, it would be faster. He yelled at me for talking back, ready to hit me, and refused to help carry groceries up the long steep stairs into the house. He often provoked arguments as an excuse to avoid work.

Another day, the kids watched in horror as I tried to flee his temper by running to the car parked in the driveway in a rainstorm. Before he could reach me, I locked the car doors, turned the key in the ignition ready to gun the engine, when he jumped on the hood of the car, sprawled out on his stomach in front of me like an animal. His maniacal eyes, his lunatic grin screamed, "Ah, ha, I've gotcha now!"

Hatred overcame my fear and good sense. I stepped hard on the gas, veering sharply onto the street. He rolled off. In my rear mirror, I saw him shouting—waving his fists—his clothes drenched in rain and mud.

I was afraid to return home or to involve police or parents. I was ashamed of him, and me for making such a bad choice. One friend had intervened in the past; one marriage counselor cringed when he saw my black-and-blue arms, but I never told anyone else, not even the pastor of our church, where Husband was a deacon, and I taught Sunday school. I had become trapped in his disease, with no money of my own, except for earning money when I painted the outside of one house, enough for college tuition for two years. I knew he'd be a deadbeat dad because he'd told me so. "You can always go on welfare or be a waitress," he'd laugh.

I drove on, sobbing, exhausted, fearful for my children, fearful for me having the responsibility of raising them alone. In Madison, Wisconsin, I slept five hours, then phoned home to say I was fine, so the kids wouldn't worry. He said he wouldn't hurt me if I returned home. I knew it was a lie. That time I phoned a divorce attorney.

The way of life that Mizinokamaigok had described to me was like one exciting continuous, changing web of connections with new people and places coming and going. In 1977 I had two close girlfriends, strong women who shared my path. They were meaningful influences. They would draw me into circles I was ripe for. We were not a threesome, even though we all had a keen interest in Indian culture. Each of us had differences in attitudes about other things, differences that would one day threaten to tear us apart.

Prior to moving to Grand Forks in 1968, I had met Maryanne at a high school reunion, during a spiritually low point in my life. I felt like a withered leaf on a tree, shy, withdrawn, lacking in self-confidence. I was miserable at the party. I grew so sick, I threw up in the bathroom, which shocked myself. An old classmate of mine brought his wife to

221

meet me. She didn't know anybody there; so I sat with her, listening to her story. She had met Jack when he was a soldier in Germany, where she was born. Maryanne spoke perfect English. She had fine features and a sexy figure. Long dark hair and black eyes framed her pale porcelain skin. I was enchanted by her vitality, the way she threw back her head and tucked her hair behind her ear and laughed freely, the way she responded quickly and listened intently. She was not only vivacious, but also well-educated; and, I would soon learn, even brilliant in some respects. She was a bit younger than me. The daughter of a father who was a German atomic physicist, she had been raised in England by her mother during Germany's post-construction years. She and Jack owned a modest home in a Minneapolis suburb, a quiet blue-collar neighborhood where the husband came home after working a union job five days a week. He was a hardworking, devoted, kind man. They had one young daughter.

Maryanne was bored. I suggested she become involved in politics; that I'd done that in 1968, that I'd met many great people.

Later, following my advice, she met Russell Means in 1973 at a political fundraiser for Democratic candidates. The American Indian Movement leader convinced her to switch her energy to his cause. She became intensely involved with the St. Paul trial of Wounded Knee.

She worked as an assistant to William Kunstler, a famous trial lawyer who was well loved by all the minorities he helped. Her telephone was tapped (according to her). She worked long hours with great devotion.

My other close friend was Doris, my Ojibwe friend from the Turtle Clan who I met in 1974 at my first art exhibit for Eddy Cobiness at the Minneapolis American Indian Center. I'll never forget her arrival. She, and her distinguished elderly escort named Earl, made an impressive pair: her olive complexion and short raven hair, his pale face and shaggy white shoulder-length locks; her formal demeanor and judgmental gaze, his casual friendliness and professorial shuffle; her ivory silk shirt and classic slacks, and the display of gorgeous turquoise-silver jewelry dripping from her body.

He followed her directly to the artist where she began a conversation in fluent Ojibwe. Mr. Cobiness was clearly delighted, yet the couple did not purchase a painting. They did invite Eddy, myself, and Roger, my friend and promoter of the event, to a post-opening visit to a home at an upscale address near Mount Curve Avenue.

Earl's wife had left him for life in a warmer climate, abandoning him to his hillside, ornate, dusty mansion stuffed up to the ceilings with rare American Indian artifacts. Inside the house, Earl gave us a tour. We descended a staircase lined with baby cradle boards. I said, "*Dikinaagan*? Cradle board?"

Doris, surprised by my knowing the Ojibwe word, replied, "*Eyan!*"

Overwhelmed by the array of museum quality items, I couldn't believe that one person could own so much. Earl led us through the rooms, stopping to point out this or that, opening a cabinet with rows of horizontal narrow shelves, each holding a woman's leather dress.

I remarked, "I bet you don't have one decorated with dentalium shells." His eyes sparkled. He opened a drawer and tenderly handed me a creamy white deerskin dress with a bodice lined with rows of seashells found only in the Pacific Ocean.

At first I felt honored to be sharing such a fine treasure with my proud collector, until my imagination kicked in, and I felt the spirit of the woman who wore the dress. Was she crying? How did her precious garment end up in this tomblike airless enclosure? What was her fate? I didn't ask, nor reveal my dark suspicions, but I didn't want to see anymore.

Within the year, I attended a dinner party at Earl's home, arranged by Doris who was a gracious hostess and an exceptionally fine cook. Soon after that, at another dinner I did not attend, Earl suffered an acute asthma attack and died. Was it the spirits, or the dust in his respiratory system that got him?

Lucky for Doris, Earl had a wonderful brother.

She had been born into poverty on a Canadian reserve, sent to work in the home of wealthy Americans where she developed her taste for expensive elegance. At eighteen years of age, she was called by her parents back to the reserve to meet her prearranged husband.

Doris told me, "A cop! He was an Ann Arbor, Michigan, policeman, and I liked his looks, and him!"

After four children things were not very rosy, so she fled to Minneapolis and found a job reading newspapers for Control Data, a large corporation, whereupon she spotted an ad for a sale of Navajo rugs on Mount Curve Avenue and met Earl, who added her to his collection.

I easily identified with powerful women searching for opportunities to reclaim their power. I felt a kinship with those who understood injustice. Maryanne and Doris were a natural fit for me at that time.

Everything seemed to happen in 1977, the year of Shungopavi, graduation and marital separation. There was also the European conference, the protest march in Oakland, California, and more.

Chapter 23

INDIGENOUS TRIBES HAVE CUSTOMS—NOT LAWS

Injustices perpetrated upon Indians by the US government will be used on all Americans someday. There will be wars over oil.

Wakpala, South Dakota

When Maryanne invited me to accompany her to the Third International Treaty Conference in Wakpala, South Dakota, I said I'd go for three of the five days, meaning I'd drive separately to the Standing Rock Reservation near the Missouri River smack in the center of both of the Dakotas. The yellow, black, and red poster for the event showed the North American continent in bright red, crisscrossed by a giant peace pipe with red feathers, and listed issues to be discussed: Treaty rights; Indian energy commission; Development of natural resources; Theft of Indian land and resources; Workshops for land-owners; Delegate selection for the UN conference in Geneva, Switzerland; dancers and singers welcome.

In June 1974, 4,000 Indian representatives from 97 tribes had met in Wakpala to form an organization to consider action on the 371 treaties entered into with the United States. It was sponsored by AIM, and they decided to open an office in New York to work with the United Nations. The goals of the Treaty Council were to work internationally to gain recognition of the treaties. In February 1977, the United Nations would officially recognize them as a nongovernmental organization consultative status—a major achievement. And I would be there.

In Wakpala, at the preplanning conference, I listened and learned. I met Indians from far and near who seemed to appreciate my interest, and also hippies who hung out, hoping to catch some rays of spiritual enlightenment. Maryanne wasn't just a listener; she was a mover, intent upon compiling a book, recording the proceedings of the conferences attended by 1,000 people from fifty tribes.

I met two amazing nonIndians from St. Paul, a father and daughter deeply dedicated to the cause. Dick Bancroft was a great photographer who called himself a "recorder of events" and would spend his life devoted to helping Indians, along with his energetic wife, Debbie. Their daughter, Ann Bancroft, would go on to fame and well-deserved acclaim as an avid arctic explorer. Sue Fourre was Maryanne's assistant, helping with the book, and Dick provided the pictures.

I felt as comfortable at that gathering as I had six years earlier at the Devil's Lake carnival and powwow. The evening drumming and dancing worked its magic on my soul. I soaked up details about the traditions of the Sioux, as many of them called themselves, and wrote them down in a small notebook, or I found a quiet corner in my car to jot things in my journal.

One day I wandered into a new metal pole barn building, away from the big-top tent where I'd been watching the dancing and listening to the old drums; but then I heard another drum inside the new structure, so I wandered in, curious. Groups of older teens had gathered there to plug in their electric musical instruments to play rock n' roll hits of the day. The juxtaposition of the old and new struck me hard as I sat on a wooden box and listened in the glare of bare bulbs hanging from cords above. With my foot tapping, I wanted to get up and dance. Alas, the electricity failed. The interior went totally dark. The fancy, status-symbolic electrified instruments died. And the musicians fell silent—all but one man. He had a wooden drum plus a formidable song that went on and on and on. There was not a warrior in that room who could have missed the meaning of that happening, including me. The old ones heard the news and grinned mightily.

The Wakpala conference was a preparation for the International

NGO (nongovernmental organizations) Conference on Discrimination Against Indigenous Populations in the Americas, to be held in September at the United Nations in Geneva, Switzerland.

Maryanne was planning to attend and she wanted me to accompany her.

Through a miracle and hard work I found myself on a plane flying over the Atlantic Ocean. Just as amazing was the presence of David Monongye, the Hopi grandfather from Shungopavi who had led the *kiva* corn ceremony I'd attended only six months earlier.

The Conference for Indigenous Populations had an unusually high attendance by NGOs, UN bodies, member nations of the UN, and the press. Over 400 came to the sessions, including over 100 delegates and participants from the indigenous peoples and nations of the Americas. The Human Rights Commission, UNESCO, and forty member nations sent observers from Latin America, Korea, Germany, Italy, France, Yemen, Iraq, Australia, the Netherlands, and more. We were all thrilled by the successful turnout.

Maryanne and I marveled at the gracious beauty, cleanliness, and formality of the Swiss. We settled into the modest Geneve Hotel Lido.

My job during the proceedings was to distribute the red books that Maryanne and others had compiled—twenty-eight pages of declarations and statements designed to inform the world about the injustices forced upon American Indians by the United States government. I also kept notes in a journal while attending several sessions and speeches.

The Hunkapapa Sioux Treaty Council listed many serious human right violations, past and present, stating that, "In March 1871, the US unilaterally colonized the Lakota Nation. That act stipulated that the US would no longer recognize the Lakota as independent. In addition, the US ceased to deal by treaty with any Indian tribe, thereby eliminating the sovereign status of Indian people."

"All tribal rights of Indian self-determination were eliminated. The US implemented a severe policy of genocide and economic independence. This policy, after the past 100 years, has resulted in the most chronic case of economic and social dependency known in the world today."

The Indians from all the countries saw themselves as completely controlled, culturally and economically, by conquerors who used such force. Resistance could mean suicide. Several examples of current and continuing exploitation were cited by all tribes during the three-day conference in Geneva.

In 1977 the US Supreme Court issued an opinion diminishing the size of the Rosebud Sioux Reservation, a decision based on a 1903 opinion supporting the US Act of Colonization of 1871. The court considered only domestic case law, not the UN treaty or UN covenants on human rights. The US also ignored the Helsinki Agreement of August 1, 1975, in which Principle 7 states that social and cultural freedoms are "Derived from the inherent dignity of the human person and are essential for his free and full development."

Further grievances were: "Genocide of tribal members; mental harm; deliberate group conditions calculated to bring about its destruction; imposing measures to prevent births; forcibly transferring children to another group."

Russell Means stated, "I come not to turn the other cheek. We have turned it now for almost 500 years, and we realize that here in Geneva, this is our first small step into the international community. We talk about human rights while my people (and in the entire hemisphere) are suffering genocide. We have brought documents that support this charge."

He continued, "The United States, the monster, and its multinational corporations have dictated foreign policy in this world.

They no longer care about the future as witnessed by the Dene, my people, by Central and South America."

He also reported, "We also have documentation about the secret activities of the CIA and multinational corporations that are now in Brazil, Ecuador, Peru, Columbia, and Venezuela, because everyone knows that the next major exploitations will be in South America."

Water rights were a big issue for all the tribes. Means pointed out that, in Wakpala, the only available water was too alkaline for use, and people had to haul it from Mobridge where the white community had plenty of good water. He warned that we would have WARS OVER OIL, but they would seem insignificant when WARS OVER WATER began in only twenty to fifty years. He predicted that INJUSTICES PERPETRATED BY THE US government onto the Indians would also be used ON ALL AMERICAN citizens some day.

Ed Bernstick, an AIM member from the Cree Nation in Canada, spoke, "When the people took over the Bureau of Indian Affairs offices in Washington, there was a contract paper that was discovered there between the Department of Indian Affairs in Canada and the BIA in the US. This White Paper policy was introduced by the Canadian government. At the same time there was a new economic development program set up called the Mid-Canada Corridor. This is the Northern Development Plan. This is a plan to take all economic bases away from Indian people. It involves the Department of Northern Saskatchewan and Northlands in Alberta, the Department of Northern Manitoba, where there is a huge hydro-development project going on, and the development programs in Northern Ontario, Quebec, British Columbia, and the Territories. "These programs are developed without consultation with the native people, who are extremely isolated and out of touch. This adds up to genocide against the native people of Canada—culturally and physically.

"IT IS ESTIMATED THAT IN THIS COUNTRY ALL OIL AND

GAS IN EASTERN CANADA WILL BE DEPLETED, SO THERE ARE PIPELINE PROPOSALS. Each province and territory exerts control of the native people within its claimed boundaries. We are affected by such laws as the Migratory Bird Act, and yet in our treaties we have fishing and hunting rights. We have court cases where our people have been put in court for shooting a duck to feed their family because it infringed on the Migratory Bird Act. In many areas, there are no jobs, and people must rely on hunting and fishing to survive.

"The government uses 'legal' tactics to keep Indian people in poverty. They try to assimilate entire reserves, and have succeeded on some in destroying the language, education, and livelihood of the people, and the Canadian government is responsible."

Antonio Millape, Mapauche Confederation in Chile, living in exile, represented 900,000 Mapuches. His story of genocide in Chile was so moving and tragic, I had tears in my eyes. He described how, after the year 1800, massive numbers of haciendas were built on their best land, forcing the indigenous people into farm labor without salaries, causing misery and sickness. During a coup in 1973, his house was surrounded by sixteen military men who invaded the area, forced his family up against a wall and called them dangerous criminals. He and 3,000 others were detained several times and some killed. Then a massive extermination occurred, leaving the living to starvation and extreme malnutrition. (Pinochet was leader of Chile at that time.) Millape said that millions of other Indians in Central and South America were being treated the same.

Indeed, I saw several from that part of the world at the conference wearing black hoods on their heads to hide their identity. They feared being whisked away by secret military men in Geneva.

Juan Condori Uruchi, a Mink'a from South America, appealed to the hearts of all when he said, "The philosophy of the conqueror is different, and they've tried to educate that in us. Now, what do we want to achieve? We want the Indian to prove that the present society has lost its human values . . . all the powers of friendship. We want you to understand that in union there is friendship and love . . . it's through our love for nature that we've learned to love . . . but the conquerors do not know this love." He also said, "The Christians say, 'Love thy neighbor.' They say so, so why don't they do so? Scientifically and philosophically speaking they say they know the truth, why don't they show it?"

Renir Artist, KANO Organization in Surinam, pleaded, "First, the Indian people want to retain their own identity. Any development will have to be in relation to Indian culture and ways. KANO is trying to help our Indian people so they may get their legal rights to their (own) land, Indian people in Surinam do not live on reservations. They live free, but have no written legal right to the land."

The Hopi, Navajo, and Northern Cheyenne called for an immediate halt of strip-mining in the Black Mesa/Four Corners area. (I had seen this and was appalled at the sight of it.) THE INUIT OF CANADA PROTESTED A PIPELINE TO BE BUILT ON THEIR LAND. The Alaskan Natives Land Claims Act was being violated. Multinational corporations were causing havoc everywhere and coal raining and extraction was a problem.

Women were strongly represented. They printed their own red book with thirty-four pages of heartbreaking stories. The Women of all Red Nations (WARN), told about a study of United States Indian Health Service practices, which proved that 3,406 women in four areas of the country had been sterilized; that few ever asked for it; that many were convinced in a coercive manner. The practice goes on in several countries by doctors who view it as a poverty control issue.

Winona La Duke from White Earth, Minnesota, an Ojibwe, wrote that Indian lands had never been so valuable and with every energy "crisis" more coal and uranium companies sprout up and get rich. She called the Navajo Nation an energy colony—like the Arabs were until they began to receive fair payments for their valuable oil. Most Navajo didn't even have electricity. It was sold to big cities by the federal government. People forced off land, work in mines. Many die from lung cancer. Winona said, "Three percent of our land is what we have left, and in order to remain as Indians we have to fight to keep that."

The indigenous people had extremely low rates of crime where the traditional systems set by chiefs were in effect, but those systems were not recognized by the US authorities. The indigenous representatives pointed out that CUSTOMS ARE THEIR LAWS.

Each day brought new revelations I would never read about in the *Minneapolis Star and Tribune*. Europe's press gave us good coverage.

And now, dear reader, imagine my astonishment upon seeing my photograph on the front page of *Tribune De Geneve*, a French language, Swiss newspaper! There I was alongside Maryanne, walking in a parade of Indians down the grand avenue at the Palais des Nations; she and I respectfully off to the side carrying armfuls of red books, wearing slacks and stylish leather jackets; she glancing off at Russell Means; me, looking straight at the photographer from under my new rust-colored felt fedora hat with a serious expression on my face.

In the background rose stately, majestic white marble buildings; tall windows/flung open to blue skies, crowded with Swiss workers—curious onlookers. Avenues were lined with people who stopped to stare and wonder at the sight and sounds of *"la indigenes Indiens."*

What a magnificent parade it was! We were near the front, close to the drum. I clearly saw who led the entire procession. It was the same little Hopi leader from my night in the kiva! David Monongye was given the greatest place of honor, between Phillip Deere from the Creek Nation and Hoyaneh Tadadaho (Leon Schenadoah) from the

Iroquois Nation, which showed the respect and esteem that his peers felt for him. I was stunned and appreciated my privileged kiva experience even more.

Resplendent in brilliant colorful costumes, the North American Indians marched proudly in their finest regalia, with eagle feathers, medicine pouches, beadwork, calico ribbon shirts, silk ribbon appliqué, fur hats, leather moccasins, silk or wool shawls, velvet shirts with silver buttons, hand-woven bands fastened over a shoulder, around a waist, hanging down a leg, and alpaca ponchos, fringed shirts, and blankets. Some had handsome bone chokers with seashell centers, while others wore round beaded pendants, some with totems. David wore a silver bracelet. Most had neat, tight-braided hair, or long, loose straight hair parted in the center.

The mood was solemn in spite of the festive sight. The mood was set by the steady rhythm of the drumbeat and the wailing cries of the strong male singers, two men. One was Russell Means.

People that I recognized were Larry Red Shirt, Lakota; Clyde Bellecourt, Pat Bellanger, Ojibwe; and a few more I'd met at Wakpala. Dick Bancroft was the official photographer for the Indians, so he was everywhere, clicking away, like many foreign photographers from all over Europe. Stories about "*La Conference Internationale non governementale*" appeared in many magazines and newspapers.

Would the papers in the US cover the event? The Indians had done their best to inform the major news outlets prior to the conference, but would they pay attention?

Arriving home in Minneapolis, I found copies of the *International Herald Tribune*, published in New York City. The September 22 issue had a great photo of the delegates in session, and a headline: Indians Claim US Stealing their Resources. The first paragraph said "Ninety per cent of the uranium mined in the US is on Indian land, an International Indian Treaty Council report claimed here today."

Further, "Rich natural resources on Indian reservations are being stolen in order that Indians disappear through 'institutionalized and systematic genocide,' the report alleged."

The story said that Indians claimed that energy projects would lead to the violation and abrogation of Indian water rights; that water from the Missouri River would be sold as if no treaties existed; that coal would be used to power jobs entirely off the reservation, and energy jobs would employ mostly nonIndians.

One line read, "A 103-year-old Hopi chief made the trip to Geneva." That was David Monongye.

A September 24–25 issue of the *Herald* had another article without a photo, and a headline that read: "US Protests That Geneva Forum Prevents Response to Indians." First paragraph: "The United States protested today that it was not allowed to reply to 'unfounded charges' of genocide and racism during an international forum on the Indian populations of the Americas."

Also: William vanden Heuvel, US ambassador to the UN, expressed his "profound disappointment," that US officials were denied the right to address the conference during the final plenary session.

In the official report following the conference, Jimmie Durham, a key organizer, wrote an inspirational notice titled: Columbus Day is now International Solidarity Day with American Indians.

One of the final resolutions called for the observation of October 12, the day of so-called "discovery of America," as an international day of solidarity with the indigenous peoples of the Americas.

Durham said, "From now on, children all over the world will learn the true story of American Indians on Columbus Day instead of a pack of lies about three European ships," and "The International Day of Solidarity with American Indians gives people and organizations a chance to do well-planned, unified actions in solidarity with our struggle. Because of our voice at the conference, people are going to take the opportunity."

On the way to Europe, twenty-four Iroquois delegates and participants traveled with their own homemade passports. They were not refused at US or Swiss customs. Three Hopis also created their passports. On the plane returning to the states, we feared trouble with US authorities, so we had prearranged lawyers waiting by the phone outside the Boston airport.

I stood behind Grandfather Monongye as he handed the startled uniformed clerk a handwritten parchment pamphlet. His spiritual Hopi demeanor was more than stately. And why shouldn't it be? He had claims to "American" soil that reached back thousands of years. To have to prove that he was a citizen was sheer nonsense. This was like a rooster asking the fox for permission to enter his own hen house. The red-faced befuddled gatekeeper-to-the-nation got on a phone.

As the line behind us grew, I thought how policy and legalese (complicated jargon) trump common sense every time. Soon, a higher official arrived, then a series of higher and higher ones, each in turn listening to our story about the Indian conference in Geneva, each wondering how to solve the problem. Our little near-blind grandfather stood patiently in the center of all the confusion and conflicting opinions, his handsome young travel partners, dressed in beautiful Hopi clothing, stood by protectively. Finally, we were allowed to pass. We didn't phone our lawyer. They apparently concluded that Grandfather was not a threat to the nation.

Perhaps the next person in line was. Her suitcase smelled so strongly of garlic that the authorities made the tiny, withered granny, who looked like an Italian peasant, open her bag for all the world to see. Amongst her personal wearables, they uncovered a long row of fat, red, hard salamis. The odor was fantastic! I wanted to nab one of them and run, but instead I scurried away, relieved for our group, yet feeling pity for the officials who had traded one aging transgressor for another. I took away the lesson that, if you are lucky to live long enough, you can get away with anything!

After arriving home from Europe and getting back into my routine with the children, I got together with my mother. I announced to her that I would be getting a divorce. Genuinely upset, she tried to dissuade me, even after I told her about the abuse. She scowled, turned away, and softly said, "Every man knocks his wife around now and then."

I was shocked. Poor Mother! Such low expectations for her daughter. I was glad my generation was fighting abuse; by improving working conditions and pay, so women could escape sick men; and by changing marketing strategies that demeaned women as sex symbols.

When later I told her the divorce was final, she sat up straight with her commendable "Power of Positive Thinking" attitude—Norman Vincent Peale's book that sat atop her Bible—and announced, "You'll need a new nightie. Here's the money."

"A new nightie?" I replied stunned, doubtful.

"Of course! You're not going to attract a man by wearing those baggy T-shirts to bed every night. You're going to have to be . . . well, you know, more attractive," she proclaimed with motherly authority.

She often had ways of rendering me speechless, but that was a real zinger! There were so many conversational taboos in my family that she'd never said anything that personal to me before. I had no idea she noticed what I wore to bed. And T-shirts hadn't prevented me from producing babies.

Just to be safe, I did as she requested, knowing she'd want to see what I bought. That pink satin number lay in my drawer as a reminder of how Mother's generation handled the problem of becoming an old maid. I would never be an old maid. Rather, an economically independent proud woman who had paid her own way through college.

Ah, well, some women get tuition. Others get a pink nightie.

Chapter 24
WE'RE OUT OF TOUCH WITH OUR ORIGINS
What is animism?

Signature Cafe

Allison grins, like someone who already knows the answer to the question they're about to ask, "Are you an atheist?" Her soft, baby-face glows with health again after her bout with the flu, "I was raised Lutheran, but I'm definitely a doubting one."

Laying my fork aside, taking a deep breath, "First, I don't like the word atheism, or agnostic, because I prefer not to use definitions that say what one is against. It's negative, and it's often used by someone who disagrees with you. Let's use words that say what we are *for*. There isn't one English word that describes my beliefs. Atheism means you don't believe in any gods. Theism means you do believe in one or more. An agnostic says it's impossible to know if gods exist. That would be me, but I never say that. Henotheism means belief in one god without denying the existence of others. That wouldn't be Catholics, but it could be Indians; except they believed in spirits, not really gods. It wouldn't be me, because I don't claim to know if any god is real, or exists."

I take a spoonful of asparagus soup, order more French bread, and continue, "Let's see now. There's animism. I believe in that."

"What's that? A belief in animals?" Allison wonders.

"Sort of. One believes that all life is produced by a spiritual force separate from matter, and that all has life and souls. However, isn't matter the spiritual force? They are inseparable."

"That sounds rather Lutheran. We believe in souls, too—souls that separate from the body and go to hell or heaven depending on God's

238

choice. You sound more scientific. Are you?"

"No. Not at all. Scientific beliefs do not include a spiritual dimension. Obviously, life derives from forces of energy. If we imagine them as spiritual, we serve a human need, one different from other plants and animals. We use our minds more than our instincts to protect and preserve that which sustains us. We are creative in different ways—a good thing too—we couldn't live without the diversity we need. A spiritualistic perspective provides me with a dimension to share with other life forms, kind of like an attitude of reciprocity: If I help you live, you'll help me live—sort of the Paleolithic golden rule of today's 'Do onto others as they would do onto you.' Problem is, today's rule only includes people."

Allison lights up, "Life is full of miracles. All the millions of creatures, trees, and flowers that cover our planet, that evolved to make life possible for us."

"They didn't do it for US. They did it for themselves—to just BE. But Mother Earth and Father Sky first created just the right conditions: fire, water, wind, earth. That's what we came out of."

"That's what made the monkeys and apes, that made us. What did they descend from?" Allison says.

"I don't know!" she makes me shrug.

"I've heard that human embryos develop like fish, or polliwogs."

"Makes sense to me. A woman's pregnant belly is like a small saltwater sea. Maybe we began in the ocean as amoebas," I suggest.

"Maybe!" We chuckle, pausing to reflect and eat. "However Christians not only despised animal spirit beliefs, but they argued mightily in the past to decide which humans are human, so they knew which souls needed saving from sin. How ridiculous! Who could not see the soul-spirit in a butterfly?"

"I think babies can, before they're taught to think like an adult," Allison replies.

"*Ahhh*. Babies—brimming with the beauty of innocence and trust."

"Yes! Babies aren't born with silly designations like: Here I am—your cute little henotheistic bundle of joy!"

Allison changes her voice to dramatize her statement, causing me to burst into fits of laughter. She joins me while other diners turn to stare. We tone down our merriment to subdued giggles.

"Don't you think, Allison, that we're all simply spiritual—feeling humans who sense animating forces? I don't believe in miracles like weeping statues or virgin births, but I do believe in the miracle of cyclical birth and growth, in unconditional love, in patterns that create change out of constancy, in human music and laughter, in the bees that pollinate my garden, and corn that grows all over the earth. Many of the miracles—heck, most of them—cannot be detected by mere humans, but rather by other animals. Our bodies respond to unseen phenomena. Our minds imagine what it looks like. To me, that's not necessary. Just respect the fact that unknown stuff exists. We don't have to understand everything. But we do have to respect it, because we don't understand it. Perhaps it's stronger than us. Most things are; but we ignore them at our peril, like the beginnings of global climate change."

Allison remains silent, sipping her coffee. She sweeps her hair back with fine manicured fingers. I sigh, slipping mine under the table, mindful of my stubby hands, crisscrossed with wrinkles—clean, but uneven nails, a testimony to my neglect, or to my age and years of handiwork. I'm not ashamed of my hands or body, but Allison reminds me of younger, better days. Becoming old and wise isn't all that it's cracked up to be, especially in America where youth and stupidity often prevail.

"I remember," begins Allison, leaning closer to me, "When we sat in Loring Park and you told me how your mentor, named Miz, instructed you to talk to trees. One day, I couldn't solve a personal problem, so I began to visit the same oak tree until I got an answer. I also learned that the oak didn't need me as much as I needed it. Trees may be smarter than some people I know—they never stop giving."

"Yes! Even after they die, they keep giving, because they never do die. They just change form."

"Don't get me wrong," cautions Allison, "The oak didn't speak any words or anything like that, but it became an example to me of how to behave myself. The relationship simplified my perspective to the point where I could see that I was overly concerned about something that was not important."

"Just being alone in the woods always clarifies things for me. In a way, nature tells us stories, if we learn to listen to them. Water and ice in melting glaciers are screaming at us to slow down. For the first time in human history, they're melting so fast, ships can now cross the Arctic Ocean," I lament, rolling my eyes, "We should pray! Cedar is one of the four sacred plants for the Ojibwe and Lakota, used in sweat lodge ceremonies along with sage. During my vision quest sweat, I drank bitter, red cedar tea, and inhaled the fumes of fresh smoldering sage. Another time, when sick with a respiratory infection I was cured after a ceremony. However, Allison, I'd certainly rather go to the Mayo Clinic in Rochester, Minnesota, for surgery and intensive care or analysis, so I'm really talking here about mental wellness, which is connected to the health of our body. And the beauty that results from that."

"Wow! A sweat ceremony," exclaims Allison, "Now that's what I call being connected."

"That's right. Because I have no sense of connectedness to the pills prescribed by my doctor. We're not supposed to cut down a jungle because there might be a cure from a tree we've never heard of, yet we haven't the faintest idea what all those pills and potions *do* come from. Pharmaceutical companies keep it a big secret so they can make an enormous profit from what nature gives freely."

Allison frowns at me, "Ohhh, like Monsanto and others? The drug pushers who churn out synthetic substances that get approved by the bribed officials in Washington? Congressmen that may go work in a drug or insurance company for more money after we turn them out of office for passing legislation that approves of swindling the public?"

"Yeah, those guys. Just dealing with healthcare has made me feel sick and outraged. How about you?"

"Yeah, me, too. Let's not talk about that," Allison says, perking up, "Tell me more about trees and how people once worshipped them."

"Ah, traditionally, all cultures believed trees had spirits, some more than others, like: the chosen cottonwood tree used in Dakota—Lakota sun dances, the Buddhist tree of enlightenment, the Maytree or Maypole of my German ancestors. Trees represented an eternal, regenerational belief that within the microcosmic order of you and me lies an eternal macrocosmic journey of generations yet unborn, and therefore the immortality of the spirit of both plant and animal."

"You mean," interjects Allison, "our bodies become plants, and plants become animals?"

"Exactly. All is connected. In archeology I learned about the Paleolithic, or early Stone Age. Around 750,000 to 15,000 years ago when humans first made chipped stone tools. During the Mesolithic time, bows and arrows, cutting tools, and weapons were made with copper, tin or bronze. That lasted until around 10000BC when farming began with advanced stone tools. After that, we have the Neolithic Age, or the last phase of the Stone Age.

"Gee, now we have the Space Age," Allison chips in, "We've progressed from shooting arrows to shooting spaceships into the sky. We shouldn't forget the Iron Age that made the spaceship possible."

"I wonder if we're not in the Biological Age now. Whatever we're in, we're out of contact with our origins," I say, shaking my head.

Allison suggests, "Our ancestors who practiced animism would have connected trees, fertility, and women in their stories."

"Let's talk about some of those stories I found in the history of the Near East, northern Iraq, Iran, Turkey, Russia, Germany, Scandinavia, Greece, Italy. Well, it seems that prior to advanced agriculture and writing, such accounts are universal. Animism was the way of life for all the world's people for 25,000 years before 3000BC, and for much longer in America. Tree spirit stories were recorded in a fascinating book written in 1922 by James Frazer. In *The Golden Bough* he traced the misty origins of gods, goddesses, kings and queens, who inhabited actual places that still exist."

Allison puts up her hand, "Do you remember one of them? I'd love to hear it, while I enjoy my raspberry sorbet with coffee."

The server clears our table. We order sorbet. A pink ball arrives in a stemmed glass dish with a vanilla wafer stuck in it like an arrowhead. I bet no one else thought of that!

"An Italian story out of antiquity tells of a little woodland lake named Neimi (or Aricia, the modern La Riccia), where the lovely Diana of the Wood resided by a water pond that was so clear, it was known as Diana's Mirror. In that wild, secluded oak grove, all the trees were sacred. The beautiful Diana, similar to the later Greek Artemis, was a goddess of nature, fertility, and hunting. As such, she was the personification of abundant wild and tamed animals, fruits and vegetables, and the patron goddess of hunters and herdsmen. Her name was connected with the moon, and she was worshipped as a goddess of childbirth. Her mate, or King of the Wood, at Neimi, was named Virbius. Their union created, as Frazer put it, 'the fruitfulness of the earth, of animals, and of mankind.'"

"And of raspberries, I'm sure," joked Allison.

"I hope so. That is my favorite fruit. Now, Frazer believes that an annual celebration took place at Neimi, in which the divine bride and bridegroom were represented by living persons, because the custom of marrying gods to images or humans was a widespread practice way back then. Such magical rituals were solemn and also merry events intertwined with the spirits of vegetation. Virbius would have been the King of the Wood who guarded the sacred oak tree that stood lower down the mountain. Frazer concludes that he was actually Rome' s later Jupiter, the oak-god, and Diana was the oak-goddess."

"I thought Jupiter was god of thunder and rain," Allison says.

"He was a supreme god, so he probably did that, too."

"I once read," Allison tells me, "about a sacred sanctuary in Greece called Dodona, which was always ravaged by crashing thunderstorms. Zeus lived there among the oak trees where his thunder crashed through the lightening, making the oak leaves rub against each other and make sounds. Zeus was the rain-god in Greece."

"Frazer says that on the Acropolis at Athens there was an image of Earth praying to Zeus for rain. And in times of drought, the Athenians prayed, 'Rain, rain, O dear Zeus, on the cornland of the Athenians, and on the plains.'"

"Who else worshipped trees in Europe?"

"The Aryans of Central Europe inhabited forests that were so immense that one German soldier told Caesar that it required his troops two months to pass from one end to the other. The Emperor Julian, 400 years later, visited the solitude and gloom of the forest, which deeply impressed him. Apparently, in the old religions of the Germans, the worship of sacred groves was unparalleled. The oak was the god of thunder among the Teutons, as it was for the Italians and Greeks. Frazer says that the chief deity of the Lithuanians was Perkunas, god of thunder, who watched over sacred oaks. When they were cut down by Christian missionaries, the people, who had always kept a fire going in honor of Perkunas, loudly complained that their

244

woodland deities were destroyed."

Allison shows her feelings with a wince, "Same thing that happened to the American Indians. The pioneers were farmers and builders."

"Trees were like persons. People offered sacrifices to them, apologized to them for cutting them down, thought of them as able to bleed and marry each other. They were treated like pregnant women during blossom time, and were planted on graves. They granted women an easy delivery; were used in sacred bonfires, were cures for sicknesses, were connected to birth and death, could have demons or evil spirits, and perhaps carried the souls of the dead.

"Pine trees were important also. The Romans adopted the Phrygian Mother of the Gods in 204BC along with their worship of a divine pine tree they dressed like a corpse, and splattered with blood. When a grandfather pine died, the Iroquois would say, 'He has fallen,' in a respectful manner.

"There was Silvanus, a forest god of woods and cattle. And Numa and Egeria. She was the equivalent of Diana, and also lived in a grove. In Athens, Dionysus, god of the vine, annually married his queen to insure the fertility of the fruit trees. The sky-god Zeus married the corn-goddess Demeter, descending into a dark place and reemerging into a blaze of light, holding a reaped corn plant to demonstrate their success."

"Did you find any Scandinavian tree goddesses?"

"You betcha, but it's fun to discover them yourself. My heritage is all German. I like to imagine that my bloodline runs through me like a river, from Hanover, Saxony, and Baden to the waters of Minnesota. Before me, like roots under a tree, are many strong women—many great-grandmothers who survived challenges far greater than any I could imagine. Certainly, my deep love for nature comes from my blood and bones. My father's people were schooled foresters in

Pomerania. Imagine my delight when reading Frazier—ancient Prussians believed there was something holy in women and even consulted them as oracles. Certain women could foretell events by studying lakes and rivers. A woman named Veleda of the tribe of Bructeri was a deity who reigned from her tower on the river Lippe, a tributary of the Rhine. She negotiated treaties through her ministers and was treated like a divine queen of royalty."

"Perhaps she was your grandmother?!" Allison quips, a mischievous grin from cheek to cheek.

"Wouldn't that be peachy!" I admit, "Anything's possible."

"Don't forget," says Allison, "Maypole dances all across Europe encouraged the tree spirits to send rain for crops in the spring."

"Yes. In Germany on May 1, they decorate the front of barns with trees or bushes, one for each cow to encourage the flow of milk. In Bavaria, bushes were placed at the home of a newly married couple for the same reason. On June 23, in the Upper Harz Mountains, the Germans would peel bark off a trunk, set it in a field and decorate it with yellow-and-red eggs and flowers, then dance around it."

"We must not forget the Yule log," Allison adds, "and the Christmas tree, both heathen traditions to celebrate the winter solstice. Of course, back in Mesolithic times, there was no tree named for Christ, but perhaps there was for Mary. Or, perhaps Mary is simply an extension of Diana. What do you think?"

"I think we should follow the paper trail! Next time I'll tell you about Gilgamesh, the hero of the earliest known epic tale, dating from the seventh century BC, who lived in Sumeria, but only on stone tablets and in the imaginations of the Sumerians."

"Well," Allison says with a smile, "Then, we'll be following a stone trail, not a paper trail."

"That's true!"

With that our pleasant afternoon comes to an end.

It occurs to me that I might mention *The Fall of the Niebelungs*, the Middle High German pre-Christian epic of the fifth and sixth centuries, part myth, part history, about Siegfried and Kriemhild, however, just because everything *is* connected doesn't mean we *have to know* everything.

Chapter 25
THE STORIES WE CHOOSE TO BELIEVE
MAKE US WHO WE ARE
Who was Gilgamesh?

Signature Cafe

"I'm studying for a test in Child Psychology, so I only have time for coffee today," Allison warns me, glancing over at a scrumptious dessert tray resting on a counter nearby. We cup our hands around fresh brewed, fair-trade Guatemalan coffee, my nose twitching from the exotic aroma escaping into the room, mingling with scents of yeasty oven-baked bread, spicy meat stew, and roasting vegetables.

Allison is still thinking about trees, "What caused the Sumerians and others to begin demonizing trees and separating themselves from wilderness, even calling trees evil," she wonders, raising both hands, looking incredulous.

"Maybe we can find a hint in the *Gilgamesh Epic*," I reply, smiling.

"I've never heard of it, but do tell me," she says, sipping coffee.

I begin to weave a thread that was first woven between 2000 and 3000BC in the rich fertile lands of the Tigris and Euphrates Rivers in a place then called Sumeria, which today we call Iraq.

Thus I begin: This is not a creation story, but rather a lengthy poetic tale like the *Odyssey*. Because it may be one of the earliest recorded stories (on stone tablets) I hoped that it would give me insight concerning the beliefs of Europeans living in antiquity. My quest to understand the evolution of humankind's attitude about their relationship with nature began with Minnesota's natives, but what about my German ancestors and their neighbors?

Gilgamesh is a story about the search for immortality, however my fascination lies with the slaying of the wild and untamed forest represented by the cedar tree, and also by a hairy, unruly hermit who refuses to be civilized and therefore needs to be slain.

Our hero, Gilgamesh, was a young, brave, and strong leader (aren't they all?) who lived in the great city of Uruk. By directing the building of the city, and displaying his civilized talents, he proved himself a great king—part god and part man. His mother was a goddess and his father, a high priest and a mortal.

Unfortunately, Gilgamesh became oppressively haughty and personally excessive, so that the miserable and exhausted people cried out to the gods for relief (sounds familiar!) . The gods responded. They decided to create another personality who could engage the attention of Gilgamesh, thereby keeping him occupied with the new diversion of an opponent.

His name was Enkidu, a wild man with long tangled hair that sprouted like grain. He was quite uneducated, had formidable strength and roamed freely over the countryside, living off the wild fruits and beasts of unfenced land, and even drank from the water of free rambling streams. It was also rumored that he enjoyed the companionship of animals.

When the alarmed Gilgamesh learned of the existence of Enkidu, he schemed to bring him into the city of Uruk—by convincing a female courtesan to enchant him into a trap (wait, where's Mother Earth?) and deliver him to Gilgamesh at his palace. When Enkidu became aware of the deception, he was so furious with rage; and so repelled by civilization that he fought and struggled to get free. However, Gilgamesh expected a fight. A great battle began as they fought in the hall, through the door and out into the streets, until finally Gilgamesh pinned Enkidu to the ground, forcing the wild man to admit the superiority of his civilized foe.

Soon, Enkidu saw the advantages of city life, thus the two men formed a mutual admiration and became close friends. The gods won, too, because Gilgamesh became occupied by further pursuits with his new companion. The two of them turned upon a new enemy—the ogre named Humbaba who was synonymous with the mountainous forest of cedar trees, for he was the unsavory guardian of the enchanted wilderness. It seemed that the god named Shamash (sun-god) wished to have Humbaba killed, for he represented evil (they still had a sun-god).

Gilgamesh and Enkidu set out for the conquest of the cedar forest, which meant they had to first slay a watchman at the gate. Enkidu killed the watchman. His hand became temporarily paralyzed as he entered the gate—evidence that the forest was imbued with spiritual power.

The two brave warriors journeyed many days within a vast, untamed wilderness until they reached the most remote spot where they finally discovered the most sacred cedar tree of the forest. Gilgamesh took out his ax and, blow by blow, chopped down the cedar tree. Alas! The noise of the chopping ax awoke the ogre, Humbaba, who was outraged and roared, "Who has come and disturbed the trees that have grown on my mountain and has cut down the cedar?"

The god Shamash suddenly appeared to the frightened and confused Gilgamesh who stood with ax in hand before an ogre full of wrath. Shamash consoled Gilgamesh by praising him for pursuing the desires of the god by cutting down the tree; and to prove his approval, the pleased god brought forth great winds from eight directions to "beat against the eyes of Humbaba" who gave up the fight and conceded to Gilgamesh who was lucky to have the help of Shamash.

Humbaba pleaded for his life, "Let me go, Gilgamesh; thou shalt be my master, and I will be thy servant. And the trees that I have grown on my mountains, I will cut down and build three houses."

Even with that concession, Gilgamesh and Enkidu cut off the head of Humbaba. They then returned to their city of Uruk as great heroes.

Allison shakes her head, "Will we ever learn? Do Gilgamesh and Enkidu stop their warrior ways?"

I perk up, "Let's finish the story and find out."

Allison stops me, "I can't stand looking at that dessert tray one minute longer. Would you share that big piece of flourless chocolate cake with me?"

"Why not? Chocolate, well, dark chocolate, is good for my heart. I should live forever. I eat a small piece most days before I swim laps at the pool. Gives me energy. And gets me out the door, 'cause the chocolate is in my car."

"What's your favorite? Hershey?"

"Yuck, no. On my first trip to Europe, I learned the joys of fresh dark chocolate, fresh roasted coffee, fresh bread, fresh vegetables . . ."

"Fresh seems to be the thing there," Allison chuckles.

"Yes. Now for a fresh start on the rest of the story:

The *Gilgamesh Epic*, which was enjoyed for more than 1,000 years, continues as Gilgamesh is rejected by the goddess of love, Ishtar. She convinced her father to send a bull to destroy Gilgamesh, but Gilgamesh and Enkidu joined forces to slay the bull. They threw the bull's right thigh at Ishtar with vulgar cursing, thus the two friends became heroes again.

Alas, things turned quite bad when Enkidu had a dream that prophesized his death. The gods had an argument over which of the two men killed Humbaba and the bull, and in the ensuing jealousy and accusations between Shamash and another god named Enlil, Enkidu was the unlucky one chosen for death, although there was no clear evidence put forth that he should die due to cutting cedar trees, or because of his transgressions. He was buried with honors.

After Enkidu became ill and died, Gilgamesh was overwhelmed

with sorrow and began his own epic journey seeking immortality, but in the end he failed. Thus, even a hero who could tame the wild Enkidu, who could defeat the bull of heaven, who endured superhuman challenges on his extended journey could not avoid death. He did manage to bring Enkidu up from the underworld so he could ask him what it was like down there, but the report was bad news, one of "devouring vermin and dust."

"What about heaven?" Allison inquires.

"There was none for humans at that time in Sumerian mythical history. No heaven where Gilgamesh could go for an afterlife in paradise. Around Uruk, there was only a sad and dark underworld. However, his spirit would last . . ."

"Just like the Indians?" Allison asks.

"Perhaps. Living relatives would leave food at his burial, and other familiar items to make him comfortable according to his rank in society."

"So," Allison adds, "No kingdom in the sky for those who were good on earth—those who had not sinned? Or those who were born sinners and managed to become forgiven by following some law?"

"That's how I understood the story," I reply.

"I've heard that the Ojibwe and Lakota have a spirit that rises to go for a walk up to the Milky Way in the sky. They make stops along the way to eat strawberries and enjoy favorite things."

"Yes, that's so. I've sewed many a special ribbon shirt for Indian friends who knew someone about to make that journey."

"Did they have a hell, or underworld?"

"I don't know, but I've not heard of one. Remember, we can't know the practices of all the Native Americans, or all the Near Easterners."

"I know," Allison agrees, savoring a bite of gooey cake, asking, "Is that how Gilgamesh ended his journey to find immortality?"

252

"No, he returned to Uruk to continue overseeing the construction of the city where he would enjoy the rest of his life in the best way he could, for the lands about Uruk were the only ones he really had."

"*Ahhh* . . . in English class we read Voltaire's book *Candide*. When the hero, Candide, returned after his quest, he resigned himself to accepting what already existed, but set himself to doing work that pleased him, kind of like Gilgamesh who settled for building walls. Candide decided to grow plants. He said, 'I know that we must cultivate our garden.'"

"I remember that, too," I said. "His friend Pangloss replies that when man was put in the Garden of Eden, he was meant to work in it, not just sit around. And another friend said they should just enjoy working in the garden and not try to make up theories about everything."

"There's lots of attitudes about how to live or die, aren't there?"

"There sure are. Humans will never stop theorizing, or so it seems," I say, shrugging my shoulders, eating my last bite of cake.

"Do you want them to?" Allison says quizzically.

Choosing to ignore her question for now I suggest, "You can read the *Gilgamesh Epic* as transcribed by Alexander Heidel. He was very interested in beliefs about life and death, which is the main theme of the epic; but I was as interested in the attitude about the wild and untamed in Sumeria, and how women were portrayed because around 3000BC, the date ascribed to early oral versions of the *Gilgamesh Epic*, 25,000 years of goddess religions were coming to an end in southern Europe. This was also when writing began, a man's occupation and the Gilgamesh was recorded on stone tablets. Domestication of animals and plants had earlier beginnings, around 11000BC, with the use of advanced stone tools.

"Perhaps the impact of writing contributed more to the decline in the treatment of females than the advances in agriculture. Mother

Earth continued to be revered in the Americas long after the cultivation and hybridization of corn. And women remained as respected figures in creation stories and myths, such as the Cree story about, the earth goddess, Omamama."

"Women suffered unbalanced humiliation and degradation with the rise of European cultures for 4,000 years while the men tromped all over the earth conquering each other—and the earth itself."

"Well," Allison proclaims, "THAT hasn't changed. But hasn't our attitude? I mean, men don't treat their wives so badly anymore, and we don't have slavery and child labor, and . . ."

"Whoa! We're talking about relationships here, and how they change for all sorts of reasons. When we begin to think of ourselves as on a journey; or life as a quest within the entire cosmos, our awareness of relationships grows. How we create relationships is perhaps the hardest part of being human. Animals have instincts that guide them, but we inferior beings have much more than that, which is why we make everything unnecessarily complicated, when we should keep it simple. Stories are human inventions that explain relationships that reflect our perceptions, and also diversity among us."

"Gee whiz," Allison sighs, "Omamama and Wasakayjack, Gilgamesh, Candide, and . . ."

"I'itoi?"

"Yes, I'itoi, the little man in the maze. They're all mythical heroes seeking answers on a journey, bringing messages to people, but each message is different from one another, isn't it?"

"Yes, they're symbols that represent who the people were, or are."

"Yes, Gilgamesh and I'itoi are very different characters, so the stories we choose to believe make us who we are?"

"I don't know, but I have more stories for you, if you want to hear them. You'd like one that dates from 500 years after Gilgamesh in Babylon. The role of women grows even worse."

"Thank God, things have changed," Allison says, pulling her jacket on, "I can't wait to get together again. Thank you so much. I mean, *miigwech*."

Chapter 26
THE SPIRITS OF OTHERS REMAIN IN MY
BLOOD AND MEMORY
Justice is highly arbitrary. Laws don't always create fairness.

Minneapolis

Allison drives home to her young children, to her future. I circle back, thinking about my past. On the car seat next to me rests a cardboard box full of yellow newspaper clippings from the 1970s about Wounded Knee, stories I am bringing to an Indian friend. A photograph of AIM's Russell Means reminds me of Maryanne twenty-six years ago.

At the conclusion of the conference in Geneva, we flew home after a brief visit to meet her family in Germany. Back in Minnesota, we were both busy. In the euphoria of our whole experience, I failed to notice that her feelings about me had changed.

I shall never forget the afternoon when Maryanne and I parted ways, a deeply shattering experience because it was so unexpected. Why hadn't she responded to my calls? But then, I was busy—busy getting a divorce. Dick Bancroft, our mutual friend and photographer of Indians, said she was mad at me, but he didn't know why. He arranged a lunch for us three—to patch things up. I wasn't worried, just curious to learn what had upset her.

Dick and Maryanne were in the Haberdashery eatery at a round table in the center of a noisy room bustling with university students. Her body language told me she was miffed. After seating myself, she began an attack on me: angry words pouring out of her mouth, narrow eyes flashing, hands flying in the air, ignoring the visibly disturbed diners around us. I was shocked by her accusations, sickened by such an embarrassing display. She accused me of being a slacker in the cause to create justice for Indian people. Attempting to appease her, I confessed that I'd not done as much as she, that her efforts were unmatched by any nonIndian women I knew.

That tactic was a bad mistake. She turned my concession into an admission of guilt. Confused, betrayed, at a loss for words, I broke into tears, sobbing. Dick tried to stop her, but she would not let up. I felt like a weak gang member, hesitant to be one of the true believers; unwilling to give my life to prove my deepest devotion to a larger cause. It was true—I didn't want to play her same role, even though I admired her unflinching dedication very much.

My reasons were good for drawing a line, reasons Maryanne knew too well. I believed in the forceful tactics of AIM. Appeasement had brought Indians nothing but impoverishment and humiliation from the US government. They'd obviously been cheated badly, and continued to be. But there were thousands of Indians who didn't back AIM. They were the ones who should be fighting for their rights. I had to prepare a new future for my children, find a home and a job.

Many Indian women resented white women or were jealous of them. Like the day I went to meet an artist (who didn't show up), in a bar frequented by a few American Indian instructors from the university. While talking to them, a black-haired young woman leaned over behind me, and in a slurred tongue, she hissed, "You ain't nothin' but a white chick in a skin bar." My friends said, "Just ignore her," but I was thinking, "Wow! That's a great title for a country-western song!"

Another time was serious. I was alone in a restroom at a conference in Wakpala, ND, when a "skin" (Indian slang used among themselves, short for redskin) woman entered the small, smelly room, pulled a knife out of her boot, saying, "You have no business being in Indian country." I simply walked away from her, but I never forgot.

Such women endured terrible suffering. Of course, I would be perceived as a privileged person. Not wanting to be anybody but myself, I was often perceived as a "wannabe."

After being confronted by the knife-holding female, I met a special individual who was a mystery to me at that time. It was a sizzling hot afternoon in Wakpala, with a dry, dusty breeze crossing over our encampment. Walking alone, I spotted him sitting by himself on a hardback chair under a shabby canvas tarp that provided little shade, next to a small table that held informational papers and pamphlets. The Lakota grandfather had a thick, head of black hair—two loosely woven braids that fell far down each shoulder on his chest. He was small in stature, wore cowboy boots, dark cotton pants, a blue long-sleeved shirt, and leather belt with a silver buckle. His face was dignified with a prominent nose, and large eyeglasses. I was eager to share my passionate feelings, yet I didn't want to be foolish.

He said nothing. I told him my name and town, and that I'd come to Wakpala to learn and to be of service. He looked at me through big watery eyes and said nothing. I told him that I believed that time alone would create so much change that Indian prophesy would manifest itself; that mankind would not realize what it had done before it was too late; that somehow Indians would survive and have their old life back.

He kept staring at me with an expression of sadness, a demeanor of not understanding, a tenuous communication. I felt embarrassed for speaking boldly and left him alone.

Later, I was told that he was Fools Crow, the Ceremonial chief of the Teton Sioux; that he wore a wig, and spoke no English. I saw him again, and he grinned at me. He was a good holy man who supported the progressive decisions of the young city Indians who were fighting for social reform and the revival of cultural traditions. Thomas E. Mails wrote a book titled *Fools Crow* that was published in 1979, a good account of Indian life after his birth in 1890 or soon after, with descriptions of his efforts to continue the sun dances on the prairie. His uncle was Black Elk.

Many thoughts swirl about in my brain: Allison, Gilgamesh, Maryanne, Fools Crow, Europe, as I leave the Signature Cafe in St. Paul, get on the freeway to Minneapolis, and drive toward the University of Minnesota to the West Bank.

My trip to Europe influenced me to start a small venture. Just like the Indians, I love to dress up. My small portable sewing machine had been in continuous use since my husband gave it to me for a high school graduation gift. It sat on a low counter in a closet nook that had a window overlooking the front yard, always surrounded with stacks of fabric, thread and trimmings. Inspiration for my clothing designs came from many sources, even dreams.

One idea provided a new spiral on my path of life, after I was inspired by a Woody Allen film, *Annie Hall,* just prior to leaving for Switzerland. Diane Keaton, actress, wore an outfit I fell in love with: a men's hat (a fedora punched up inside), a loose men's white shirt, baggy khaki pants, and leather sandals. A wide necktie completed the playful ensemble. Annie was a smiley, seductive scamp. Seated in the dark theater, I felt my brain light up. A voice said: *YOU can dress like that, TOO! Create a whole vest out of neckties.*

So, I did. Clearing away the leather scraps left over from making my own medicine pouch to take to Geneva, I sat down to stitch together rows of silk pieces from Uncle Chester's funky old ties in muted, conservative tones from the 1940s—flat colors, mostly browns and blues. I laid the quilted pieces down and traced a pattern on top to cut out two fronts. The back and linings were cut from navy blue taffeta. An antique buckle in back, old bone-colored buttons from my button collection, no label, and almost done.

259

Oh, oh, I discovered a small hole in one piece of tie, so I covered it by sewing on one of the labels from the discarded scraps. It read: Dayton's Department Store. I added two more labels for balance.

La, dee, daaa! During my travels in Europe, women stopped me in the street, wanting to know where they could buy my vest. Soon, I was in business!

That's when the child labor began. We set up shop in the living room where the kids couldn't watch TV unless they ripped open their quota of ties. Lisa ironed them flat and piled them into rows according to color. They could earn a free dinner after the first 100 ties, so it was a fun fall day when we all headed to Hastings to the Dinner Bell for a supper club treat. We joyously celebrated our success, offering a toast to Woody Allen and *Annie Hall*.

Necktie vests were good for my pocketbook and ego, but they would not last forever, nor would the financial support from my separated, soon-to-be divorced husband. Becoming a serious sculptress was becoming a dream further and further out of reach, however, I'd had a taste of representing other artists and enjoyed their association and the world they created for themselves. Wouldn't it be cool to be a part of that?

Driving my car through the University of Minnesota's West Bank shopping area, a bustling commercial downtown section of Minneapolis, I pull over to park on Cedar Avenue near Midwest Mountaineering, an outdoor retailer. I long to get out and walk, but my legs won't let me.

Nostalgic, haunting images call me back to 1977: Me, a college graduate about to be divorced, walking along the street feeling energetic and hopeful, each step drawing me toward a new beginning. What would that be? How would I reshape myself? My auburn hair is long and straight. I'm clad in bell-bottom jeans and a necktie vest. A

Civil War brown leather saddle bag swings at my side. Sauntering across the street I wander over to a small Indian art gallery called The Raven, featuring Canadian, Alaskan, and Inuit sculpture and prints. I knew that two women had started The Raven art gallery on their own.

I stood there thinking about my great-grandmother and her sister who each owned their own resorts. Aunt Ethel owned a greenhouse. Aunts Alice and Lorraine were accountants for large businesses. And my mother became a territorial manager for Avon cosmetic products.

A vision formed in my imagination. The Raven sold Inuit art from Alaska. Perhaps I could sell Indian art from the Southwest. Wouldn't it be pleasant to have a reason to visit New Mexico often?

The truth is, I was terrified to ask someone for a job. It seemed less daunting to start my own job than to fill someone else's expectations of me. Why would anyone hire me anyway? Who needed an expert on Indian art who was not an Indian? I'd given a successful lecture at the university, but didn't want to learn about Indian philosophy from books, like an academic. I wanted to be free to personally meet my mentors. Owning my own Indian art gallery seemed to fit all the things I wished for. However, I'd not be an artist myself. Maybe I could do that in my spare time. Traveling to Georgia O'Keefe country—warm, sunny and exotic, to a Minnesota girl. Yeah! Big skies, greasy tamales, pink adobes, turquoise jewelry, happy brown faces. Wouldn't it be fun? On my trip to Santa Fe I'd already met many sculptors and painters who created in modern expressions. They were already widely respected. Some were still students with tremendous talent and promise. I had good instincts for good art (and clothing), and trusted myself—to choose good sellers. And, as for running a business, I'd figure that out, too.

All I needed was money; money, and a storefront. The necktie vest production line went into full gear. Quilts of silk pieces lay draped over the living room furniture. (Bless the little children for they shall

261

inherit their mother's dreams.)

Letters went out to selected artists inviting them to join my venture. Each one gave me more names to contact. Some were in California where Leonard, my oldest son was staying. We enjoyed a reunion while viewing art. Len was living with pals in Newport Beach while recovering from a snowmobile accident in Minnesota.

At the University of California-Davis, I met a Navajo artist who had been one of the famous code-talkers during WWII. Carl Gorman had a son in Taos, New Mexico, who was famous for his drawings of women. The son was R.C. Gorman.

During an art opening in Manhattan Beach, I met a jolly nonIndian woman doing watercolors of Hopi villages that were so gracious and moving I had to have them. Sari Staggs became a friend.

Russell Means had told me to stop in Oakland at AIM's western headquarters. They issued me a yellow card with the AIM logo in red, making me a member. I still have it, signed by Ted Means. My heart was still with them, and they knew it, which is why I agreed to march with them that afternoon to protest against a major newspaper that was criticizing a religious organization called the Peoples Temple, led by the Reverend Jim Jones.

With hundreds of people of all colors, I marched. Carrying a sign for more equality, I marched. Imagine my shock when on November 18, 1978, about one month after the event, they willingly became a mass of suicidal cyanide Kool-Aid victims who horridly died with their kids, in the jungles of Guyana, South America—900 of them, who convinced each other that Jones was the messiah to follow to heaven. Jones however, didn't plan to die himself, not yet anyway. Those swayed by bad religious propaganda have catastrophic consequences. Communal sharing can be healthy, or sick if led by one authoritarian power-seeker. A liar like Jones disgusted me. His promises about a better life, love, and compassion killed children who had no choice and who trusted him.

I've never forgotten those poor people with whom I rubbed shoulders on the streets of San Francisco. Lying leaders seemed to be rampant. Men with strong convictions and no conscience, believe their own lies when they send others off to die for a false cause that only the perpetrators profit from handsomely.

My list of dead suckers includes some deluded people who "die for honor and glory": Mayan Indians who died for a sun-god decked out in gold on his throne atop a stone mound; soldier slaves who followed European or Asian egomaniac generals into battle century after century; willing victims of capitalistic, corporate greed who fight modern wars that are invented by those who profit from military contracts. I shake my head and marvel that so many are duped by psychopaths—followers willing to do what they don't understand. One only needs to read *The March of Folly* by Barbara Tuchman, a 1984 publication. Every American male or would-be soldier should read this book.

I start the engine on my car and drive away from the West Bank. Nosing my car onto Washington Avenue, maneuvering twenty blocks away to the north side of downtown, I remember how, in the 1970s the north side was known as the Warehouse District, a dying manufacturing center where immigrants had once found factory work. Later, women sewed items for World War I and II. After that they made coats, jackets, hats, pajamas, and all sorts of clothing for Sears and Roebuck, J.C. Penney's, and other US stores. Then they all left.

Did this same faction of Americans vacate the garment district and move to new modern facilities in the suburbs? Did the corporations care about the income of those who lived in the USA? No. The exodus of jobs to poorer countries became a great "sucking sound" just as candidate Ross Perot predicted. Service jobs followed manufacturing jobs overseas, taking with them the American Dream—the middle class, union security, pensions, health insurance, long-term employment, and eventually affordable housing.

I knew it was the beginning of the war on America when Ronald Reagan's policies (1981–1989) attacked Franklin Roosevelt's New Deal which had formed Social Security. Reagan was elected to destroy our "bloated welfare state."

Within two years of his election, defeating Gerald Ford, he cut $41.4 billion from Jimmy Carter's proposed budget, dropped the capital gains tax from 28 to 20 percent, while increasing defense spending, creating a deficit of $100 billion (twice the previous record), and an unemployment rate of 10.8 percent. Yet, his affable personality, and a vigorous TV campaign defeated Minnesota's Walter Mondale, his Democratic opponent in the 1984 election. Reagan's folksy, down-home fundamentalist spin on reality captured the South from the Democrats. As the marginal tax rate plunged from 70 percent to 28 percent, the largest percentage reduction in tax rates in United States history, the poor cheered on the Republicans who rallied against social services as higher taxes, and who led the charge for military "Weapons for Peace"—a program to build shields against missiles.

The rhetoric never matched reality, which turned citizens into cynical critics, opponents of their own government that gave them social security, job loss help, veteran's services, public parks, roads, and waterways; plus fire and crime prevention; emergency funding for natural catastrophes and, most of all, public education. With the wealthiest Americans supporting Reagan, he limited their personal income tax while at the same time, taxing the rest of the people more to make up for it. Thousands of mothers entered the workforce to maintain a living standard that could formerly be earned by one partner. At the same time, conservatives shouted from the pulpits about family values. Who needs soap operas? We have Republicans.

The Judith Stern Art Gallery began in 1976 at 416 First Avenue North. I signed a lease for a street level storefront with 3,000 square feet that needed to be completely gutted of office cubicles. It was in a multi-story brick building of empty upper floor spaces that would one day become hip artist's studios. My rent was not cheap, but my space was adjacent to an already established gallery named the Women's Art Registry of Minnesota. They called it WARM.

Above my art gallery space, empty floors begged to be explored. Two of my teenage sons found a creaky old wooden elevator. Like cave snoopers, we wandered among the dusty rooms lit by unwashed windows with small square panes. A hazy thickness settled upon everything. No sounds disturbed us, except a mouse scurrying to find a hole. The sewing machines were gone, but I could still hear their humming. The cutters were gone, but I could see their patterns spread out upon long sturdy oak tables. Those who pressed, tagged, and boxed garments were gone, too; but there were the boxes, the labels, a pot of glue, spools of string, and a scale. Scattered about were cones of faded thread, scraps of filthy fabric and odd pieces of furniture. We rescued a work table for me, and a solid heavy office chair like the one Grandpa had in his home office. My Ojibwe friend, Joe Geshick, helped me. He was a trouble-shooter who solved problems for Control Data Corporation, a computer manufacturer. My son, Heath also cheerfully labored to renovate the gallery area into its original vast open space, creating a beautiful display room for modern fine art created by living American Indian artists. There was also an office and a back room for my design and sewing work.

Thank God! The messy divorce was final. My parents provided help for housing closer to downtown. The boys and I often did "big city" days—movies, art shows, museums, foreign food, and powwows at the Indian Center on Franklin Avenue where I enjoyed gathering with my Indian friends, like Doris and Dayshun, and my "wannabe" friends like those I met in the group formed by our mentor, Mizinokamigok. They shared my excitement about starting an art gallery.

My two youngest boys and I made plans to move, while the oldest one went off to college. My daughter insisted upon going to live with drugster dad who was "cool." This broke my heart.

My ex-husband took me to court for not vacating the house fast enough. I was shocked when the judge ordered me out in two weeks. Me, with kids and no income. He, with a job and pension. He, the abusive bully. Me, the devoted mother. Why hadn't I called the cops on him more? My compassion for him had been received as a weakness to be manipulated. Women who protect our sons need to be protected by our men, an unspoken covenant since humans began. No written laws should be necessary. We need better customs.

I would never have to be a chump again. Or would I? I found myself defending my body again on moving day. Snow fell the night before we began loading the U-Haul truck. The bully entered the house, grabbed me in the kitchen and threw me against the washing machine, wrenching my back as I collapsed. He yanked me up before I could catch my breath and hurled me against the back door, smashing the glass of the storm window with my head—my hair getting caught in the door frame, as I buckled and sprawled on the floor, screaming, begging, "Stop! Stop!"

Then the hot-brained husband ran upstairs, and right back down. He ran outside to the truck as I locked the house door and watched him through the window. Tiny bits of blood mixed with heavy tears fell on my sweater as I clutched my throbbing back. The rascal raised the hood of the truck, ripped wires from the engine, then moved around to the back. He opened the doors and forced his way in. I ran outside to protest, afraid he would smash my furniture, but he found my dresser, opened a drawer, and removed the only piece of jewelry he'd given me in eighteen years—my precious Zuni turquoise-silver needlepoint bracelet. Like a plundering thief he plunked it into his pocket.

A car drove up. It was my helpers, three husky Indian men who remained in their car. The bully jumped in his car and drove away. I wheeled around stumbled, and called the police, who arrived as I was explaining my dilemma to my friends. The police said they could do nothing because they hadn't witnessed the act themselves, even though they saw blood and the ripped wires. They said I could go to the station and sign some papers; however, if I did that, I'd lose my moving helpers who had to get to work. So I did nothing. We moved. We celebrated with dinner at a Country Kitchen. I felt safe in my own place that night—finally. But my spirit mourned the loss of my dear Zuni bracelet.

Thus I learned more about justice for women in domestic abuse. There really was none unless my husband agreed to let the officers watch him beat me up! I also had to fight my insurance company to keep my insurance, because I could not demonstrate any former income that I had earned myself that was sufficient enough to pay the premiums. I won on the basis that they'd have to drop every mother with kids who ever got a divorce and hadn't worked outside her home. No bank would loan me money to buy a van for my gallery before I began to earn my wages. Dad provided me with a loan so I could buy a new Ford Econoline van, dark green with beige leather seats. Back then, vans were for commercial use only—for plumbers, grocery deliveries, carpenters—definitely not for women! I was in the front of a very big trend that Ford hadn't invented. Millions of moms took to the freeways in vans. I couldn't wait to get back to New Mexico.

Chapter 27
STRIVING FOR COMFORT AND MEANING
CREATES MANY PATHS
Do you want to die for things, or live for reality?

University of St. Thomas

"Think outside the box. That's what Bob Erickson, your social studies teacher recently heard from a speech by the writer Thomas Friedman, who wrote *The World is Flat* about our current global economic trade structure. He believes we need more innovation and competition," I tell the students in my Indian Art class.

"I say, think inside the circle. Innovation is killing us, or shall I say, extreme innovation does us more harm than good. We continue to compete with nature as if it is separate from ourselves; as if we will be happier if only we can defy her every attempt to make us healthy and beautiful.

"Where is ugliness in nature? I have never found it. Where is ugliness in human creations? Everywhere, or so it seems to me. Why is this? Does anyone know?"

Kathryn answers slowly, "Is it because we create so much trash?"

Barbara adds, "Is it because we produce so much in our consumer driven culture that is just junk?"

"That's part of it, but why do we behave like this in the first place?"

Facing the class, shifting in my chair, I continue, "Attitude, values, philosophy—call it what you want, the perceptions of the Hopi traditionalists consistently create beauty because they live simple, reciprocal, predictable, conservative lives. They are the opposite of Thomas Friedman's conjectures. Black Elk told us that a circle is stronger than a box, and that balance creates more abundance than competition. I'm starting to wish that all the experts would jump back in their boxes and leave the world to the rest of us.

"The world is quickly becoming more complex and difficult to understand for many people. Change has to support balance or it's not healthy for the system. Forcing people into complexities they aren't ready for, or that they see no great benefit in, only causes insecurity and fear. These fears are well founded."

Drawing a diagram on the blackboard, I proclaim, "We cannot create enough energy today to run all of our inventions without endangering the continuing evolution of humankind.

"Notice, I didn't say planet earth. The earth will go on. But we will be just another extinct species. All because we lost our way—we forgot how to imitate the patterns of the earth—to live in harmony in the circle, rather than outside the box." I then ask, "If most Americans did simplify, would the world follow suit?"

Kathryn pipes up, "Isn't it the other way around? Others already have a smaller imprint on the globe. It's time that we followed them."

"Yes! Didn't the creator make us all with strengths and weaknesses? Leaders are at the top of the line and others come from behind. A box is four lines, but a circle is one. We need to stop thinking in straight lines, and instead think in curves, like the shapes of the planets. Then, the weak and the strong, the old and sick, help each other."

Sarah raises her hand to speak, "Do you mean that if we make as much energy, like electricity, gas, oil, and so on, as we need to sustain our lifestyle, we'll all die from extraction of resources and the pollution that results when we use them by converting them to our use? Is that what you mean?"

"Yes. That's what I mean by extreme innovation. It's the same as saying 'unsustainable lifestyle.'"

269

"Well," says Lindsay, looking doubtful, "Nobody's forcing me to live in a certain way. I like it. I certainly don't want to live in a mud house in the desert like the Hopi or anyone else, yet I don't need a McMansion in the suburbs on a private street with a gate. I don't like feeling guilty because some people are smarter than others. Some simply earn less money, or don't want to work."

"Sounds to me like you've chosen a moderate path within your means. That's good. I, too, prefer living in Minnesota in a wood house near a river with more choices to enjoy," I pause for a minute, "And so do all the Indians that were forced onto the most difficult lands so we could enjoy the best.

"Let me ask you all this question. How many use a computer?"

All hands rise. "How many drive a car?" All hands rise.

"How many eat food bought in a grocery store?" Laughter, as hands rise.

"How many have a cell phone?" Big laughter as all hands go up.

"You think that nobody forced you to use these things, but in a sense you are addicted to them. According to the dictionary, addiction is a physiological dependence on a drug, OR to abandon oneself to something compulsively or obsessively.

"You see, in a competitive, dollar-driven society, culture revolves around creating needs.

"*Ahhh*, I see you nodding. You agree with me. Everything is designed for comfort, pleasure, and most of all, to addict you to use or do things you really don't need. Workers once provided services for our needs. Now we invent wants and work for things that make us sick. This is an attitude change that creates waste, ugliness and sickness for people and the planet.

"Did you know that the happiest, healthiest people on earth live in other countries? Many of them, like me, have no computer, no cell phone, no TVs, no junk food, and they grow their own food. I think they're more free than we are. We work our entire lives to buy many things because we're addicted to them. And what do we have? Half of our youngsters are obese, unfit to serve in the military, suffer from depression and diabetes (all preventable problems), and many may wind up in jail, all preventable problems.

"I'm not personally criticizing any one of you. I simply hope that you will consider thinking in alternative ways about what really matters to you as an individual and how you're connected to others and the earth.

"There are a lot of lies spread by marketing, but you can step back from them and imagine a bigger picture that encompasses a richer life, a reality in which people had fewer choices. Do you want to die for things? Or live for reality? You don't have to live like a Lakota in a teepee, but you can learn why they do what they do, and maybe you'll discover something useful for you.

"People like the old Lakota or Ojibwe believed in many things that seem downright silly today, like rituals or dream catchers. They believed that imitation of nature provided protection in many ways. Remember nature was personified as members of the great family of life. The hoop of the dream catcher reminds us of grandmother spider.

"Most Indians created meaning in everything to remind them of where they came from, and where they were going. They copied animal behavior in rituals, made masks, drew pictures and sang songs. There was a practice of behaving in prescribed ways to produce a desired effect far away, as when men went hunting or warring, women observed certain taboos to aid their men by an act of sacrifice or restraint.

"In 1993 I taught a class named Exploring American Indian Spirituality in Contemporary Society with a Lakota author named Ed McGaa, who wrote a book that has become a classic in Native American literature. Ed's written several instructive books, but I

271

suggest you begin with this one, *Mother Earth Spirituality: Native American Paths to Healing Ourselves and Our World.* He writes about Lakota ceremonies and rituals, Black Elk's vision, women as spirit guides, and the history of the destructive attitude and actions of the Pilgrims. He states that his people traditionally had 'an advanced governmental system that afforded far more democratic privileges than any existing (European) system.'"

Holding the book up for the class to see, I continue, "McGaa, or Eagle Man, his Indian name, teaches us that Europeans were ruled by autocrats, while the Lakota, Ojibwe, Iroquois, and others had an elected council, that was copied by America's founders who took credit for the idea, then were too narrow-minded to recognize the benefits of the Indian Way, even after it had saved their very lives.

"He says the most important lesson of Indian teachings is the holistic value system they demonstrate, and respect for Mother Earth, each other, and ourselves, because all are sacred.

"You should buy this book and place it on your shelf next to *Black Elk Speaks*.

"I can see by the clock that you must go on to your next class.

"Your assignment is to find pictures, or examples of Indian art that demonstrate two different attitudes: that of restraint and cooperation and that of excessiveness and individuality."

The room empties. Allison pops in the door between classes and approaches my desk smiling, "Do you have time to stop at the Signature Cafe on your way home?"

"I must leave early today to pick up a package, but I could do lunch at 12:30. Would that work for you?"

"Sure. Say, you look a bit weary," she cautions me.

"I'm just wondering why we citizens of earth haven't learned more from each other by now. I suppose we learn only what we choose to learn."

"*Hmmm*. Maybe we've learned too much. You said innovation can be bad."

"Yes. Sometimes, too many exotic, rich spices spoil the soup."

"You mean we need to study the art of the bland?" She teases me.

"Oh, not that! Perhaps the art of the subtle. Life should be like rich buttery soup in France—like good wine, like vichyssoise soup made from fresh garden leeks and potatoes, like chewy, crusty French bread."

Allison chuckles, "Not like beet borscht and pumpernickel bread with beer? Not like Pilsner Urquel beer?"

"Well, I suppose one must strive for balance between being bourgeoisie and becoming proletariat," I say coyly.

"Good grief! Not many would stop to consider it a mere choice. Most Americans strive to be as high class as they can," Allison retorts, then adds, "What if all Americans chose to live like peasants?"

"The stock market would plunge as people downsize homes, cars, travel, medical bills, and their bodies," I say dryly.

"Gosh," Allison says sprightly, a sparkle in her eyes, "You make me want to live in France in a mountainside cottage!"

"What? Not a villa just outside Paris?"

"No! A cottage with a big garden."

I sigh, "It never hurts to dream. See you in a few hours at the cafe. Maybe they'll have sweet fresh strawberries. Winter is over."

Springtime in Minnesota. The bears are stirring in their dens while I'm staring out the window at skyscrapers. How many generations have passed in my German lineage since members of my clan entered a sweat lodge, venerated bears, and acted upon the visions of a Holy Woman? Surely my people did all that. Surely they sought the spiritual along with the physical, the intellectual. Surely they worshipped the trees in the solemn dark forests inhabited by spirits. And didn't they

273

dance with dream-filled motions to assure meat and berries for their babies? Surely they used names, symbols, and stories for actions that provided comfort, meaning, hope and order in a mysteriously infinite, yet bounded world that knew no logic and science, nor human control over phenomena. Surely they gave thanks, sacrifices, anger, and awe to the forces that controlled them. Surely they desired to influence them with their will and words; thus was born motivation for striving with progress. Thus was born the imaginative creativity of predictability: tool making, symbolic representation—oral, or etched.

Inventions that made life more comfortable grew in complexity, for it was the natural inclination of mankind to make his clan or tribe powerful by living in harmony with nature and by competing with other humans, for they understood that harmony and discord are the ways that nature creates balance.

Most of my Germanic ancestors didn't seem to question the consequences of limitless progress, or life without taboos. They didn't pause to consider the future implications of the impact of their inventions, or they did think about such things, but chose to ignore certain possibilities that could become unfavorable to humans as we continue evolving. Many humans viewed their new knowledge as a gift extended from a deity. They saw their special treatment among earthly life as an invitation to create even more special gifts for themselves, at the expense of people like Lakota natives, who saw inventiveness as not only a gift for everybody, but equally as a burden, or a responsibility; and by increasing the amount of comfort or convenience for humankind, their burden should increase proportionally, because that's what balance means.

Striving for comfort and meaning took a variety of paths, like spirals of wind spirits sweeping the prairie. For some, the path never led far astray from the sweat lodge door, but there were others who would ride rockets to the moon. Nobody will know where the path of the Ojibwe, Hopi, Iroquois, and Blackfoot might have led, if they had not been subjugated or acculturated.

In America, prehistoric towns were built that far exceeded the villages found by the earliest white explorers, but we can only speculate why they fell into ruins and were largely abandoned. The city of Cahokia near present day St. Louis once had a population of 20,000 on the banks of the Mississippi River, larger than London in 1050AD, with 3,200 acres of homes, corn fields, temples, and mounds—one pyramid was the third largest in the New World. By 1400 the Mississippian, or Cahokia culture had dispersed across the South, Southeast, and into Midwestern river valleys. The Cahokia story reminded me of how I'itoi became too powerful, so Earthmaker destroyed his tall house with an earthquake. Did power hungry rulers kill Cahokia?

Chapter 28
CUSTOMS WERE BASED ON SACRIFICES
What is the Babylonian genesis?

Signature Café

Spotless glass window panes reflect sunbeams across the brick patio, now free of ice. No shadows darken the view of the street, for leaves on the elm trees have yet to unfurl. A lone robin sings atop a maple, a perfect companion to cheer the heart of any winter-weary soul. Twittering sparrows light upon dormant alpine current bushes. Closing my eyes, I raise my head as if I can really move closer to Grandfather Sun.

Sunshine on my face feels so loving, like a gentle force nourishing my spirit. Still wrapped in woolies, my snow-white body waits to emerge like a butterfly from a cocoon, or a bear from her den. Seasons of nature are great teachers. Reemergence of life forms are important lessons.

My gloves lay on the bench beside me. My bare hands wrap around a mug of steaming hibiscus tea that reminds me of my months spent in Haiti. So many places I have yet to see, but if I don't, that's okay.

Here comes Allison, sauntering down the sidewalk, swinging her arms like a free spirit, smiling like a happy cat, "Hi!" she calls cheerily, "Can we eat outside?"

"Management says, 'Not yet. Still too early,'"

"Oh darn—not too early for me. I'm ready to trade my snowshoes for hiking boots."

"Lucky you. My ankle hurts too much for any hiking these days."

Allison frowns, "Have you learned anything new about that?"

276

"No. And we won't talk about it, because today we're celebrating spring."

Allison agrees, "Finally. It's been a long winter."

I shrug my shoulders, "Why do people always say that? Winter is always long in Minnesota. Nobody should ever be surprised."

"That's true," she says, adding, "I'm looking forward to hearing another story. I want to know why people—well, Lutherans and such—don't say the terms Father Sun and Mother Earth anymore."

We choose a table, select our beverages, and discuss Allison's future plans to teach in an elementary school. She suddenly bolts up in her chair, exclaiming, "I almost forgot. I'll be right back."

She runs out the door and returns with a gift for me. "I almost forgot. I brought tulips for you. Don't they smell sweet?"

"*Miigwech!* I love fresh flowers more than anything. I'm delighted."

After our server loans us a vase, Allison proudly arranges the scarlet and gold Turk's caps. All those around us can share our joy for the festive spring posies.

"Did you know," I begin, "wild tulips come from Asia Minor, the Caucasus Mountains between the Black and Caspian Seas, and the Mediterranean region? I've planted some Turkish species tulips in my garden. They're quite small—a few inches tall—with pointy splayed petals, white centers and purple edges. There are other wild tulips that appear more like the hybrids in our vase, but none so large. You should come see my garden this summer. I planted 300 bulbs last fall," I say, adding, "Tulips make me think of the Babylonian creation myth, my next story for you today. Are you ready?"

"I'm all ears. Please start."

"First, a few reminders: Remember that around 3000BC began the end of goddess worship in the old world, after lasting around 25,000 years; and that *Gilgamesh Epic* wasn't a creation story, but rather the earliest known epic recorded in writing in that part of the world—Sumeria, during 3000 to 3000BC. Great tribal migrations were moving east to west, influencing thinking among Indo-Europeans."

"Can you tell me," asks Allison, "what's an Indo-European? People from Europe and India?"

"Yes . . . ," I begin.

Allison stops me. "Well, where did they come from, after humans came up from Africa?"

"You're going to have to read Karen Armstrong's books about the foundations for religion in the West. She came to speak at Macalester College, and I was lucky to meet her. She was a Roman Catholic nun until 1969 when she left to get a degree at Oxford University and teach literature. She's living in London and has written more than sixteen books. I strongly suggest *A History of God* from 1993, and also *The Great Transformation* from 2006. Her work is thoroughly researched and presented in a very readable format, in spite of an amazing amount of detail. I love her because she's a spiritual writer with a curious mind, an unusual openness toward theological history. She writes without personal opinions or proselytizing."

"Does she write about American Indian religion?"

"Not that I know of; however she traces religious ideas way back to antiquity, to the Aryans who lived where these tulips originated on the Caucasian steppes in Russia. The Aryan tribes had a common language that became many subsequent languages for those who came to inhabit much of Asia and Europe—hence the term, Indo-European. Eventually the population grew and expanded, to the east and west, becoming separate speaking groups, either the Avestan dialect or Sanskrit, yet the people maintained similar living patterns of farming and raising animals. Their relationship with the forces of nature were very much like the traditional Ojibwe and Lakota, for they thought everything had a spirit."

"Did they also have something like the Great Mystery, like our American tribes?"

"The Avestan speakers called it *mainyu* and the Sanskrit people used *manya*."

"Gee whiz," Allison says, "both words start with ma, like mama, or mammalian, mammal—even Mary. I bet their great mystery was based on a female ideal. Maybe they had a Great Mother goddess like Omamama."

"I believe so, but it's interesting that the natives of Polynesia and Hawaii have a spiritual great mystery, too, called *mana*."

Allison adds, "Isn't the Ojibwe word for this *manito*?"

"Yes, and the word *mater* is related to mother. Mater in Latin is related to trees, and Demeter, the goddess, was like an earth mother for the old Greeks."

"This suggests something universal going on, doesn't it?"

"Yes. Aryan peoples came to create more complicated systems of gods, but not like the one in the Bible. Aryan gods had much less power and were more like humans in their need to behave in proper ways to assure stability and harmony, so that nature would continue to provide for the humans. The customs were based on sacrifice."

Allison suggests, "Again, like the Indians."

"Armstrong tells us that the Aryans believed that, without sacrifice, there could be no life. They thought the gods rightly made the world in seven stages: First the sky, that was like a big round shell like a stone; then earth, a plate that sat on water in the shell; then came one plant, one bull, and a man; lastly, fire."

"*Hmmm*," Allison muses, "Earth, water, fire . . . what about wind?"

"My guess is that wind was the sky. Or maybe sky and sun were alike, but nothing was animated until the gods performed three sacrifices."

"What were they?" Allison asks, sipping her coffee.

279

"They killed the plant, bull, and man. Then circular motions began the seasons. Then, plant, bull, and man came to life, each one producing appropriate plant foods and trees, animals, and humans."

"So humans understood that they depended on what came before them in order to enjoy life on earth. Pretty simple, isn't it?"

"I think so. They didn't understand the scientific explanations that we have today, but they were far more wise in recognizing what was required to survive. They were practical, rooted in a reality without an afterlife. It was a peaceful life, like the Hopi Indians are known for. The Aryan rituals remind me of my participation in the *kiva* ceremony in which every action represented prayer and sacrifice, and in a very real sense every day was a form of ritual."

"What changed all this? Were they invaded by people like Columbus, Cortez, and Pizarro? Did disease kill them? What happened? They had to have survived because they became US!" Allison wonders.

"Well, yes, us and the people of India, and so on," I remark.

Continuing on, I explain, "This perspective of balance, rhythmic, nurturing patterns of life slowly changed when some of the wealthy members thought they, too, should join the gods in a rich afterlife."

"Oh, not again! Sounds like I'itoi of the Tohono O'odham tribe in Arizona. I'itoi forgot that he had only the power to do what Earthmaker wanted him to do; but I'itoi became arrogant and so Earthmaker moved the sun further and further away till ice and snow covered the earth. All the people got punished because of him."

"*Ahhh.* Lots of lessons there. Not only about arrogance, but also about dangerous individualism. I'll talk about that another day. But now, I'll tell you what Armstrong says about the Aryans: Around 1500BC they were trading with more technologically advanced people like the Mesopotamians and Armenians who had bronze weapons, wooden carts with wheels that were pulled by oxen, and carts pulled by horses, or chariots. When the Aryans adopted these devises they could be warriors like the southerners and raid their neighbors' farms on the Russian steppes, forcing everyone else to defend themselves.

"All this violence resulted in competition among the strongest men; chiefs searching for fame and glory; and new gods that exemplified the actions of the killing robbers. Indra was the battle-hungry hero who slew dragons and rode through the clouds in a chariot, who encouraged the Sanskrit-speaking Aryans to wield their spears while being guided by spirit-gods.

"This caused much confusion because the godlike life of the heavens had always been a model for earthly behavior, so the Aryans wondered who the spirit-gods were warring against. They also must have been exposed to the stories from Mesopotamia, today named Iraq, and firstly Sumeria.

"Beginning about 4000BC, these dwellers of the lower valley of the Tigris and Euphrates Rivers had a mother—god named Inana, who was more important than their sky-god. The Sumerians invented writing laws and architecture, advanced for that time, but were conquered by Semitic Akkadians, who were conquered by the Amorites, who were conquered by the Assyrians. Babylon was the capitol which practiced traditions that influenced the people of Canaan, which became the Promised Land where the Israelites lived."

"But, what happened to the Aryans?" Allison asks, looking confused.

"Let me finish that story after I tell you an even older one, because they all tie together eventually. Gilgamesh was a myth from the cuneiform-writing Sumerians who also started the Babylonian creation myth called *Enuma Elish*, also celebrated by the Assyrians, but according to Heidel it was popular from 1500 to 1000BC. Heidel's book, *The Babylonian Genesis*, is an actual translation which I'll do my best to recall for you. The Babylonians were like the Avesta-

Aryans when they were concerned about the lives of the gods and how to interpret them for meaning, linking the divine world with earth. Babylonians wished to prevent the original chaos from returning, thus they sacrificed to the gods who had brought them order in the beginning. Being civilized was thought to be difficult to retain. Remember Gilgamesh who tamed the wild Enkidu, then the two of them slew the keeper of the forest named Humbaba, who symbolized the untamed and uncivilized."

"Do ideas in these accounts," Allison asks, "end up in the Bible later? I know that the Bible represents thousands of years, and hundreds of conflicting beliefs that originated in different ancient cultures, and that only scholars can understand the writings."

Allison is trying to comprehend how Sumerian myths could ever be relevant to her life, to the Biblical curriculum she has been taught.

I tell her, "Today's scholars want everything to be precise, factual, and proven—even scholars of mythology, apparently, because they never cease arguing over the separation of myth and fact. I think it's quite amusing. Our literal minds, which are almost absent of any reference to personal spiritual recognition, are not equipped to understand the world of our ancestors. To me, the Bible, or any comparable book, is a source of poetic insights as to how people once thought about the world. It is not a book of laws to be followed, nor even a guide for behavior, because so many stories are examples of perpetuating war, violence, cruelty, and so on."

Allison looks away, tips her head, and says, "If the people wanted a kinder, more compassionate society, why didn't they tell stories about love, sharing, being connected, and so on? Why don't we just take the violent parts out of the Bible and leave Jesus with his message of 'love one another'? Maybe then we'd have fewer wars."

"*Ahhhh*. Wouldn't that be nice? You asked me why nonviolent stories aren't told. Well, they are. And have been for thousands of years, by native people who live peacefully as farmers and fight only when their existence is threatened, just like the Aryans who defended against the Mesopotamians who had weapons first. Just like the Hopi who in 1680 organized a Pueblo mass resistance and chased the Spanish Christians out, led by the defiant medicine man, Pope, killing 400 soldiers and burning all the new missions they hated."

Allison remains quiet, thoughtful.

I add, "If you ask my opinion, I don't think the most aggressive humans among us are civilized any more than Gilgamesh was, because aggression as an offensive act is really just a lack of control, an inability to check one's impulses, like a child who hasn't yet learned to behave responsibly. Babies aren't born killers of people. An adult has to teach them."

"Well, that's not a hopeful message," Allison murmurs, shrugging her shoulders.

"Animals kill each other to eat. Humans kill animals to eat. Why do humans kill humans when they don't have to?" I ask, frustrated.

"I don't know, unless it's to defend themselves. I don't know."

About 2000BC, oral Indo-European storytelling included the Babylonian genesis story, *Enuma Elish*, a fictional poetic explanation of how life was created. The Babylonians spoke and wrote a Semitic language; built a city amazing for its time-famous for wealth and luxury; had extensive agriculture, domesticated animals, kings, queens and slaves.

"Excuse me," Allison says, "I don't mean to be rude, but what is a Semitic language?"

"Semite people of Caucasian stock are mostly Jews and Arabs, and there were others of the eastern Mediterranean Sea."

"Wasn't Jesus a Semite, and not an Aryan?" Allison queries, her blue eyes meeting mine.

"He was, and so was Moses and Mohammed, founder of Islam."

"How strange. I never thought of it before, but our Aryan, Scandinavian ancestors, who worshiped gods like Thor, god of thunder and war, abandoned them for a Semitic god from the land of camels, turbans, palm trees, and olive skin with brown eyes," Allison marvels.

"It's quite remarkable, yet religions come, and religions go. We choose them to match our needs as conditions change."

"You make it sound like buying a car!"

"Really? Many Americans would choose a car over any religion, don't you?"

"Depends what kind of a car it is! I might swap for a bright-red Porche—just kidding."

Laughter.

"No more interruptions till I finish this story. This is my summary of the Babylonian genesis. A soupy, undefined mass, probably quiet and watery, existed without earth and heaven. Then the universe was made by two divine parents, Apsu (male/sweet water ocean) and Tiamat (female/salt water ocean). They had a son named Mumu who represented a mixture of chaos and rising clouds. Heaven and earth still didn't exist, but in time Apsu and Tiamat bore two pairs of brothers and sisters. The first pair seems to be insignificant. The second pair, named Anshar and Kishar, had a son named Anu, the Sky-God. Anu created the Earth-God named Ea, also god of wisdom, strength, magic, and skilled authority over all the divinities, even over his father's.

"The older and less active parent and grandparent gods became distressed about the increasing noisiness of the younger gods and tried to persuade them to cease their antics. They refused to cooperate peacefully. Apsu, the first male god, took Mummu his son to Tiamat, his wife, and told her he wished to destroy the unruly gods. Tiamat, her motherly instincts aroused, protested that they should not destroy that which they themselves had brought forth.

"Apsu said he would do it anyway. When the young gods heard this, they quieted down and called on Ea, who used his magic to slay Apsu, and then he imprisoned Mummu, but since Tiamat was not in sympathy with Apsu, she was spared.

"Ea married Damkina. They lived in wealth and had a son named Marduk, who was a sun-god. He sucked the breasts of goddesses; and, because of this, he became head of all gods and was the most wise. Meanwhile, Tiamat missed her husband, became restless, and allowed herself to be convinced by the gods that had been against the murder, that she should avenge her husband's death. Tiamat and the rebel gods schemed to overthrow Ea. She gave birth to eleven kinds of evil serpents and dragons who could help her planned conquest."

"Gosh," says Allison, "another female associated with snakes, like Eve in the Garden of Eden, in Genesis."

I grin and continue, "When the battle finally occurred, Marduk the youthful male, decided the older female, Tiamat, was frenzied and unreasonable, deserving of a violent end. He split her skull open, spilled her blood, then split her body in half, creating sky, earth, and laws. Next, Marduk fixed the calendar and the workings of all the cosmos.

"Tiamat's second husband and leader of her troops, Kingu, was also slain, and out of him Ea made mankind. Marduk set the gods free if they had sided with him. Now that mankind existed, Ea could take over the task of keeping bad divinities in order and concern himself with feeding all of them. Marduk divided the 600 gods into 300 for the earth, and 300 for the sky. Then the grateful gods built Babylon and gave Marduk fifty titles.

"The Babylonians had other, similar genesis stories. There's one in which Mami, a goddess of birth, joins with Ea to create man out of clay and the blood of a slain god."

Allison grimaces, "I like Omamama better than Tiamat, an

285

unfeminine, scheming female who birthed evil serpents and dragons and got her skull smashed."

"However, out of her body came a new world, a better one. Over and over again, gods used creation to improve upon what was, so they built new temples, wrote new laws, found new gods, formed more powerful centers of spirituality—sacred places. Remember, the gods were partners with the people, living among nature, not far up in heaven somewhere. But the gods had something humans could only imagine—immortality."

Allison adds, "And the ability to fly, become invisible, and stay young—maybe even see the future."

"Gods could do anything humans could imagine them doing."

"But the people didn't really believe that the gods were actually building walls and stuff, did they?" Allison asserts, doubtfully.

"Millions of people today still believe these things," I answer, "Like gods that walk on water, fly with angels, sit on a throne in the sky, provide you with a palace if you die, and so on."

"Or provide you with hell if you're bad. I get the picture. Boy, this religious stuff sure is complicated. But I find it fascinating, also."

"Wait till I tell you about Zoroastrianism. The same themes occur, but with a new twist, and new characters. One thing remains the same, the bad image of most women. Persian women were not better off than the ones in Babylon."

"Poor Tiamat. She was a goddess, yet ended up like a sacrificial animal. Do you think she ever got to eat chocolate brownies with chocolate sauce and vanilla ice cream, like I want to right now?"

"Tiamat only got to taste chocolate if she flew to South America, because it was unknown to the Babylonians. However, since we are celebrating with tulips on the table . . . ."

"And spring in the air . . . ."

"Let us rejoice with food for the goddesses!" we pronounce.

Merrily we raise our water glasses and signal the server. Another meeting ends with full hearts and full stomachs—and full heads, too.

Chapter 29
LIGHT AND DARK ARE BOTH GOOD
Nourishing my soul with wonder

Marine On St. Croix, Minnesota

Color! The miracle of spring that never ceases to amaze me. Scarlet tulips, tall and wavering in my backyard. Awe and wonder, tulips peeking green pointy heads out of black, soggy earth warmed by March sunshine, patches of snow remaining in the shade.

Comical black-capped chickadees singing joyously, although they've been home with me all winter at the log cabin bird feeder, vying for seeds with cardinals, nuthatches, snow buntings, finches, and crows. Red and gray squirrels survive on messy stores of black walnuts hidden under the woodshed, while deer munch my baby spruce trees.

Bundled up in wool, I'm on a white wicker chair on the deck, for the sun always warms my heart. I think of summer as nurturing, growing, creating—all light and giving; whereas winter reminds me of reflecting, consuming, rotting—qualities of darkness. One is not good and the other bad; for without one, we couldn't have the other; and life would surely be impossible. Thus, light and dark are both good, but one makes me feel happy and the other mellow.

Excitement grows within me as I contemplate garden plans and seed planting. However, for most of my life, I only dreamed about a garden. As I pour another cup of Earl Grey tea from my red thermos bottle, into an elegant English teacup, I lay my book aside, *The Left Hand of God* by Michael Lerner; close my eyes and think back to that wonderful first trip when the gallery was ready to open, yet the walls were still bare. Oh my God, that was fun, and so liberating!

288

Spring meant a trip to Santa Fe and the Southwest to buy art. Each excursion in my van was an educational adventure, but the best trip was the first one prior to opening my store in 1978. Some artists, like Sari Staggs from California, rode back with me for an art opening, but I bought plane tickets for others. Shipping costs for large pieces of art are expensive, so I made two trips per year, visiting the artists and transporting their work back and forth. All other art arrived by airplane.

I can see myself driving along that first time; my youngest sons, John and Heath, taking turns in the passenger seat, in our new "Mean, Green, Fighting Machine," the name my daughter gave to the extra-long Ford van. It had a window in back on one side and a seat along the other, big enough to sleep on. It had a wide white stripe all around the exterior, a shiny chrome grill on front, and forest-green paint. I sat so high in the seat, I could see over all other cars, an advantage in mall shopping lots and backed-up traffic. It had a big motor and an automatic transmission. I'd always preferred a "stick shift," which was a lot more fun. I was the only girl in my high school who took her driver's test with a stick shift. Dad had owned a car lot, and we always had a Cadillac, but he brought home old clunkers for Mom, ones with a stick shift. I felt like a queen who had escaped from the guillotine. My women friends called my unique van The Freedom Van.

We merrily sped across Highway 80 through Nebraska, windows wide open, tunes on the radio by the Rolling Stones and Creedence Clearwater Revival. We stopped in Denver to visit my brother's family, then drove on, into the Rocky Mountains to the tiny town of Raton, and then Eagle's Nest, elevation 10,000 feet; temperature, freezing cold. We slept in sleeping bags in the van and ate a rancher's size breakfast in a log cafe. Everywhere we felt and saw the beauty of spring.

Taos, New Mexico, was a picturesque village of Spanish-style mud adobe homes, surrounded by vacant lots and modern convenience shops. Willows, sagebrush, grass, and powdery earth defied any serious kind of gardening. A feeling of grace fell upon the annoying poverty that one could not ignore. Natural decay has its own charm, whereas man-made deterioration is ugly. Hence, I don't like rusting trucks and cars in yards, or cement block buildings, or broken, faded plastic.

We were thrilled with the sunny T-shirt weather. I eased the van off the road to change into a dress before parking near an adobe studio-house-gallery complex where artist R.C. Gorman had an art opening that evening. I was going to arrive late, so instead of finding a restaurant, I gave the boys some money to buy tacos at a nearby shop, warning them to remain in or near the van, and told them to come in to the show only if they had trouble. They were happy.

Soon after joining the crowd, I met several fascinating guests, including the owner of Hand Graphics print shop where R.C. had hundreds of hand-made lithographs printed. He invited me to join himself, and R.C., and R.C.'s boyfriend for dinner after the show in a dining room in the compound. I said I'd love to, if my sons approved. I left at the end of the party to go ask them, knowing they could snooze in the van because it was soon bedtime.

Back at the van, trouble had been brewing. I found them in growing darkness, sitting on the curb, tossing pebbles at the street. Seeing my approach, they both jumped up, accusing each other of one mean act after another. They were covered with dirt. No, they hadn't been fighting. Yes, they got something to eat. Was it tacos? No, it was candy bars and ice cream. What did they do with the rest of the money?

John, older, brown-haired, scrupulously honest, the peacemaker in the family; and Heath, blond, fair-skinned, cunning, the provocative charmer, fighting for rights; both faced each other. Silence. I waited, wondering if I'd hear two different stories, or one. More silence. You boys better tell the truth. You know I trust you. Firecrackers? What!? Where? By the taco shop. You didn't! Don't worry, Mom, It's legal in—New Mexico!

Where are these explosives now? They're gone. We found a vacant lot a few blocks away and blew them off. What? I didn't hear any noise during the art show!

That's because we stuck them in the ground.

Why? Why did you do that? Silence. Giggles. Because we dropped them into big ant hills and blew them up. More giggles. That's not funny—those poor ants—you know that's bad. Giggles stop. Is that why you're so filthy? Look at you! They look at each other, then back at me, guilty faces smeared with dust.

You boys just get in that van and get some sleep. I've been invited to dinner in that door there. You can meet R.C. in the morning and see his art. He said so. Silence, then Heath said, We can't get in the van.

What? Why not? Because John locked the keys inside. I tried to pick the lock but the stick we used broke off inside the lock.

Oh, what next!? I'm going to that taco shop to use a phone to call for help. You mean, the police!? Yes, the police!

Now that's a rich memory! They looked so scared! A nice officer opened the other door for us, and they dutifully crawled in like two dirty, hungry dogs, and went to sleep. I hurried back to R.C.'s place where I was led into a cozy room where dinner would be served.

I loved the contrast and texture of the architecture in R.C.'s Southwestern house: Low ceilings and small rooms with heavy, dark handcrafted rugged furniture, soft pastel colors on smooth plastered walls, deep-gray uneven natural stone floors, and sparse, comfortable furnishings. The home embodied the same qualities as R.C.'s extraordinary lithographs of Navajo women.

The round oak table was set for four beneath a black wrought-iron candelabra hanging from a chain from an oak beam. Pink adobe walls, Spanish-style chairs, a sideboard buffet with drawers, square windows with small panes and bars, two corner tables—one with a sculpture of a seated woman, and the other with an urn spilling over with fresh flowers.

We all sat down together as walls danced with shadows formed by flickering candles. R.C. sat opposite me, paying me no special attention, appearing to be in high spirits, exuding warmth, and a gentle demeanor. He was dark, with Navajo features, heavyset, wearing a long-sleeved white tunic shirt, woven belt, red headband, and slippers. I was fascinated by his boyfriend—thin, blond hair, blue eyes, young, Swedish looking, wearing jeans and clean shirt. I couldn't stop watching him and his interaction with R.C.

Never in my life had I met a gay person, nor dined with a Navajo, nor a black person! Ron, from Hand Graphics, sat to my left. He was average in stature, short black hair, brown eyes, wearing Western-style clothing, making jokes with R.C. while the boyfriend moved back and forth between our table and the kitchen where fabulous smells made my mouth water. He filled our crystal glasses with fine wine, then served fresh fruit and salty crackers on peasant pottery plates.

Had some magic bird plucked me out of my cold Minnesota nest and plunked me down on a Hollywood movie set? What good fortune had brought me to partake in such a rare, beautiful experience? Did Ron think I was going to spend a fortune buying his prints the next day? Did R.C. wish to acknowledge his appreciation that I was opening a gallery in Minneapolis, featuring Indian modern art, including him? Maybe, but there was no talk of business, except for a few questions about my new Judith Stern Gallery and which art I would be selling in my new shop.

No, the evening was a post-opening celebration, one of many they had. Perhaps it was my knowledge of Indian art that had seemed to impress Ron and R.C.

As the party progressed, I did figure out what it was.

The boyfriend proved to be an accomplished chef. Each fresh ingredient he used came with a story about where he got it. We were served a mixed salad of greens, goat's cheese, and pinion nuts from pine trees. Next came home-baked bread, smelling sweet and earthy, ivory-colored, crunchy crust, and soft as a pillow inside. Even the butter was home-made in a butter churn. Next came a platter of roast leg of lamb that had come from the Navajo reserve, grilled till crispy with secret herbs, juicy, rare and tender. I could cut it with my fork. I stuffed myself with abandon, never refusing another glass of wine.

That's when I realized that R.C. had been observing me closely, with interest and approval, a big smile on his wide face.

He asked me about my dress. I told him my story about the European conference in Geneva and how one day I found a bazaar in the back streets where people from many countries came to trade their wares, and that I fell in love with a genuine Afghanistan dress. It was a very traditional cut: a heavily stitched bodice with a deep slit on the chest, long full sleeves, and gathered under the breasts in a skirt that fell to just below my knees. It was all patchwork in vibrant reds and blues, solids and florals, with hand-stitched braid on the hem, all homespun cool cotton. I always wore my Zuni needlepoint bracelet with it, till Husband stole it back. I also wore tall, high-heeled, sleek black leather boots, like the Illinois Curling Club had worn back at the Grand Forks curling championship, six years earlier.

Then I realized why Ron had invited me. R.C.'s interest wasn't portraying landscapes, nor making political statements, nor shocking his viewers with bold new techniques. He liked people, and he loved to

293

draw women, an interesting paradox since he was openly gay. I was different. They enjoyed my Minnesota stories. Yes, especially the one about the boys, the firecrackers, the lock, and the police.

During the following week, we were based in Santa Fe at a Motel 6 where John and Heath, who had never stayed in a motel before, swam in the pool so much, they became sunburned. We ate cheap, tasty Mexican food, trying to stay within a strict budget. We visited museums, hiked on mountain roads, went to Shidoni Sculpture Garden, enjoyed Indian Market on the square in Santa Fe, and most importantly we met with artists and collected art.

Finally, the time to return to the North Country came around, so we drove back through Colorado on Highway 285—spring in the Rockies. P.S. The lock on the van never worked properly again.

Arriving back in Minneapolis, we prepared for our grand opening, the first of many. Just before opening my gallery, I had a distinguished visitor, Martin Friedman, director of the Walker Art Center, the largest modern gallery complex in the Twin Cities. He paid me a fine compliment, saying that my space was the finest yet, for art, in the area—very "New York." He liked my choices of contemporary art, too, giving me more confidence than anyone before, although it would be the Minneapolis Institute of Art that would buy some work from me, and include my artists in one of their shows.

After my opening, I counted my money. I was going to be in trouble. My rent was too high, and I had no reserve funds. What seemed to be a nightmare turned out to be my good fortune. I sublet my space to Forecast Gallery, the dream of my friend Jack Becker who envisioned a center for large works of locally made sculpture. Then I moved around the corner to a much better location next to The New French Café, an extremely popular, chic restaurant with gourmet food. It became the anchor in the warehouse district, serving meals all day to those who could afford it. Just the people I wanted to meet.

My new space was one-third the size, not as nice; but what the heck—location is everything. My dear friends from Miz's Indian learning group helped me get ready. My kids were terrific. Barbara Flanagan, the columnist who knew everything about anybody, wrote about the Judith Stern Gallery several times in the *Minneapolis Star and Tribune*. Students came from the Perpich Center for Arts Education, doing class assignments, which gave me many opportunities to teach about contemporary Indian art. Mother was helpful, too, teaching me how to make a sale. I was too shy. She watched the store, so I could have lunch with a friend, go to the dentist, or simply rest. Good thing that the New French had the first café latte and espresso machine in the Twin Cities, because I needed caffeine.

The demand for necktie vests continued. I was given a power sewing machine and a serger by an elderly woman who stopped in the store and took pity on me when she saw my tiny portable machine in the corner. Bessie was one of my regular visitors who never bought a thing, and who taught me so much, such as the 1914 Ladies' Garment Workers Union song she sang with passionate love. She made us both cry.

I had to feed two growing teenage boys, and I had to spend money on lawyers to collect from the deadbeat dad, who was proving true to his words. Hennepin County provided me with assistance in collecting what was due me, until Dad moved to another state where no reciprocity laws existed. I never got a nickel out of him after the first year. Good riddance.

The most difficult part of my new life was that I ached to be outdoors.

My gallery hours were designed so I could be a hockey mom, home on Sundays and Mondays and never open past 3:00 p.m. I had time to return to nature by cross-country skiing and long-distance hiking. Alas, that didn't last forever. I gave up the artist's studio space where I hoped to do sculpture, took shorter walks in my neighborhood, and was lucky to go fishing with my parents and sons in the summer.

New friends opened up a whole new social world. I met and dated several men, but nothing "stuck" for long. I was focused on my interests, and most men I met expected me to be focused on their interests before mine. I was too busy to do both. Doris, my Ojibwe friend, became a constant companion, although she got a new job as an Indian advocate in welfare work, and was pursuing a relationship with a gentleman from out of state, and caring for grown children.

Never in my life, except for school, had I felt so ruled by time and indoor tasks. My gallery front windows faced south, but tall buildings prevented much sun from entering for most of the winter when the sun was low in the sky. There was one memorable day each spring when a bright flash of light would flood the room, then vanish, like a spotlight switched on and off. That day marked the beginning of warm days, hot un-air-conditioned ones, for the sun rose higher and higher, and the gallery grew brighter and brighter.

Near my new home, I discovered a wild area among suburban houses, that was a one-hour hike from home each way—not a park, but a neighborhood public forest and grassland, rolling with sweet, green meadows; streamlets with banks wreathed with wildflowers under which toads and trout hid; wet, rich cheerful puddles; bogs and thickets; cold snowy silence, winter's solemn sleep; seasonal changes, autumnal leaves, spring buds opening. A place of renewal where all the secrets of my heart flew into the sky as prayers, while the worries of business and children fell behind on the path.

Only in such unclothed, un-landscaped beauty could I truly nourish my soul with the wonder of life's meaningful mysteries. All other concerns were soon put into proper perspective.

Why was I drawn to cultivate that place within me that was connected to the primal conditions out of which I had come? There was no doubt that I was born with it. My first memory at two years old was of the Mississippi River flooding the ground, running over the banks near Anoka, Minnesota. I walked toward the encroaching water unafraid, till Mother snatched me up and carried me away.

I remember sitting alone under a grandfather oak tree during lunch recess in kindergarten, watching dried red leaves fall at my feet. The other children played tag. I felt like the tree was my best friend, but I couldn't tell anyone that. They would laugh at me.

I missed the school bus for most of my first days back to school in the fall. I left the house, then just walked the other way! It wasn't that I hated school. I just loved being outside much more. Maybe I was seven or eight when, one day, I decided to walk home during recess at Lee Avenue School. The building sat upon one square block of land, and I thought I could find my way for five miles to my house. But I got to the school-ground corner and was afraid to cross the street. I wasn't afraid of the street, or the walk. My fear was punishment from my teacher, and the shame I'd bring my mother.

When the grade school had the oak grove cut down because of insurance issues, I was physically sick for a week. I learned to not talk about my feelings, because there was a reason that the other kids were not (or so it seemed) bothered by such losses. Nonetheless, I never doubted the rightness of my instincts. I just needed to develop my understanding more, so that I could give voice to my feelings in ways that made sense to others. Therefore, I would grow up knowing that there is a difference between those who experience spirituality in nature, and those who don't.

Mother told me that I changed from a happy-go-lucky girl to a serious thoughtful one after kindergarten. She didn't know why. I know why. School was a process by which I learned new and useful skills to prepare me for a world in which nature was primarily to be exploited as a resource. Of course, I didn't realize that in grade school; but I did know I didn't like the way men altered my town and state to suit the desires of industry. I liked *my* new house, but I didn't like the one they built on *my* cattail marsh where I could hide among the blackbirds; nor the playground they built after plowing over and filling in *my* Mud Lake and woods.

There was plenty of alteration, and little, if any, preservation.

Chapter 30

COLORS OF THE RAINBOW DISAPPEARED

What is the book called Avesta?

Signature Cafe

Allison has arrived at the cafe, however my attention is elsewhere. What do you see?" she inquires, following my gaze, "A bird?"

"*Shhh!* No, it's Garrison Keillor—over there!"

Shadows crossing the outdoor brick patio obscure a couple dining in a far corner in the trees, carrying on a hushed conversation.

Allison seats herself, "I wonder if that's his wife? Have you met them?"

"Not her, not his wife, but I've sure met him—Minnesota's favorite bard and radio host of *Prairie Home Companion*. I was at a small party in his New York apartment when he was still married to the Danish lady he met in high school."

"That's rather interesting. I love the *Prairie Home Companion* show."

"Me, too," I agree, while the server hands us water and menus.

Allison wears a long print skirt, red sweater and baseball cap that says "Audubon"—the name of a naturalist. She is so cool and sweet, like a refreshing spring cocktail. She tells me about her cap and taking her kids to a nature center. Talks about school. And home.

Clouds pregnant with rain approach from the west. We glance up at the sky. I'm cozy in my warm chartreuse jacket, slacks, and coral wool tam. I cease sneaking looks at the gal with Garrison.

"Soup and salad special for me, today," I pipe up.

"Same for me, and coffee."

"You'll need it for this story," I quip, grinning.

"You were going to tell me more about pre-Christian religions, one in particular about Aryans living in the Caucasus Mountains. I looked on a map. That region borders today's Turkey and Iran in the north. Above that is Russia, where tulips grow in the wild."

"Now for our story. The Near East was a boiling pot of religious activity, wars, or preparations for war. Waves of barbarians from the North weren't interested in proselytizing religion—they wanted land and wealth through conquest. Religion changed along with politics. Perceptions of spiritual absoluteness were formed and spirituality began its transformation into institutionalized, hierarchical, dogmatic belief systems. Nature-based polytheistic spiritualism declined.

"In the seventh century BC the Assyrian Empire of the Arabs dominated from India to Egypt, to Asia Minor. In the sixth century BC the Persian Median Empire annihilated the Assyrians and moved even further East, ruling the Northern Near East. The Babylonians, under their god and ruler Marduk, and the Chaldeans, ruled in the South.

"In 550BC King Medes was overthrown by King Cyrus, another Persian who was an unusually tolerant ruler who allowed his enemies to remain somewhat intact. He defeated Marduk who praised Cyrus that he let people continue their polytheistic worship of idols, although during his reign, the empire, 600–529BC, adopted a new official religion called Zoroastrianism. This was close to the time of the Buddha in India (563–483BC), and Confucius in China (551–478 BC)."

"Where," asks Allison, "is Persia?"

"Persia was renamed Iran In 1935."

"What happened to the Persian Empire and King Cyrus?"

"He was destroyed by Alexander the Great, a Grecian, in 324BC. Remember *Inuma elish*? The Babylonian creation story? It was an oral story until written in Semitic cuneiform on seven clay tablets around

2000BC. This is also true of other ancient oral stories like the Bible, and like *Avesta*, the book of the religion of Zoroaster. Those texts were written or collected in about 226AD, after 800 years of oral telling."

"Wait, *Avesta*? As in Avestan language—Aryan speakers—not Sanskrit?"

"Very good! Yes, the oldest branch of the Iranian, *er*, Persian, language. During the reign of Cyrus the Great, Zoroastrianism spread far and wide."

"Wait—what is the oldest recorded spiritual scriptures?"

"The Indo-European, or early Persian, around 4500 to 1500BC. The Hindu Vedas had thirty-three gods and goddesses of nature that they divided into three groups: earth, atmosphere, sky. A strongly naturalistic cosmology."

"Another polytheistic belief system—like belief in many gods?"

"Yes, like *Avesta*. I'll tell you about that next. I didn't study Eastern Asian religions. I was searching for the roots of religions that came to Minnesota. Not too many Hindus here."

"Who started Zoroastrianism? How was it different?"

"The mastermind was Zoroaster, a Persian. His religion is still practiced in part of Iran and India. He was born in 628BC, died in 551BC, lived during the beginning of Persia's empire before Alexander the Great, influencing people in Egypt, Phoenicia, Asia, and the Indus Valley for 800 years."

I hesitate before continuing, knowing I'm about to inject my own personal opinion. Oh well, somebody has to do it—in this society of manufactured consent and fear—as my acquaintance Noam Chomsky would say. He's my hero of intellectual dissent.

"I think Zoroaster's ideas, well, some of his unique ethical ideas, made their way into Western thinking through Hebrew and Christian religions, also. His precepts were radically different than previous religions, such as Mother Earth spiritual beliefs in the old European cultures and those of the American Indians.

"Even if one is not affiliated with any church today, I think Zoroaster had an influence on modern culture, a permanent stamp on the Euro-Western psyche."

Allison observes, "It's kind of scary how much one man, one idea, can have so much impact. Everything really is connected, isn't it? I love to learn how ideas converge with each other. I wonder, did Zoroaster have a vision like Jesus and Moses?"

"Certainly! All prophets are intercessors between the Divine Power who tells him or her his or her will. Each prophet wants to be the main spokesperson for that divine inspiration. Thousands of people have had such messages or visions, but few become known or influential. I think it's interesting that people today who proclaim personal powers like this are considered nuts, yet millions of us continue to believe prophets who lived hundreds of years ago.

"Zoroaster was born in Azerbaijan or Medina. At the age of thirty, he had a vision of two male gods, Ahura Mazda (Ormazd), good god of light and truth; and Angra Mainyu, evil god of anger and darkness. Ahura created the world and man to help defeat Angra. Life was a struggle between two, dualistic, absolute, nonrelative forces. Although an ultimate triumph of Good was assured, men would have to help Good achieve that goal by virtue of their thoughts, words and deeds. Good had told Zoroaster which ethics man must pursue: justice (truth), good thought, obedience, immortality, prosperity, piety and dominion.

"The Zoroastrian genesis story was and is considered mythological and not historical. It tells in the Avesta that while Angra Mainyu, the god of evil, darkness and the like, slept and waited, Ahura Mazda, the god of good, light, and truth, created good mind and sky. Out of Ahura came the light of the world, the good religion of righteous order, perfect sovereignty, divine piety, excellence, and immortality. Next, Ahura made the galaxies, the four captains in the four quarters of the

302

universe, the moon, sun, water, earth, plants, animals, and man.

"Ahura had enjoyed nothing but unchallenged goodness and light for three thousand years. Then Angra Mainyu ruined everything by appearing out of the light, creating darkness and defeating Ahura. The manner in which this was done was through a villainous female character. The hag awoke the sleeping Angra by screaming at him to awake for it was time for her to help him create misery and injury upon Ahura and on the angels by poisoning righteous mankind, laboring oxen, and all the rest of creation. Angra was so pleased with her wickedness that he kissed her; and she became polluted forever with blood, or menstruation. He then granted her one wish. She said she wanted a man. So, out of a lizard, he created a young man, and she was thrilled! The jealous, temperamental Angra continued his desecration by making a road to the center of the earth where there would be hell. This place is described in great horrendous detail in *Avesta*, in page after page; and truly, even Dante could not have made it worse than Zoroaster.

"In the scriptures, Zoroaster says that man should recreate the earth into an attractive cultivated series of gardens so that the evil demon, Angra, would be incapable of resisting it and would appear on earth and try to enjoy it, but when he did, he would be caught in a trap. Thirty gods, six protectors, angels, and all humans would work together to that end.

"*Avesta* also instructs man to bear many children and encourages polygamy, concubinage, and incest, all of which would be rewarded. A man needed children in order to enter heaven and, if he failed at that, a proxy marriage could take place after his death, and any offspring could then be attributed to the departed one so he could receive salvation. There were privileged wives who inherited, and wives who didn't and were servants. If a woman married above her class, she became a servant. She may or may not have needed permission to marry, but if she married a second time, the first husband would still always have control over her.

"Women were to be submissive, to be controlled, and to consider their husbands as lords.

"Humans had a body and a soul, and the soul was divine and immortal; and upon death, it received three days of either heaven or hell before it went to be judged by three angels who instructed the soul as to which path it would ultimately take. If there was indecision due to the person being as good as he was evil, he would wait in a third place for twelve thousand years after creation until a divine descendent of Zoroaster's would resurrect all bodies and rejoin them to their souls before purging the whole of mankind in molten metal for their sins. Finally, all could enter Paradise for eternity and be as one together. Ahura asked men's souls, before they were born into their bodies, which path they chose; therefore it was man's own choice to determine his fate as a free man. There were, however, some things that belonged to fate: life, wife, children, and wealth.

"Ahura was the deity of the heavens, and had six holy assistants who were immortal and represented: good thought, fire, metals, country, health, and agriculture; who, in turn, had the help of thirty more gods who represented each day of the month. Zoroaster was the supreme mortal, a worldly sacred prophet. There was a third pantheon of angels who were neither celestial nor terrestrial. There was to be a last judgment day when Good would decide who would attain immortal heavenly entrance, and who would go to eternal darkness due to their sins.

"Zoroaster was slain by invading tribes, but his religion spread quickly. Zoroaster lived in a region of farmers and nomads.

"The farmers had settled down to till their fields, whereas the nomads continued raiding excursions and worshipping many gods to whom they sacrificed. Zoroaster saw the ways of the people as sinful, chaotic, and evil; saw their gods as demons; and their rulers as wicked. The pastoral farmers were a contrast to the wild nomads and although both were of the same Indo-European migratory stock organized by tribal lineages, each group felt superior to the other. Some of the farmers prospered more than others and built cities and gained political and military power. Monarchies grew out of villages with chiefs and formed hierarchies that were divided into classes of priests, warriors, and peasants, all living and dressing differently, and separately; and stuck in one class for a lifetime. Eventually, the farmers at the bottom became slaves, while chiefs of the tribes became kings. It was a harsh life with no equality and no freedom for the majority.

"But Zoroastrianism was about competition, hierarchies, authority by males, subjugation of women—not new ideas, but new combinations."

Allison raises her hand, "Wait a minute. What's wrong with trying to balance good and evil? Isn't balance what it's all about?"

"This was a dualism, but not a dualism of earth and sky, of earth and wind, or fire and water, or east and west, north and south. It was one of moral principles, and . . ."

Allison says, "But the four directions represent moral principles, don't they?"

"Sure they do—but different moral principles, which means even balance is a relative term, isn't it?" I muse.

Allison murmurs while listening carefully, and twisting her hair in her fingers, "Explain more, please."

"I understood Zoroaster's vision as not complementary opposites that together create a whole, or harmony; but rather one of adverse opponents that cannot exist together at the center, for one always has to dominate the other. It was not mankind's duty to balance the two forces, but to subvert one at the expense of the other. There was a line and on one end was good, and on the other, evil.

305

"When Ahura assigned the captains to the four quarters of the universe, he had no thought of an orderly, interrelation concept of the American Indian four directions. He mentions that the demons came from the quarter in the north and the kings came from the south, which suggests that even the metaphysical universe was a field of opposing forces, not a harmonious one.

"This was about competition, not fairness or equality; an either/or proposition.

"The colors of the rainbow disappeared and only black and white remained. Light and dark. True and false. The god of goodness, Ahura Mazda, was good because he had chosen the RIGHT spirit for behavioral guidance; but the other deity, the twin spirit, had chosen the WRONG spirit of evil, and the spirits were divided into divinities or demons. Heaven or hell. God or Satan. It was the fault of the spirits themselves that they became demons; because of course, a benevolent god such as Ahura couldn't be responsible for evil-doing. Yet, it *was his* devising that man would choose evil! When the spirits and man chose wrongly, it was the beginning of the great war for dominance and superiority.

"Real chaos was the result of such ideas. No amount of consensus could fit into such a plan, for there was no room for agreement or tolerance of a differing perspective. I can recall my first class at my university in art appreciation, and the professor said, in an adamant tone, 'If there is art, then there is 'not art.' I was perhaps born as a rainbow thinker, for I at once felt discomfort rise within me, but I dared not disagree for I was only a beginning student. I tested that remark by applying it to several other things. For surely, if something as ethereal as art could be so absolutely defined, then other ideas or concepts must also. It was a hopeless game for me, for my brain would only work in degrees of being.

"Zoroaster was not the last to divide the human body into body and

306

soul. Many years later, we have even more divisions!

"We have body, soul, and mind. We have anatomical terminology. We have psychic terminologies of consciousness and the unconscious. We have reality and unreality, and on, and on, and on. The divisions we create don't seem to end. Only Euro-Western man divides conscious and unconscious as though aware and unaware. But a Lakota would be aware of either at once because for him, all parts are inseparable. Indeed, they are different components of one dimension. Just as the body evolves from everywhere in the earth, the mind evolves and works throughout the body. One lives his dreams through his body, while awake.

"If the view is that there are right and wrong parts of something, then the perception becomes one of purging the wrong to make the right. The larger the purge, the more righteous will be the result! Thus, Zoroaster's holocaust for the earth and mankind will be the final purge, and then all men will live in perfect peace; and the god of evil, Angra, will have been revenged and vanquished. World War I was supposed to have been a great purging of man's evils, but then along came World War II.

"What about the notion that doing enough good will finally create good forever? Or no amount of good will ever be enough, so a great purge of evil will be necessary? What's troublesome about thinking that those who believe righteously will triumph, and those who disbelieve the right god will perish? Should we really cast the wicked into hell? Should ethics and morals of intelligent men be the supreme law of the land?

"During the entire reign of Darius, the last king of the Persian Empire, his goal was to force moral righteousness upon all enemies of Ahura Mazda; for if you weren't with him, you were against him. Compare his attitude with that of Cyrus the Great. To Darius, you were as good as on the demon's path to hell, even if you had never heard of

Zoroastrianism. Especially, if you hadn't!

"In the world of good and evil, nature is seen as in conflict with itself as evidenced by the good and evil in nature. Mother Nature is seen as in continuous disorder and the only way to set it right is to create order out of it. One over the other. One instead of the other. What will happen to nature after the great purge? It will become placid, still, tame, and even the mountains will become only gentle rises on the landscape. No more storms! No more rot and decay! No more death! All will be immortal.

"The prophets could not blame a god for nature's ways, so natural catastrophes were also the result of evil human deeds. In Zoroaster's mythical view, the world was sinful, not because of nature, but because of human intervention which accidentally, thoughtlessly, foolishly and wrongly debauched it.

"Zoroaster does not forget the little animals of the earth. For he gives them a role to play in hell where they live in the bodies of women who have been abusive to their lords. I quote the prophets words: 'Many (women) who hung by one leg, through all their apertures of whose bodies frogs, scorpions, snakes, ants, flies, worms, and other noxious creatures went and came, who, in life, had been untrue.'"

"*Wow!*" Allison exclaims, "Better to be a Lutheran than to be stuffed with scorpions into a rotting woman's leg in hell, in the Near East!"

"Probably even better to live in the Garden of Eden as a snake, than in the soul of a Zoroaster man, 'through whose fundament a snake went in, like a beam, and come forth out of the mouth; and many other snakes ever seized his limb.' Yes, better to be grandmother spider of the Ojibwe, rescuing the sunshine for the woodland creatures and spinning dream nets, than to be in Zoroaster's hell.

"The prophet's words also remind man that he is made up of dust, but not the loving elements of earth, air, fire, and water, or of renewable trees and flowers, for dust is a punishment that man becomes unless he performs pious deeds. I quote, 'He alone mingles *not* with dust who in the world, gives praise to piety and performs duties and good works.' If nature was good, it was also full of evil. It even extended into hell where rivers were those of tears, and animals were used to torture men. Nature was not interpreted by her own standards, but by rules imposed upon it by humankind."

Allison has long ago finished her lunch. Mine has grown cold, but I don't care. I glance over at the corner, but Garrison is gone.

"They left a long time ago," Allison says gently, "And I won't ask you any more questions. Zoroaster certainly diminished equality between men and women, if they ever had any. Manly characteristics fill *Avesta*, don't they? Man! Competition between man and man, men and women, man and nature, good and evil, and everything else. Geeze—only the male human alone was supposed to prosper, and that too was full of pitfalls, wasn't it? They all had a bad attitude."

Allison sits back thoughtfully, hands folded in her lap. She says softly, "I feel like I've been away—on a long journey to a different land."

"You have been. We all have been. Most Americans, except natives, have no idea who they are, because their roots are not here, and they don't know the stories from back there. We're all like rootless trees," I say, slumping in my chair.

"Now I feel like I'm part of an occupation of a foreign land."

"The Indians would probably agree with you. They're probably still waiting for us all to leave," I say, chuckling, shaking my head.

"Do you really think so?" Allison exclaims. She thinks I'm kidding.

"I'm positive," I answer with a positive attitude.

309

Chapter 31

YOU HAVE TO LIVE

Go for a walk. What is the meaning of life?

Minneapolis

Life as a gallery owner started out with a bang—almost. I was threatened with robbery at gunpoint. Feeling more angry than afraid, I talked my way out of it!

Another day, my son Leonard came by to pay his first visit, only to stop in the doorway and watch in astonishment as I darted out the building in pursuit of a suspected thief, whom I chased down the street, caught in a traffic jam then reached under his long overcoat to retrieve a painting he'd stolen.

I hotfooted it back to the store, waiting for a bullet in my back, "Thanks for watching the store!" I gasped, hanging the picture back on its hook. The dumbfounded expression on my son's face made me laugh.

"Do things like this happen often?" he wondered, his big brown eyes bigger than ever.

In truth, they did. Inner-city business ownership as a "pioneer" in the fledgling artsy-fartsy warehouse district, came with ample weird challenges: buildings decaying and being rescued, exotically dressed and mentally insightful artists with a variety of sexual preferences, a lively music scene, exciting cuisine, and the well-dressed rich who supported the artists, joined the parties, pretended to be less happy than the poor, and drove home to the suburbs in their Porches and Mercedes Benzes, giddy with wine—with stories to tell.

I cultivated the patrons who became collectors. I offered reserved compassion to those who never bought anything, but who were lonely and just wanted to talk. I turned away Indians who were not good artists, who sometimes became upset when I didn't buy their work on the spot. I sold clothing designs from the boutique room in the rear of the store, and paintings, sculpture, jewelry, and weavings in the front.

A new friend! The day that Deanne walked in my door, my life changed. She became a family member for life. It was the necktie she wore with the hand-painted robin on pale-blue silk that first caught my eye. I sewed her a custom-made vest of ties to match it.

Deanne Kamiel was a bit younger and shorter than me. Her wavy, long dark hair lay on her shoulders, framing smooth ivory skin, large dark eyes under schoolish glasses, fine nose and lips. Her voice and articulation were so perfect, she was paid for doing radio and TV ads, and documentaries, which she also produced for Minnesota's KTCA-TV, our public station. On the day we met, she was new to the Twin Cities, arriving from Toronto, Canada, her hometown. Searching for life's meaningful answers through art, we felt lucky to share that rare chemistry that grows through mutual interests with trust, sympathy, and love.

With Deanne, I kept my spark alive—the fire through which I desired to understand the world and my role in it. I was creating a modest living, but I didn't believe clothing design was art. I was selling other people's art, but I wasn't an artist myself. Deanne saw me as an artist, and respected my secret dreams. We shared our conversations and discoveries over many cups of *cafe au laits* and croissants with apricot jam in the New French Cafe. She introduced me to books like *The Book of Tea* by Okakura Kakuzo and *The Tale of Genji* by Murasaki Shikibu that led to my collection of works by Lafcadio Hearn, an American with Japanese sentiments. We attended all the classical films at the Walker Art Center, and the avant garde flicks at the Bell Museum—thanks to my friend, the remarkable Al Milgrom, the indefatigueable founder of the Minneapolis and St. Paul

International Film festival.

Two of my favorite directors back then were Les Blank: *In Heaven There Is No Beer* and *Garlic Is As Good As Ten Mothers*; also, Werner Herzog, a German: *Burden of Dreams* and *Fitzcarraldo*.

We discussed books about Colette, Simone DeBeauvoir, Jean-Paul Sartre, Gloria Steinem, Dorothy Parker, and other strong women. We went to meet Patricia Hampl, St. Paul poet, who was reading from her first non-poetry book, *A Romantic Education*, at a Czechoslovakian Hall. Hampl became my most admired writer.

Andrei Codrescu, a regular on National Public Radio, was one of the many prominent persons who Deanne met through her work. Through my store, I met Joel Grey, actor, who bought my first published gallery poster; Gary Busey, who brought his filming friends to buy; and Prince, singer, who paid me to keep the gallery open late into the night while they filmed *Purple Rain* across the street.

On sojourns to New Mexico in the Mean Green Fighting Machine, I sought out poetry readings and art openings. I began keeping journals again, imagining a day when I could try writing or continue my interest in creating sculpture.

Deanne introduced me to KTCA people, which is how I met Marian Moore, and her friends: Ted Mondale, the son of Vice President Walter (Fritz) Mondale, and Ted's friend, Ted Yates; all from Washington DC. I was on a date with Marty Keller, a music reviewer for *Sweet Potato Magazine* (renamed *City Pages*). The magazine published a story about my gallery. When Marty and I were at the Prom ballroom, Marian showed up with the two Ted's and joined our table. Yates was a striking figure with a strong presence. An aura of self-confidence oozed from his athletic Nordic-looking body. Tall, casual, fine featured, with neat blond hair, fair skin, pale-blue eyes, wearing clean jeans, a white shirt, sport coat, cowboy hat and boots. I liked the looks of that guy—a lot!

He had a woman by his side, but I don't recall anything about her.

Standing next to our table, he took no time in addressing me. I tried to remain cool, to appear gorgeous in a long, fitted, slinky yellow rayon 1930s dress, black-satin high heels, black velvet elbow-length gloves, and a matching hat with sequins and feathers. The dress was a prize I found in a Taos antique store, and had been worn by the wife of a New Mexico governor. Yates stood tall and proclaimed, in a drawl, "My name is Ted Yates and I come from Lander, Wyoming, in the great Wind River Range where I live in a cabin and do surveying work in the mountains."

I was immediately smitten, but I couldn't let him know that!

We all went to two more parties that night. By the end of the evening, Marty and I had switched dates.

Yates invited me to Washington DC, to meet his family. His talented, Minnesota-born mother was at that time, the producer for a popular TV news show that aired on Sunday morning, CBS TV, named *Face the Nation*, featuring interviews with political figures. Yates's father had worked with Mike Wallace on a show that would later become the format for another show, *Sixty Minutes*, but Ted Yates Senior had been tragically shot in the head while setting up his camera atop a building in Israel at the beginning of the Six-Day War.

While Mary Yates handled the recovery of her husband's body, she placed her three sons in an underground shelter, which turned out to be pummeled with gunfire and bombs. The boys survived, but Mary tried to carry on—mourning for ten years, until *Face the Nation*. She later married Mike Wallace.

Yates finished his Wyoming surveying and returned to Washington DC, while we began a long-distance relationship. He warned me that his goal was to move to Montana as soon as he could. I planned to sell him on the marvels of Minnesota.

313

The gallery continued to prosper just enough to meet expenses, keep the store stocked, and feed growing children. Hmong women were sewing designs for me; Miz was knitting sweaters that sold as fast as I got them; an artist named Lonnie Lovness asked me to try to sell her silk scarves and later her jewelry; and Mary Ellen Stewart brought me her fabulous jewelry. Mother was an ace saleswoman and loved to help out from time to time. My daughter had a job working in Yellowstone Park. Oldest son was in Grand Forks at the university, then in California, while the youngest ones were with me, prospering at Hopkins High School with great teachers, the youngest playing hockey and going on trips with me.

My art gallery artist openings were festive affairs for which I got ample publicity and good attendance—regulars who became collectors of the art of David Bradley, Sari Staggs, Doug Hyde, Emmi Whitehorse, Presley LaFontaine, Lala Lapeshkin, Walter Piehl, Jaune Quick-to-See Smith, R.C. Gorman, Fritz Scholder, and others. My sons helped me set up a refreshment table with a kitschy centerpiece— a Mexican pottery bust of an Indian chief painted in gaudy colors with red pepper twinkle lights draped over his head—watching over the punch, wine, cheese, and crackers. Yates was there along with Joan Mondale, Marian, Ted, Deanne, Doris, also Jim and Susan Lenfesty, art supporters and writers. My name list for mailings soon grew to over two thousand.

The Minneapolis Art Institute borrowed select art for a show, and later bought paintings for their collections, which gave me selling points for sales.

Deanne looked after the boys when Yates and I took trips to Haiti to vacation in his mother's seaside house, which came complete with two housekeepers—a Creole cook, cleaning woman, and her husband, who did yard work.

The Landmark Center in downtown St. Paul was the location for a fashion show I organized to show off my latest designs, an expensive, laborious affair that served my ego much more than my pocketbook. But it was fun, too, and my three youngest each got involved by helping. My beautiful daughter Lisa was there to assist me.

Yates moved to Minnesota. He lived in Marian's house for one summer—"party-central," a wonderful, happy time. Till the inevitable struck. Yates was leaving for Bozeman, Montana, hoping to become a building contractor and wanted me to go along, with my sons who loved him. Deanne and I had long talks. I told Ted I'd help him get settled and see what it would be like for me in the college town of Bozeman with cute shops, terrific skiing, hiking, and scenery.

We traveled to Montana to get him settled. I got him his first job with an old Grand Forks connection. Then, I went home. The long distance romance continued. After three or four years, I got a phone call from Montana. The love of my life was not going to wait any longer. He was going to marry another woman. I cried convulsively, but I could not bring myself to beg him to change his mind. My freedom meant more to me than love. My dreams were not his dreams, and I would have spent the rest of my life fulfilling another man's vision of who I am. It wouldn't be easy to uproot two sons who had been through so much and were now establishing a new life. I loved my gallery, my designing, recognition, independence, and earning my own way. And as much as I loved nature, I discovered I was fond of urban culture, too. I lost ten pounds, mourning for my love, but years later we would meet again.

In 1984 I took my son Heath to San Francisco to the Democratic National Convention where he was generously given passes to have access to any place Ted Mondale went. And since Fritz was running against Ronald Reagan for the presidency—that was everywhere— even the "smoke-filled rooms" where the real convention took place.

Fritz lost. Heath took his video camera, and award-winning

315

expertise, and flew to Washington to interview Walter Mondale. This work and other documentaries got him a scholarship to George Washington University, where he worked as a waiter at night. He graduated with a degree in journalism and earned a masters degree at New York University.

After a trip to Europe my son John got a job in a union print shop. Later he worked his own way through Hennepin Technical College earning a degree in computer science and graphics. My son Leonard enrolled in the aviation program at the University of North Dakota. However, after he was half-finished he was injured in a serious snowmobile accident. He moved west to live in California. When he returned to Minnesota he began his own home decorating and landscaping business. Lisa traveled far and wide, eventually settling in with her father.

I was alone for the first time ever. Plans to remain in the gallery business were doomed when my building manager, Bob Thomson, tripled my rent. He had owned his gallery around the corner from the New French Cafe. Popular among the artists, I was not one of his fans. He'd done petty acts that made my job more difficult. I searched for less-expensive spaces, but a new Vikings' football stadium had been built nearby, and artists were moving out as chic restaurants moved in to pay the higher taxes. One artist commented that their next refuge would be abandoned shopping malls in the suburbs.

While I was searching, I also found time to do things I hadn't as a mother: hiking in parks, cross-country skiing, days at the U of M Landscape Arboretum, Sunday drives to small town festivals in the Minnesota farmland. I discovered Jesse James Days in the small college town of Northfield, adored the sexy long-rider coats the actor-bandits wore, and decided to sew myself one. I met Chip DeMann who played Jesse, borrowed his duster in return for making him a new one, created a line of patterns for men and women size six to forty-four, got my Hmong lady seamstresses to sew two hundred dusters, placed ads in magazines, and closed the gallery, with a profit.

Deanne, Doris, and I were at Doris's plush downtown high-rise apartment one night when they asked me what I was going to do now that the kids were on their own, and my store was closed. I heard myself say, "I'm going to write," surprising even myself.

"What? That's a hard decision. Not a good idea . . ."

"I'm going to keep designing in my home, *and* write."

"We don't agree with you, but it's your choice."

Driving home that night, I recalled many years earlier when I'd been canning tomatoes all day, then went with Husband to a party that night, a going-away party for a popular woman journalist from the *Minneapolis Star and Tribune* who was leaving for bigger and better things in New York City. I asked her writer friend, a male book author whose name I've forgotten, "What does it take to become a good writer?"

"First, you have to LIVE!"

Apparently I looked dead. Or I had tomato seeds stuck in my teeth. I knew preserving vegetables and changing diapers were not something Simone DeBeauvoir, Virginia Woolf, or Dorothy Parker spent much energy on.

Becoming a businessperson had challenged my strength and sapped my spirit. I'd made some money, fabulous friends, and life-long connections. Most important of all, I had raised my kids without any alimony or child support (legally due to me) from the deadbeat dad. But something inside me was missing. A sense of loneliness tugged at my heart. I heard voices from my past: Talk to the trees. Go for a walk. What is the meaning of life?

I still didn't know.

Chapter 32

ONE MALE GOD, ONE HOLY SPIRIT, ONE WORLD POWER

Yahweh defeats kinder, gent'ler gods and goddesses.

Gasthaus Bavarian Hunter, Stillwater, Minnesota

A hot, muggy summer afternoon in the lush-green hills surrounding the red brick river town of Stillwater. Wearing cool cotton, my I'itoi pendent and a wide-brimmed straw hat; carrying a computer print-out copy of an ancient writing titled *Germania*, I climb the wide plank stairs of the Gasthaus Bavarian Hunter, glancing at the view—waving farm fields and wood lots edged with towering old white and red pine trees, reminiscent of Germany.

Resting on my crutches, with each new step, I reach the top. Tugging on the heavy wooden double doors, I step into cool, old-world charm: a family-owned restaurant, soft creamy plaster walls, dark oak posts and beams, deer antler chandeliers, windows with small panes framed with lace curtains. I recall Oktoberfest events in the pine sheltered grove out back—revelries that rocked the big-top tent; real, or would-be Germans guzzling pints of Spaten, Paulaner, Haaker-Pschorr; wild polka dancing for all ages; lustily sung songs accompanying Artie Schaefer's *oompah* band; everybody raising their beer mugs in unison as Artie shouts, *"Ticky-tacky, ticky, tacky, oie oie oie!"* (Imagine my joy when I discovered he is my cousin. When I told him, he thought I was just flirting with him! Oh, that male ego!)

For many years Mother loved to leave Minneapolis and drive us out to Stillwater for lunch at the Lowell Inn where she honeymooned in 1938, a quiet landmark reminding me of Mount Vernon with a far more stately ambience and elegant reputation than the Gasthaus. I

318

preferred the gaiety of the beer hall, while loving the beauty and formality of the other.

Mom had cooked many Easter dinners before she died in 1990, when our family began a new tradition eating German food on Easter at the Gasthaus.

A glass of wine or iced tea? I'll wait to see what Allison chooses.

All the servers at the Gasthaus dress prettily in Bavarian costumes—be they lederhosen shorts for the men; or white blouses, full skirts and sleeveless, laced vests girded tightly, on the women— their bosoms sweating from the August heat as they scurry about with fantastic-smelling sausages, red cabbage, potato pancakes, liver soup, veal cutlets, and more. Many have been employed here for several years, surely a testimony to owner Kim Schone who carried on after her husband died. The Gasthaus always emits a sense of *gemutlichkeit*—good heart, good soul, good guests.

I never feel lonely here. It's so easy to feel connected. So much easier than trying to connect myself to Zoroaster's strange beliefs, but if I really think that everything is connected, then I want to understand how he, Moses, Jesus, and Mohammed affected my life. And, why are those heroes *all* single men? Why didn't they worship Mother Earth?

I had learned that the historic Germans were tree-worshippers, but did they worship Mother Earth? Tacitus, a Roman historian, wrote the earliest account of Germans late in the first century CE, in *Germania*. This remarkable writing includes his Roman observations on the vast numbers of people sharing a language, divided into warring tribes, living not in cities but in individual homes scattered about the fertile land, swamps, forests, groves of trees—the most revered being the oak. The Suevians, according to Tacitus, were the most ancient and noble. They were divided into several nations led by the Semnones, inhabiting one hundred towns, and claiming a sacred grove, the

319

dwelling place of a deity or supreme goddesses, or the place of original being, consecrated by "publicly sacrificing a man, they began the horrible solemnity of their barbarous worship."

On the contrary, among the Suevians (who covered much of today's Northern Germany), the Langobards were the smallest nation, and two of their members were the Reudignians; and the Angles (English) who invaded Britain in the fifth century by crossing the North Sea. Langobards were smallest in number, but famous for adventurous deeds and battle. They were otherwise remarkable for their worship of Herthum, or Mother Earth. These people were large, healthy, dressed in skins, raised cattle, hunted, grew grains, lived in wood homes protected by rivers or forests. Their Mother Earth was a goddess who intervened in the affairs of men and visited countries. From *Germania*, "In an island of the ocean stands the wood Castrum: In it is a chariot dedicated to the Goddess, covered over with a curtain, and permitted to be touched by none but the Priest. Whenever the Goddess enters this, her holy vehicle, he perceives her, and with profound veneration attends the motion of the chariot, which is always drawn by yoked cows."

The story continues, saying that when Herthum visited a place, only rejoicing, feasts, and recreation abound: "They do not go to war; they touch no arms; fast laid up is every hostile weapon; peace and repose are then only known, then only beloved, till to the temple the same priest reconducts the Goddess when well tired with the conversation of mortal beings."

The *Germania* account mentions other goddesses and female leaders.

Allison finds me in the cozy dining room, "Whew! It's so hot outside, I could fry an egg on the hood of my car! Too bad we can't eat out on the back deck overlooking the pine grove, in the shade."

320

"Next time—if you like it here. I hope you do."

"What should I order? Allison says, searching the menu. Black Forest cake sounds good, but I want lunch, too. Oh, Mom always made goulash at home. I'll get that."

"How did she make it?"

"With hamburger, noodles, canned tomatoes, and corn."

"This is real goulash—not the American version most kids know. This is fat chunks of beef dredged in flour and braised with fresh colorful red bell peppers, then simmered in a sauce heavily flavored with Hungarian paprika and tomatoes—like a meat stew—spicy and totally delicious. Eat it with dark rye bread slathered in sweet Minnesota butter and an amber Spaten ale in a chilled glass pint mug, of course."

"Gosh, how could I not do that? And cake. Do you ever make goulash?

"I have to do something with sixty-five beefsteak tomato plants, so I freeze goulash, can beet borscht, tomato juice, soup, whole stewing tomatoes, spaghetti sauce, conserve, and salsa—lots of vitamins in tomatoes, and peppers."

"I don't have time for gardening or much cooking. I've decided to postpone looking for a teaching job. Dad continues to need my help, and I can save my money for a year if we stay with him. He pays me well, more than I'll make as a teacher. I want to take the kids on some trips and enjoy them more."

"*Ahhh*—sounds like a good plan, but I hope you use your education."

"I will." Big smile, "Your stories are the best education ever!"

I order the liver pate' plate with crispy crackers, chopped red onions, hard-boiled eggs, fresh tomatoes, rye bread, and lettuce.

"Before you arrived today, Allison, I was thinking about German goddesses in mysterious groves at the end of the first century, and about Zoroaster's influence, his religion of absolute opposing values of good and evil. So many religious choices at that time!"

Allison says, "I wonder what the Germans were doing at the time of Christ."

"They were living much like American Indians, without the use of iron; at war with neighbors; hunting and gardening for food; clothed in skins; proud of their horses; raising cattle; using spears for weapons. I brought an account called *Germania*. Take it home if you wish.

"The Germans were not then called Germans, but by many tribal names, people all speaking a related language.

Allison asks, "Are we going to talk about Germans today?"

"No, today—the story of the Israelites. Their roots lay in a dark time in the Eastern Mediterranean—drought, famine, roaming bands of starving, depressed people. Canaan was the land between the Jordan River and the sea, also called the Promised Land, or Palestine, where a gathering of tribes all speaking distinct languages—different than their neighbors and enemies— moved in after the Egyptians left."

"A Semitic language," Allison adds, "What period was this?"

"Around 1200BC. The rise of the Israelite tribes develops roughly at the same time as Zoroastrianism, 1500 to 550BC. After the first villages, another 800 years would pass before the birth of Jesus."

We pause when Jean, our server, returns, so I can request bratwurst sausages and red cabbage. Allison orders goulash, black rye bread and warm potato salad with bacon.

"Back to the Middle East . . ."

"Excuse me, but when did the Gilgamesh story occur, compared to this?"

"That was in Sumeria about one thousand years before the first Israelite tribes. There are few similarities between the two.

"The Hebrews lived a humble, but fearful, tense life. Stories and rites bound them together with tight kinship rules giving them courage.

The Northern land was far more fertile than the South which they called Judah. They both lived a simple life of agriculture, had temples in different towns, and worshiped many gods and goddesses. Among the gods was Yahweh, a divine warrior who defeated cosmic powers of rivers and seas and who carried their most sacred object, the Ark of the Covenant, when they went into battle, which was often. Prior to Yahweh was another stronger god named Baal who was extremely popular, a favorite of a woman named Jezebel, who defended him."

"Wait a minute," Allison remarks, "Who was Baal?"

"An ancient god of the Canaanites. The Israelites arrived adopting many of their rites. Life was much like their neighbors. Oral traditions were stories: Abraham was the first father of the Hebrews, and Isaac was his son. Moses was the lawgiver who led them out of Egypt. These stories still contained a spiritual energy inherent in nature and humans, not an energy conferred by gods, as Karen Armstrong points out in her fabulous book, *The Great Transformation*, which is my best source for religious history. Long plays, in the Middle East were reenactments in which people played or performed military victories as if they had happened in sacred, mythological time, way back in the mysterious beginnings of time. Eventually, according to Armstrong, this changed, and the stories about Abraham and Moses and others, were told as if they occurred in historic time about real people—not gods in time. This was an important alteration of thinking by the Israelites, and continues today.

"A kingdom was formed to unite the tribes, but it was split later. David was king of Judah, considered a divine figure, a son of a god adopted by Yahweh, his father. It was David's job to defeat earthly foes in the same manner that Yahweh destroyed the heavenly ones.

"These early people couldn't have understood the idea of having only one god for everything, or that one god could contain all that is spiritual, holy or sacred. Divinity could be found in mountains, lakes,

323

and women, too—just as it had been for thousands of years.

"King David of Judah announced that the newer historical festivals would change back to the former mythology, but many didn't want to return, causing an increase in divisions of thinking that helped lead to the worship of one god—Yahweh. But Yahweh was a warrior god. Jezebel was a woman who defended Baal, god of agriculture and fertility. Elijah argued Baal was an outside god from Phoenicia, so he set out to slaughter all the Baal prophets, and Jezebel. He grew sick and afraid, so he hid out on Mount Sinai, Yahweh's shrine, seeking guidance from Yahweh. Jezebel was dead."

"She understood the important connection with Mother Earth and was trying to save it, don't you think?" Allison offers.

"Prior to Yahweh, female goddesses still existed. Thousands of big-bosomed female statues are found in Hebrew ruins prior to the one-man, one-god invention. Archeologists say one female named Ashura may have been Yahweh's wife!"

"*Hmmm*. Really?" Allison's mouth hangs open, "Well, I wonder what horrible ending SHE had? What was her fate? She was probably called an evil witch."

"What happens next to Elijah on Mount Sinai became a turning point in the role of nature in religion, in my opinion. He waited on the mountain for an omen—a message from a god, or Yahweh. Such messages had always appeared in the form of a natural event—a huge thunderstorm, an earthquake, a flood. But not this time. No god appeared! Elijah concluded that Yahweh had separated himself from nature; that Yahweh had ruled his divine council of gods in their assembly, but he decided he didn't need them any more either, so he killed them off."

"Elijah wanted one god," Allison says.

"Yes, and he had help from others. Joshua had always preached that Israelites should stop worshiping gods that came from the eastern side of the Jordon River, and whoever didn't stop would be destroyed by Yahweh. But the one-god idea frightened people. They would have less power without their old familiar deities that favored them. Armstrong points out that the Israelites were about to embark upon a way that would set themselves apart forever on a 'lonely and painful path that would take them away from the ways of myth.'"

I pause. We gaze silently at our plates, the burdens of the Jews weighing upon our shoulders, visions of future persecutions to come. My unfinished meal reminding me of the stories: the white oval plate now red cabbage juice—the Red Sea. The fluffy white dumpling—now Mount Sinai. The bits of parsley and spices swimming about—now dead bodies. Was the little chunk of asparagus Yahweh? No, he was beyond nature.

Jean, our waitress, startles us, "Say! You two need a cup of coffee!"

"Too hot for coffee," I reply, fanning myself.

"How about iced coffee?"

While I consider, Allison pipes up, "I'd like *apfelkuchen* and iced tea. Oh, and vanilla ice cream on top of the cake, please."

"*Kuchen* for me, too. Hold the ice cream. Do you have sour cream? And please bring iced coffee. Thank you, Jean."

Allison slumps down, "Too bad for humankind that Yahweh won. What if Jezebel had won?"

"Indeed! There were kinder, gentler gods and goddesses, peace-loving ones who cared more about fertility and growth. Yahweh destroyed the cedar trees of Lebanon. Joshua said all people had to worship Yahweh alone, or Yahweh would maim or destroy them, too."

"Geeze—history sure repeats itself. I mean, remember the Gilgamesh story when he goes into the sacred cedar forest and cuts down the tree, and the guardian Humbaba is outraged; but the god Shamash comes to the aid of Gilgamesh who is confused and scared, and tells him, with great praise, that he is doing the will of Shamash. The god then sends winds from eight directions to beat down Humbaba." Allison stops for a second, "I guess anybody thinks they can do anything, if they think some god has told them to do it. I mean, gods tell sicko people to do some really horrible things."

"I don't disagree at all."

Jean serves our coffee and cake—the sweet, spicy scent of warm apples fills my head. "I wonder if these apples came from Aamodt's Apple Farm down the road. The barn, which is now a store, was built by my great-grandfather who learned engineering at Heidelberg University in Germany."

"I'll have to take the kids there this fall."

"Fall will be coming soon," I reply, savoring my first bite of cake.

"Let's now return to the Israelites. Assyria became a super power which hurt the Hebrews, mostly in the north. The south recovered faster after the war—744 to 612BC. There was extreme poverty and wealth, and a new idea that prophets shouldn't only promote their own interests but those of the poor, using justice and equality. This was different than mystics in India who studied yoga and went on internal quests. Hebrew prophets only had an outside power that left them feeling stressful. Some acquired a feeling they were speaking Yahweh's words, not their own. They felt Yahweh's joy or anger, not their own. Also, they saw that God liked to test his followers, causing people to do crazy things against common sense, like when Abraham was ordered to kill his own son, on faith. God sent him a lamb to kill instead, but apparently God could be cruel or kind and do meaningless acts. The god of Abraham didn't relate personally to human circumstances. He didn't even require any energy from them, yet could demand anything.

"The gap between ordinary people and the divine world of gods was becoming a wide one.

"Another thing. Yahweh wasn't satisfied being ruler of Israel. He said he was ruler of the world! Isaiah was told by Yahweh not to worry about the transgressions of Assyria, because it wasn't an army that would defeat them. Yahweh could control the gods of other nations.

"At that time, there was extreme inequity between the rich and poor. On the bottom were the peasants laboring in the fields for the wealthy land owners who took whatever they wanted, including men and boys for soldiers. And then there was a king who ruled over the unjust system. Now, the king was supposed to be taking care of the poor if he was following the dictates of the gods. When this was not the case, concerned prophets, Amos and Hosea, were upset and they began to record prophetic oracles.

"Around 800BC writing had been used in the Middle East to record business transactions, but there was a growing sense of people feeling more pity for the less fortunate—for their neighbors. There was a growing sense of justice in matters. Some were writing down ethics."

Allison sips her coffee, "I still don't really understand what it was that influenced the Israelites to create their unique idea of worshipping one god. I mean, wasn't that revolutionary? Why did they want to set themselves apart like that?"

"*Hmmm*. Why did the Christians adopt the practice of monasticism and celibacy? Why did the Mormons decide to record the birth of every single person on the earth? Why did the Hindus invent the exercise of yoga?"

"I'm sure I don't know," Allison replies.

"I'm sure there's a reason why; however, each practice helps to create identity and therefore strong bonds that hold a group together. For instance, the Israelites practiced circumcision for males."

Allison says, obviously upset, "Some tribe in Africa actually does something like that to girls. They cut their clitoris. Isn't that awful? Is it necessary to do such barbaric things to create identity? Do we have to keep doing dumb things just because our ancestors who lived in uneducated times did them? I don't think so."

"You asked me what it was that most influenced the Israelites to worship one male god. I don't know, however, when the Babylonians invaded Jerusalem and burned down the most holy temple of all, and people were dragged off to be slaves in Babylonia, they asked themselves, 'Why did Yahweh do this to us? Why are we being punished? Is it because he's a jealous god who wants us to worship him alone?'

"They held secret meetings and began to worship in groups. They kept the Sabbath while they were in exile. They learned they could follow the commandments wherever they lived. This was a new idea—one did not have to be physically connected to land—to a sacred place that was spirited, to be able to worship. And, very important—Yahweh becomes an invisible god."

"Gee whiz," Allison says, "If gods and goddesses had always been the model figures for humans to follow, this left women without any mentors. They must have been furious, like Jezebel. If you think about it, this may have been the beginning of not valuing women for womanly behavior. I mean, the female heroines, like Joan of Arc and Judith of the Bible, are famous for being warrior goddesses."

"Yes, and then they burned Joan at the stake for witchcraft!" I exclaim.

"Who was Judith?"

"A Hebrew woman who rescued her people by killing an Assyrian general."

"Oh. You said there began a disconnect with the land—a severance of sacred ties, at the same time female goddesses were phased out."

"Yes. It's easier to justify the destruction of something or someone you have demonized. It was okay to rape the earth. It was okay to slaughter animals. It was okay to not teach women the skills of reading and writing or the knowledge in the sacred texts."

"What a scam! Being invisible made Yahweh more mysterious I suppose."

"The Israelites had to compete with King Marduk and the Babylonians. Yahweh was one—not two fighting gods representing a cosmic struggle between good and evil; Yahweh slew a sea dragon, but not in a war in which the sea was a hideous goddess. Marduk had to remake the World every year, but Yahweh had done it once in six days and had the seventh day to rest, and the job was done forever. The exile to Babylonia was another separation from their homeland, but Yahweh was wherever they were because he was the world over. But the people were to blame for their troubles because they had not been holy enough, or because they had not enough empathy for those who suffered."

"You mean like love and forgiveness?"

"Yes, some wanted revenge; but others didn't, which was something new. Now, during this exile, most of the Torah, the Hebrew Bible, or, the first five books of the Christian Bible, was compiled or written from earlier writing. Eventually, the people returned to Israel. There were about 1,000 years of changes before a final Bible version was accepted."

"What happened to the Israelites after Marduk let them go home?"

"Cyrus did that. He was Marduk's son who lived 530 to 450BCE. The people had a monotheistic one-god idea, but there were opposing views of what it meant. A Judean prophet described it as a one-god messiah who would save the sins of those who suffered; while Isaiah thought it was a harsh, warrior god like back in the old days. Meanwhile, the people built a new temple in Judah that was modest and unimpressive. But the land was full of strangers who were not Jews, and the Jews who had remained behind did not relate to the new religion."

"More coffee anyone?" Jean cheerfully inquires.

"No, thank you, Jean. Almost time to leave."

Allison pulls her shoulders back, tips her head up, and proclaims, "I think the Jews and all of Mother Earth's people have suffered, not because they're sinful and deserve punishing, but because they denied equal rights to female goddesses, like Herthum and Ashura. Can you tell me more about them?"

"According to my *Brewer's Dictionary of Phrase and Fable*, Herthum, or Nerthus, was goddess of fertility, or Mother Earth, worshiped on the island of Rugen by Germans and Scandinavians. She corresponds with Cybele, Mother goddess of Phrygia, goddess of fertility and mountains. Rugen is in the Baltic Sea. Phrygia, an ancient Indo-European country in the area where Turkey is now, was settled in the thirteenth century BC."

"I don't think," muses Allison, "that Americans understand their European history or roots. Heck! They don't even know their American past anymore. How can people know who they are if they don't know where they came from?"

"That's so. However, it's amazing how often people in the old world moved about, adopting new ideas, teaching new things, changing languages, altering identities. People are anything but static creatures. Perhaps we long for predictability so much, because we behave in so many unpredictable ways. We forget when we study the past that life moved far more slowly than it does now. We've accelerated behavior in extreme ways. We can't keep up with our own inventions."

"I know," says Allison. "It's quite stressful, isn't it? Who has, or makes, time to even think about who they are?"

"I learned that Germany is a Celtic or English name chosen by a Roman, perhaps Tacitus. And Britain is full of names from Germany. German means cousin in Latin.

"It seems," I add, "that humans like to choose their own identities, and give them to others at the same time."

Allison is the first to leave the Gasthaus. We agreed, it was a wonderful afternoon, and we should meet in the fall at Aamodt's Apple Farm.

I linger for a moment.

Mom had cooked many Easter dinners before she died in 1990. After then, Dad came to the Gasthaus on Easter. I could almost hear Dad's voice. His unabashed and powerful singing would delight diners as he accompanied Ed, the Polish accordion player. Dad and Mom taught me to sing, *"Du, Du, liegst mir im herzen, Du, du liegst mir im sin . . . .*

Indeed, I've been known to stand up at a party and yodel! I wonder if Herthum knew how to yodel.

Chapter 33
SOME PEOPLE BELONG IN JARS
Only humans invent reasons for nature's behavior.

Marine On St. Croix

Alone in my garden. Allison has promised to join me for lunch tomorrow at my home, her first visit to Marine. Hopefully she will like heirloom tomatoes. I'm dragging a tomato bucket behind me that may be woefully too small. The sun heats my back. Growing food nourishes my spirit.

I cherish working alone in my garden; on padded knees, crawling on soft, warm black dirt, between five-foot-tall tomato plants, sharp leaves brushing my tan face, narrow eyes squinting. *A-ha!* A tomato lying against the fence. I pluck the Brandywine prize, a monster as wide as my hand, shiny, smooth, and scarlet red. Retreating to the stone slab path, I admire the fat beefsteak gem, a gift from a seed planted four months earlier: forty to sixty seeds punched into potting soil, the best heirloom varieties from the Seed Saver's Exchange in Iowa, where I purchase all my vegetable seeds. Early in the spring I set black plastic trays in the kitchen window and carry them in and out of the house, until transferring the wee sprouts into two-inch pots. Later I move them to the garden shed window, carrying them in and out, until an early day in June when they safely rest in a raised garden bed rich in compost and minerals. I've protected my babies from dryness, hail storms, frost, and hungry critters. Like children, they are a serious commitment.

In a silent gesture of thanks, I glance up at the sky to the high noon sun for this is surely a glorious day. My heart swells with satisfaction. My mind fills with visions of future meals with tomatoes, all organic, all economical, all vitamin-rich and tasty.

Upon closer inspection, my Brandywine prize, the object of my affection isn't perfect—a slight crack in the side, but unlike some others, there's no black beetles to shoo away. Anyway, "cracked" tomatoes are "put up" into quart jars. And they're not imperfect—only different. They're perfect for different roles similar to people (some who belong in jars!).

The early, smaller succulent Stupice tomatoes have the best flavor. This year's experiment, the Gold Medal tomato, may become a regular, having good flavor, size, and a fair yield. Nice color, too. I'll discontinue the cute little perennial Golden Pear brand. It looks pretty, but the taste is boring.

Setting the heavy, full bucket aside on the old sugar-house bricks in the circular garden center where four narrow paths come together, I sit to rest. The circle is ten feet in diameter, defined by a low wall of gray and yellow Lake Superior stones mostly hidden by rambling golden California poppies. Escaped purple Bowles violets sneak into the cracks where I leave them happily in the sun. Such incursions are common in my garden, since I often allow the plants to decide where *they* want to grow. They tell me where they grow best. I'm not so egalitarian with most weeds that settle in to drink the water and sop up the nutrients, telling myself, "There's plenty of room for you guys wherever you came from. Your purpose lies elsewhere—other than to teach me a lesson or two!" The stone circle is surrounded by four raised beds that measure four-feet-wide by twenty-feet-long, each bearing so much vegetation, I can almost hide like a rabbit in the comfort of my lair.

The neighbor children, on the other side of the white painted fence, make me laugh. They're so much like my plants—the lilies, roses, iris, daisies, bleeding hearts—over 200 flower kinds in my yard. Like the funny kids, they're healthy, free, independent-minded, moody, happy, forgiving, unpredictable, generous, and beautiful. Today, these kids and plants are my best friends. I'm a rather private person these days, perhaps due to my long period of seclusion as the result of a bad accident in my recent past.

No, my life wasn't always so quiet as this. People of my kind, who fancy they have something meaningful to tell others; or who feel they haven't been listened to; or who think they haven't had a chance to express themselves; or who have a big ego and think they're important; or who simply love to share stories, or preserve traditions— well, they sometimes end up like loners if they're not careful. The temptation to write things down is like a disease. A writer is like an addict—a word addict who can't get enough of writing down thoughts.

What a peculiar habit this is! No other critters waste their time thus. Written words were first scratched symbols, then utilitarian marks. Long groups of symbols became words that gained the status of magic! Then holiness! Because someone wrote words on a sheepskin thousands of years earlier, it must be the truth. He who wrote them must be holy or a hero—god or Gilgamesh. Is there ONE holy book written by a woman? We praise books that give us new ways to think. The key word is new. Anything new is as important as something old—one reflects change; the other one values preservation. Most natives haven't bought into the idea that just because something is in a book, or it is new, it is right or superior. They were brainwashed and swindled by writings on paper and retain a healthy skepticism of information, or laws.

The worst part of all this gibberish and jotting today is the proliferation of laws that leaders concoct for the political, financial advantages for a few of the wealthy, while making life hell for others dumb enough to follow them—laws they didn't participate in writing. Rule by decree! Rule by law!

There's more justice in my garden than in the US Senate. More ethics in nature than in the House of Representatives. More kindness in peoples' hearts than in current "kinder gentler Christian" policies forcing folks into destitution in our land of laws.

Carrying the bucket of tomatoes—almost too pretty to eat—up to the house, I turn on the water spigot, spray the fruit with a water hose, drain the water on the grass, and one by one I fashion a tomato parade on the edge of the wooden deck. Sitting in the shade of the back of the house in a white wicker chair, relaxing with a cup of tea, admiring my work, I count the Brandywine babes that lay shimmering, saucy, and voluptuous. Why? Why count them?

I don't know. Why do we count everything? What difference does it make how many kinds of plants are in my yard? None, whatsoever. Why do we have a natural instinct to believe that more is better in every instance?

Because we had to hoard food to survive as a species? Because if we have more than our neighbor we are better? Friends ask me why I plant so much for only two people. The truth is I try to give seeds away, but my friends are too busy to use them, and they don't want to work as hard as one needs to, to raise a garden.

They know I'll give them some tomatoes. I can't throw away a seed, so I plant it! I admit it's kind of crazy.

I lie in the sun, my skin absorbing the same nutrients that grew my heirloom honeys. Each tomato appears different, yet the same. Each one is like a planet or star dependent upon rhythms, harmony, chaos, connectedness, separateness, motion, stillness, and so on. Everything grows and decays according to nature's rules.

Isn't it amazing that the romaine lettuce, Empress green beans, Detroit Dark red beets, the chard, parsnips, and leeks—are all created out of millions of years of life without much writing or numbering? Plants don't need us bungling ones, who mess up nature's perfect plan. Yes! Perfect! Plants instinctually know how to be formed, expand, create, integrate, separate, conserve energy, live, and die. They do not do any of this because they want to feed us nice people, or because god directed them to live in our behalf. Only humans invent reasons for all of nature's behavior—justifications for how we wish things to be for us. We rarely consider the integrity or needs of the plants that feed us. We often do not respect their right to live in peace with dignity. We should treat them with as much love as we do family members, like the Indians love Mother Earth and Father Sun.

The evolution of diversity is accomplished without writing.

Nature, which is very selective, avoids waste and plenty of mischief, unlike us who choose to be wasteful and live with the debilitating consequences of poverty and war—government sanctioned circumstances.

Does this mean nature is always clean and peaceful? No! It's always clean, but there's always a tension between forces of energy that create a stable living environment. My garden is anything but a haven of tranquility. Brown fungus rot attacks the tomato leaves. Beetles bite through the splits in the fruit. Fat frogs catch the flies. Robins devour worms. Monarch butterfly cocoons are gobbled up by bluebirds. Jennifer the cat stalks the wrens, the mice, the song birds, and the moles who upset the tulip bulbs, the plant roots, and transform our lawn into a tunnel system more vast than New York City's subway routes.

Is it a war out here? Is it a competitive world in which winner takes all? Not at all. It's simply Mother Earth trying to maintain balance. Balance—that which makes all worlds possible—the best ones, and the worst ones.

The herbs are planted close to the back door for quick picking, and fragrance. Lying on my new chaise lounge, sniffing the mint, dill, tarragon, rosemary, chives; soaking up the sun; feeling drowsy; my mind wanders.

After closing the art gallery in the 1980s, I didn't hear from my mentor Mizinokamigok for a long time. Our Ojibwe study group, which she had led, drifted apart, but of course she was often on my mind.

I began devoting more time to Indian philosophy during my long walks, challenging myself to use what I'd learned in my personal life as much as possible. I became arrogant enough to think I may have something to teach others; but I wasn't sure, and I knew I had a long way to go. The Indian name that Rose, the old Mille Lacs Lake Ojibwe teacher, had given me was *Aabitawayi'ii Ikwe*, or Halfway Woman, because when I was in her class, she thought my learning was halfway. Miz's group class called me Mang because I said, if I could be an animal, I would be a loon.

I phoned Miz one summer day. She agreed to meet on a certain bench in a shopping mall in suburban North Minneapolis where we could sit outside in a quiet corner. She was pleased to see me and know that I'd not forgotten her. She hadn't changed. I was glad she was so pleasant, because she could be quite moody and testy if you displeased her, and I had done so at least twice.

After an appropriate exchange and a bit of silence, I revealed a few pages of writing, an outline of sorts, with key topics. I wondered what she would say after reading it, for her opinion mattered a great deal to me.

She quietly finished, laid the paper in her lap, and with deep intensity in her black eyes, she met my hopeful gaze, "This is what you must tell THEM; because if you don't, it will be too late. If people don't get this now, they never will. This is what my people would want you to tell YOUR people."

"However," she added, admonishing me in a low tone, "However, just remember that 'mankind' in this writing doesn't always include

MY people, because we didn't do all this destruction and polluting that you talk about, yet we are part of mankind, too." She paused as if to emphasize her next thought, "Be sure that you make a distinction!"

I thought to myself, *But, THAT'S what it's all about—distinguishing between two disparate cultures.*

My friend Doris married the brother of her boyfriend who had died of an asthma attack due to his enormous, dusty Indian artifact collection in his mansion. The brother was a prominent banker from a Minnesota family. I attended the wedding reception held downtown in the venerable Minneapolis Club, a small celebration where I met a charming, lively gentleman named Waring Jones who was a book collector and founder of the Playwrights' Center on Franklin Avenue where the Loft, a writing school, also resided. I joined the center and wrote two plays critiqued by my teacher, Lee Blessing. He said it was extremely difficult to write humor and dialogue, but that I'd done a great job of it. I was devastated because I was trying to be serious, yet pleased that I could do something.

Waring introduced me to Frederick Manfred from Luverne, Minnesota, nominated five times for a Nobel Prize in literature, author of many excellent novels based in his *Siouxland,* including *Green Earth,* which absolutely deserved a Nobel Prize. We became long-time friends. Not far away in tiny Minneota, Bill Holm lived and wrote award-winning books. A group of Minnesota authors, including Robert and Carol Bly, started *Corn Stalks* in a church basement, so that writers could gather and read aloud in a social, informal setting—noted authors mingling with fresh young students from the University of Minnesota at Marshall. A potluck supper, plenty of red wine, good beer, and a great time was had by all—sometimes ending at the Silver Dollar Saloon, or a sleep overnight at Bill Holm's crowded house. I had to sleep on the floor underneath his harpsichord!

338

As usual, I was pulled in several directions at once, as if my path were a triple spiral. My close friend and confidant, Deanne the documentary film maker, and I still met for movies and talks; but she was not a nature girl, and hiking was not in her DNA. She had talked of moving to New York City for a long time. Sadly, she finally did it for career advancement. New York was the last place I wanted to be at that time. I was dreaming about a log cabin in the woods.

Another friend, Dick Bancroft, who I'd met at an AIM conference in Wakpala, South Dakota, was all excited because his daughter Ann was planning a trip to the North Pole with explorers Will Steger, Paul Schurke and others. Their expedition would walk, ski, and use sled dogs. I joined a committee to help raise funds for the trip, a joyful experience because it renewed my deep connections with Northern Minnesota, although I'd never missed my annual summer fishing vacations with my family at Rainy Lake or Nelson's Resort near Voyageurs National Park. Plenty of canoe trips into Quetico Provincial Park, too.

One year later, in 1987, I participated in my first John Beargrease Sled Dog Race along the north shore of Lake Superior from Duluth to Grand Marais and back, by volunteering to be a dog handler at one of the checkpoints. It was colder than hell outdoors all night. But I was really living!

When I told Doris and her new husband, John, I thought it would be great to live in a log cabin, they offered me their summer house at the Beaver Bay Club, close to the tiny town of Beaver Bay and Split Rock Lighthouse. My devoted friend, Dick Wilson, the "Jingle Man" who wrote the Minnesota Twins tune and advised me on my P.J. Penguin Publishing venture, gave me a fancy new electric typewriter and loaned me his all-wheel drive Subaru car.

Like a dream-come-true, I settled into a low-roofed log cabin huddled on a hillside dotted by towering pines, overlooking frozen

Lake Superior. It was December first with a temperature below zero. Firewood was stacked high by the wood-burning black stove. Electricity provided light and cooking facilities. I hauled water in three-gallon jugs and used a slop pot like a pioneer. Nobody else had ever spent a winter at the club, but I felt totally secure and happy in my snowbound abode, watching the season change and the lake in its many moods while reading American nature writers, especially Emerson and Thoreau. Each day I wrote in my spiral notebook journal and explored the woods on skis. I'd wax my wooden skis, secure my backpack, which held hot tea in a thermos, chocolate, and dried fruit. *Swish-swish*—off I'd go. Trails through the forest ran everywhere.

The best part of that winter in Beaver Bay was the wonderful local characters who befriended me. I was so curious and interested in their lives, that they shared story after story with me, about lumbering, fishing and hunting, laboring in a taconite plant, unions, cancer, parties, smelt fishing, dog sledding, Finnish heritage, music, and each other. I felt like I'd left the ethereal world of art and fashion and joined the earthy world of reality. I was different from them, but in their "us against them" insecurity, they accepted me. I never felt so free in my life. But then, I wasn't beginning to worry about money—not yet.

There was also the need for healing a broken heart. My Montana cowboy had married a cowgirl. Then I met and fell for a married man who was very rich and a very good liar; and when it came time to choose, of course, he chose his wife. I thought I could run away and wipe away my shame by becoming a hermit. Instead Mother Nature and the Northwoods' folks kept me entertained and happy.

My Beaver Bay escape had been a busy series of adventures. But, alas, it had to end. Spring came. Buds formed on the fragrant balm of Gilead trees. Icicles drip-dripped onto the deck. Dark storms swept the lake, stirring up brown sediments. When a white-throated song sparrow sang to me, I knew sadly that the club members would be returning soon, to open their rustic summer cottages: my friends the DeLaittres and Joneses. I would miss the empty Pillsbury abode which perched on the nose of the beaver for which the town was named, a prime location atop a cliff where wicked waves crashed far below. Exhilarated by wind howling through my hair, I would raise my arms to give thanks to the four sacred directions and *Gitchi Manito*. Far below *Gitchi Gumme,* my watery witness, always reminded me of the infinite wisdom of west winds and the flapping wings of thunder beings.

On June 1, I gathered my memories and left, my tattered broken heart nicely mended—thank you.

While living in Beaver Bay, I resolved to live a more outdoor lifestyle thus I had explored possibilities of moving to Beaver Bay, Grand Marais or Ely, about as far north as you can go and still be in the USA. I came to the conclusion I would not move that far up.

One blustery winter day, during my visit to Ely to see a friend named Jessica, an actress, a new opportunity occurred, because we chose to eat lunch in Vertin's Café. A local author wearing a fur hat, and a red-and-black checkered shirt was dining in the next booth with another woodsy man. We all got together in our booth. We talked about his new book titled *Wilderness Visionaries* in which he included the lives of Henry David Thoreau, and someone I'd never heard of, Calvin Rutstrum, a Minnesota wilderness skills author.

I was thrilled to converse with Jim Dale Vickery about Thoreau. We both knew friends from Rush City—a former Minneapolis bookstore owner and his wife who were active in preserving the St. Croix River, the river that comprises the border between Minnesota and Wisconsin, a wild and scenic gem saved by Walter Mondale and Gaylord Nelson who sponsored the Wild and Scenic Rivers Act in Congress, saving it from high-rise apartments and bridges.

Jim invited me to partake in the Thoreau Excursion, a canoe trip on the Merrimack and Concord Rivers, celebrating the 150th anniversary of Henry and his brother John's voyage from Concord, New Hampshire to Concord, Massachusetts, in 1839. During the week-long voyage, we heard a different speaker each night in a hall or church, from experts who were paddling with us all day, who knew more about Thoreau than any others, like Dr. Walter Harding and Tom Blanding of the Thoreau Society, and Linck Johnson from Colgate University, an authority on Thoreau's familiarity with American Indians. He was my canoe partner for two days.

There were others, including Vickery, who delivered an exciting, fresh account of Alexander Henry, an explorer who wrote *Travels and Adventures in Canada and the Indian Territories Between the Years 1760 and 1776,* a book Thoreau read the year before his big canoe trip, when he was the age of twenty-one.

I designed T-shirts for the excursion; learned a ton of information and got my name in the *Boston Globe* when my canoe tipped over, because my partner's big-brimmed sun bonnet flew off her head, and we both stupidly lunged for it. Everybody was grateful to me for proving that if you fell into the river that nobody ever swam in, you would not die. The cloudy water was not like the almost pristine Boundary Waters Canoe Area Wilderness in Minnesota, near Ely. Thank goodness the canoe trip occurred during a time of much needed revival for our eastern rivers.

Vickery was a proficient woodsman. He served as one of our guides, by patrolling the brigade in a kayak, as did Parker Huber, a Vermont authority on Thoreau's Maine travels, and a spiritual soul who led an expedition into the Grand Canyon each spring.

The road map of life Miz had described, the spiral path in the maze that the Tohono O'odham lived, and the Good Red Road of the Dakota were all continuous connections I was creating—making choices both independent and universal. My goal to live *in* nature was actualizing in ways I could not have imagined. How could I possibly continue on this path, while earning a living in a capitalistic society?

Chapter 34

YOU DON'T NEED A SAVIOR TO HAVE A GOOD HEART

Who needs goddesses anyway? In place of magic, we now have miracles.

Marine On St. Croix

"So this is your little slice of heaven on earth?" Allison tilts her head, an impish grin from ear to ear on her baby, bronze face, a glint in her eyes, her sandals clicking as she follows the yellow brick path to the center of my garden, her long gauzy skirt snagging on the marigolds, leeks, and poppies, her sleeves brushing up against the tomato plants.

"Earth *is* heaven to me. I'd rather live on a real planet I can smell, see, and touch, than on a fantasy. This is all there is, so we better take care of Mother Earth. We make many choices in life. However, I believe that's the most important."

Allison smiles, "I agree with you, for the sake of our children and grandchildren."

"Iced tea or lemonade? I'll serve lunch whenever you wish."

"Lemonade now, tea later?" she says, her teeth perfectly white next to her golden suntanned face.

"Sounds good to me," I say, suggesting she sit on one of the white wrought-iron chairs and me on the other. Setting my notebook on the matching table between us, I answer her questions about the extensive deer fence, the chattering wrens, gladiolus in varying heights and hues, young plum trees, organic vegetables, storage sheds, wood fired sauna, and the modest 1880 vintage house that was remodeled.

Allison tells me she's sorry that I could not join her family for fun at Aamodt's Apple Farm. She likes Honey Crisp apples best. I prefer Haralson. She describes her recent canoe voyage on the St. Croix

River with a group of friends, including a young man she seems interested in. Perhaps that explains her sweet, spicy demeanor—an extra swing in her walk, something I don't have just now. My crutches lay on the stone wall in case I need them to reach the house. Allison offers to fetch the beverages for me.

When she returns she says, "I cannot believe you do all this gardening on crutches. I mean, most of the yard is under cultivation, and I hardly see a weed. You also teach, belong to clubs, take care of a house, and travel!"

"I have to keep going. If I don't, I may never walk again, and that is unthinkable to me. I concentrate on what I have and try not to think of what I'm missing."

Allison shakes her head. She detects that I don't wish to speak about it, and changes the subject, "Your Indian learning must give you strength and courage."

"It has, many, many times in my life."

"I appreciate all the stories and the caring you share with me, but I confess I'm finding it harder to recall so much information. You told the class one day not to take notes. You said Indians never took notes."

"That's right. If it's important to you, you'll remember it. I don't expect you to recall all the dates and names and so forth. Heaven knows, I can't! You'll remember impressions, patterns, characters, lessons. Your mind will accept some and reject others. We all find ways to fit new information into previous perceptions, which is why we need to be sure youngsters receive healthy lessons from us. Not just things they hear and see, but things they smell and sense."

Allison's thinking about her children, "They hear the story of how the earth was made, and another of how people were made, from the Lutheran perspective, but I don't know if those stories teach them how to behave in today's world. *Geeezee*, how could they? Everybody ignores the Ten Commandments. Kids can see that. There must be some moral guidance common to all races in all religions."

"There is. You just said it: morals, or ethics."

We enjoy our icy lemonade, distracted by a flitting bluebird on the lower branch of the elm tree.

"Jesus, like some people in Hebrew society during his upbringing, had the notion of compassion for the sick, poor, and women, which made him very popular, but also got him killed. The stories surrounding him were mythologized, adding to his appeal. When the Jews refused his offer to provide himself as a savior, some Jews began a new religion, which contributed to further confusion over the writings in the Bible."

Allison throws up her hands, "So many authors! Over such a long period of time. Contradictions were inevitable. Interpretations many."

"I agree. We'll never have a universal religion because each society or nation prefers their own cultural beliefs, however we do have worldwide ethics that humans agree upon, very simple values that any normal person knows, like: sharing is better than greed; kindness is better than being mean; saving is better than waste. You know what I mean."

Allison stops me, "I have friends like myself who choose to ignore the Bible and live by what Jesus said, 'Love one another.'"

"*Hmmm*, that's one way, but what about loving Mother Earth?"

"Oh yes . . . ," Allison exclaims, "Last time we met, at the German Restaurant, you talked about the Israelites and all the interesting changes that they made in their religion that still influence us today, including a departure from nature-worship and polytheism."

"Do you remember how Elijah waited on Mount Sinai for a message from nature, which was still associated with the gods, but nothing happened because now Yahweh was above—beyond all else, even nature?"

"Yes, I remember."

"Moses especially revered the Israelite god of thunder and storms who ruled the high heavens to whom the shepherds prayed and sacrificed for life, breath, and light. Previous to Elijah's experience, Yahweh had appeared with a message on ten tablets bearing ten laws for the Jews, during a rainstorm, a gargantuan tempest."

"So, I think," begins Allison, "that Moses still had a healthy respect for nature, and probably thought of it as a messenger from some mysterious higher being that wasn't necessarily in human form. However, Elijah wanted to make a god more powerful than nature."

"Do you remember Jezebel? How she tried to keep the god named Baal? And how other tribes in Europe and the Near East had worshipped female gods, but how Hebrew prophets chose a male warrior god who would be the only god with all the power over all? He alone would be omnipotent."

"Yes, I recall the story about Joshua. He thought the Hebrews should not worship stranger gods from the east. Those who did not stop this should be killed by Yahweh."

"Do you also remember how the Israelites lived in Babylonia in exile, had no permanent land base marked by boundaries, yet they believed in holy sites to return to? Then, they decided anyplace they went could be holy. Religion didn't have to be connected to a place because their laws were with them and those transcended the local laws where they lived. Yahweh was everywhere, or as we say, omnipresent.

"Then there's the one-god revelation. Who needs goddesses anyway? In the monotheistic Christian genesis, one male named God is the divine principal independent of all other life forms. He exists in a void alone, except perhaps for some angels or fairies, with no other gods or spirits before, or above him; because there could no longer be competition—he encompassed all in his ONE being. He would be a god over those who didn't even know him, who had never heard of him! What do you think of that?"

Allison adds, "He would be omniscient!"

"Right-o!" we chuckle, as I say, "I actually think women are much more omniscient than men are, don't you? I mean, I wonder if motherhood gives us a stronger sensibility toward nature. We create and sustain life, while the men go off to fight wars and kill the babies we raised. How many of these wars actually create more good than bad? All of them kill Mother Earth, too, . . . the food source for all of life."

Allison observes, "*Gee!* We now have a god who is omnipotent, omnipresent, omniscient—does all, sees all, knows all! With a god like that on your side, what could go wrong?"

"Oh, plenty! That's why they had to invent sin. They couldn't blame all the human suffering on a loving god, and they couldn't make him a mean god, even though he actually was in the stories," I declare, raising my voice, "So they claimed we are ALL bad, born that way."

"This is too complicated. Why do we need gods at all?"

"Before humans became creative enough to invent them, there was simply nature. We were just another part of it. We were not reinventing nature."

Allison and I continue chattering throughout our lunch of fresh-from-the-garden romaine lettuce, green beans, tomatoes, chives and red onions, all dressed in grated parmesan, olive oil, and fresh lemon juice topped by previously grilled Copper River wild salmon steaks. Slices of buttered cranberry orange bread accompany the salad. A carrot cake with cream cheese frosting waits in the kitchen by a pitcher of icy mango tea.

Allison rests her fork, "I'm puzzled. There are two origin stories in the Bible. How do you interpret, or understand them?"

"The Judeo-Christian genesis may be interpreted in more than one way. I will relate my understanding of the event as I learned it in my Lutheran church. It is as follows:

"In the beginning, there was nothing but darkness. God's will and word created water and matter, which was firmament in the middle of water. He also created heaven and earth. Then he created the sun, moon, and stars to separate day, night, and seasons. Then he created man in his image. Next he created woman, with or without Adam's rib, depending upon which story one believes. Then God created all the animals, including the birds and fish. The earth was formed so that it may serve man, and man was formed to serve God."

Allison nods, "That's very familiar to me, of course. I'm thinking back to when you told me the Cree origin story about the Mother Earth creator named Omamama, a beautiful, kind loving woman. We sat together in Loring Park. Then, early last spring at the Signature Cafe, you outlined *Enuma Elish* , the Babylonian genesis with Tiamat, the awful schemer, like an evil she-spirit. Let's not forget *Avesta*, with Zoroaster and the two opposing gods fighting against good and evil."

"Today we discuss a monotheistic god who had three religions formed after him: Judaism, influenced by Moses; Christianity, by Jesus; and Islam, by Mohammed. Let's talk about the stories and have fun comparing them with each other. Would you like that? Do you have the time?"

"Oh yes! I would like that very much!" she says, sitting up straight.

"We'll continue to explore Judeo-Christianity now. Perhaps we can better understand how the human relationship with the earth became disconnected, and how I believe we are more and more disconnected with each other, too."

"But not everybody on earth has brought on this change, have they?" Allison asks.

"My mentor, the Ojibwe woman named Miz, warned me, 'Don't blame my people for the havoc—all the destruction. It's mostly your people who are responsible.'"

"What about the Asians and . . ."

"I'm only talking about Anglo-Europeans and Americans, because I want to know the role my ancestors played in this drama; and how they evolved into people so different than the indigenous natives like the Cree, Ojibwe, Lakota, Tohono O'odham, and so on."

Allison nods, "I understand. Do go on."

"The Christian god knows everything, including what we are thinking all the time. He even knows what we will do before we do it. Which means, he had to know that Adam would remind Eve that God had warned them not to eat the apple of good and evil, and that Eve would tempt Adam and they would both eat, and because of her mankind would be full of suffering forever. Like Tiamat, the Babylonian goddess, Eve is associated with the evil serpent.

"Part of Eve's penance would be to bear children and to be subservient to her husband, for she was 'cursed above every beast of the field; upon thy belly shalt thou go, and dust shalt thou eat all the days of thy life.' Adam was also punished, for listening to his wife, 'cursed is the ground for thy sake; in sorrow shalt thou eat of it all the days of thy life' and, 'Dust thou art and unto dust shalt thou return.'

"God decreed, 'Let them have dominion over the fish of the sea, and over the fowl of the air, and over the cattle, and over all the earth, and over every creeping thing that creepeth upon the earth.'

"Christians believed that men and women (especially men) should rule the earth, sea, air, and all else because God decreed it so. They were bound by duty to turn the soil and grow fields which God would make fertile with the rains he sent. Mankind (The English language is brutal on women with its obsessive, egotistical penchant to use masculine pronouns; thus, I awkwardly propose mankind and womankind. They were responsible for tending the Garden of Eden, preparing it for people of God.) Man's and woman's destiny was to cultivate the soil. The Bible says, 'The heavens are the heavens of the Lord, but the earth has he given to the children.' Tell that to NASA's space team!"

Allison and I break into giggles.

"The garden was not perfect. It needed man's and woman's help to be useful and productive. Unfortunately, spirits in nature had been eliminated through a magical alteration in Christian thinking, such that the soil could now be disturbed and no spirits would be bothered. The only sacred places left were grave sites, where those with white skin lay in peace, unless their spirits had gone to hell. Indian graves contained spiritless pagan bodies. Digging them up to plant corn was no cause for concern or guilt for the Europeans.

"Farmers didn't deem the soil as teeming with interconnected spirits of trees, worms, flowers, and stones that were sacred. Soil was material to be reshaped, tilled, fertilized, planted, harvested, dug up, moved, or buried under stones, concrete or asphalt.

"We Anglos separated the earth into useful or useless components. The useful ones were studied to determine how they could benefit man, or the men who *owned* them. Gold, silver, oil, coal, limestone, copper, and so on. Each was identified, bought, sold, traded, and finally, fought over in wars between nations (corporations next). Mother Earth progressed from being worshipped, to being respected, to becoming a resource and a commodity.

"Adam and Eve were punished by God when he sentenced them to eat dust, be dust, and return to dust. Perhaps he was using a metaphor; but either way, the intention was that becoming dust was negative and undesirable. However, the Great Mystery's cycle of dust is how the American Indian views the circle of life.

"Unlike the Great Mystery, the Christian God has a personality. He uses spoken words, not only signs in nature, to create life, proclaim laws and extend his power to will. He is inherently good, and he created man in his own image. But due to Eve's foolishness, mankind became sinful and evil. Thus the good-intentioned God has to punish wayward humans, all of us—even those who didn't mean to do bad, because we failed to abide by his laws.

"The good thing is, anyone can reinterpret the Bible to change the intent of God's word and start a religion they like better."

Allison: "That's been done over and over again!"

"*Hmmm*. I wonder how many times? Has anyone ever counted?"

"I don't know. I wonder, too. Continue. This is fascinating."

"God has no external threats to his position—no competitors. The guide for human behavior is his words. The Bible, an external source, differs from internal seeking within one's self for enlightenment, and is unlike observing signs in nature's behavior for knowledge. This God does no negotiating or compromising with other gods, nor with a wife! No planning between a male and a female. No succession of leaders who came before. He enjoys unlimited authority at the top of a hierarchical pyramid: God the Father, Son, and Holy Ghost. He's actually not at the top because he IS all three. But it's important that he is *not* four—an even, equal number that suggests balance and harmony. He has a succession of followers, just like the general of a great army of soldiers marching to a distant drummer."

"Just like Yahweh—god of war," Allison observes.

"Early biblical scriptures had no reference to a last day of judgment, a final holocaust, angelogy, paradise and hell, Satan, resurrection of the flesh, messianic delivery, all of which became part of the Jewish eschatology, and also the Christian. The latter also adopted the Persian ideas of drinking the symbolic blood of the Son of God as a sacrifice, and later influences stemming from an offshoot religion, called Manichaeism, gave the Christians the ascetic practices of abstinence from sex, meat, and alcohol.

"Gone were the ancient dreamers—the priests whose magic herbs, sacred objects , special words, and healing rites could heal the sick and change the weather. Kings were no longer sacred, nor the son of a god. They became ordinary people who gained lots of power. Tribal elders became state judges where they gathered at the supreme court in Jerusalem—men who could read, appointed by the king.

"In place of magic, you now have miracles, like the miraculous birth of Jesus Christ, although Mother Mary never experienced sexual contact."

"Geeze!," Allison groans, "We still have taboos in today's crazy culture, don't we? I mean, it makes sense to me to have one sexual partner after marriage to raise a family, but it seems weird to me that religions invent unnatural ideas about sexual behavior, like conception without physical contact, or abstinence from all bodily contact for life, or punishing women, but not men, for the same sexual desires, or removing a girl's clitoris. Why all this mean-spirited punishment toward our mothers, daughters, and wives, who are after all, the ones who carry life in their wombs? All they ask for is protection from harm, a safe home, kindness and opportunity to be the person they want to be."

"Perhaps," I begin slowly, "Men feel guilty because they are less able to control their emotions or desires, so they accuse women of the very thing that they lack. Their competitive ego, also a problem, suffers in a capitalistic society where jobs define manhood, and if jobs don't exist, men express anger more in many forms. Family roles are in great flux now. Technology has redefined everything without consulting whether change is all good for all people."

Allison nods, walks to the kitchen to fill our glasses with refreshing mango flavored tea. When she returns, she reports that we can expect rain tonight. That's good news. The garden needs water.

Allison, stirring sugar into her tea, remarks, "I've always wondered how we know what is true, or not true, in the Bible."

353

"We don't know for sure, but many biblical scholars spend their whole life trying to solve that mystery. Very few lines are actually ascribed to Jesus. It required hundreds of years for men to decide what should be in the Bible, and what should be left out.

"Remember this: Judaism gave us the 'Out of one comes everything' theory. Out of one, not two.

"Allow me to remind you of Zoroaster, or Zarathustra in Persia, who wanted to reform the world in his image so it would return to its original state of pristine calm and order. The mythological Garden of Eden concept runs throughout Western and Eastern literature. Behind this was a universal wish to control suffering. Buddha thought this was a useless endeavor because there were so many forces outside of one's individual self. He preached tolerance and acceptance, but Zoroaster wished to defeat evil by following the right rules of ethics. This emphasis on religious ethics became politicized in the hands of ruling kings, as organized theologies tend to do.

"War was more justifiable when it became a MORAL obligation to uphold righteousness. Somehow it became more noble to conquer other nations under the name of one's god, than one's own name. There were no god-sanctioned wars among Algonkian-Siouxian people, because there were no gods—only a Great Mystery. After the Persians conquered their enemies, they then named themselves gods.

"Zoroastrian laws to restore order were in opposition to nature because they were meant to correct it, not preserve it. They had two opposing gods: Angra Mainyu—darkness, ignorance, deception; and Ahura Mazda—truth, light, righteousness, order. The good god is also called Ormazd and considered the chief deity, while the bad god is also called Ahriman. Their book is *Avesta*. Some ideas that went beyond Persia, today's Iran, were a universal war in the future, a pure female virgin, a second coming of Zoroaster, and the end of the world. And, the righteous dead could be resurrected with their families."

Allison stops me, "Wait! I'm trying to remember something you said."

"*Hmmm*. Was it about gods and goddesses?"

"Yes, the name Ahura sounds familiar. Wasn't she a female goddess?"

"Perhaps you are thinking of Ashura who was found in the form of statuettes in excavations of Hebrew ruins, and who may have been Yahweh's wife, but they were Semitic speakers, and the name Ahura comes from Aryan speakers, and Ahura was not a female as far as I know."

"But, what if thousands of years ago Ahura was the wife of Angra? And what if she was adopted by early Israelite wanderers?"

"Allison, what an interesting theory! Maybe you should be an archeologist. You certainly have a curious mind."

Allison laughs as I tease her, "See that display on the rock wall behind us? I dug up all those pieces of rusty metal, bones, stones, and glass while tilling the soil. You can begin your career by interpreting what they are—or were. The neighbor kids call them treasures. They love to come and dig in the dirt with the little rusty shovel I uncovered. I've begun burying my old costume jewelry just to increase the excitement for them."

Allison picks up a fake pearl necklace, "This must be a cheat-piece?"

"Oh no! That belonged to the Shiny Pearl Fairy that used to live under that climbing rose bush. One day, she refused the wish of King Silver Frog who lives under the brick walk, and he stole her pearl necklace and hid it forever—well, until Nora discovered it last week."

I briefly peek at Allison who's frowning. Remaining serious, I add, "What was the wish of the silver frog? I told Nora it was a kiss, but between you and me, he wanted to have sex with her."

Allison's mouth drops open, then turns to a belly laugh.

I'm chuckling, too, but I say, "What's so funny? We aren't laughing about virgin births, end times, sinners in hell, and all the highly imaginative stories that form serious beliefs around the world."

"Nora must think you're great."

"I doubt that—but she did say, 'I wish you weren't a grandma, and you could come over and play with me every day as if you were a little girl like me.' I replied, 'That's the nicest thing anybody ever said to me. Thank you, Nora.'"

Allison returns the necklace to the rock wall.

"Next, the beliefs of the Babylonians. I already told you the creation story, but I need a little break. I got up early to bake. Are you ready for a cup of coffee and a fat slice of carrot cake? I made it fresh this morning. It's all ready on a tray in the kitchen."

"Sounds good. I brought a little surprise for later. I know you like chocolate—dark chocolate. Gosh, we're going to get fat before you get to the end of this saga of everlasting narratives."

"Gardening and swimming keep me fit. But it's not like a few years ago when I could hike fifteen miles in a day—with a backpack. I still go canoeing, even with crutches, in the Quetico-Lac La Croix area in Canada. Did it last summer," Pause, "Please go get the carrot cake. I can't wait to serve it."

"Now for the short version of the polytheistic Babylonian myth: First came the material and spiritual, then eternal matter and water. Equal to these were two primary god and goddess creators. The goddess, Tiamat, made heaven and earth while out of her slain husband came mankind. Six hundred gods were deities of nature who lived in a hierarchy of divinities.

"Babylonians had an animate view of the cosmos for they felt that everything had life and spirits, however, spirits were manifested in the multiple gods who lived in the sky, water, and so forth. Their gods often had mythological human forms, such as Anu, the sky god with a human personality who could be bad or good and was therefore not morally perfect.

"*Ahhhh*," Allison exclaims, "Just like Wasakayjack, the trickster of the Cree who could change form at will—any animal shape, good or bad."

"Yes, I'll go on. The Babylonian genesis story has two distinct sexes as equal creators, however the female has dragon-serpentine-monster characteristics, whereas the male does not. She has overtly negative ways of being chaotic and unreasonable and comes to a violent end at the hands of the male gods. Yet, in her defeat, she is made over into heaven and earth, by the male gods. She's an evil female who doesn't simply give birth to life, but whose body is *used* by the males to create heaven and earth.

"The myth suggests there was no time when there was absolutely nothing. Even the two creators had ancestors. Even the material and spiritual had always been there.

"There's no suggestion that Babylonians denied the existence of other gods for other peoples, such as Egyptians or Assyrians.

"Like all other tribes at that time, they believed in sacrifice. Man was created to partake in everything to satisfy the gods: to serve them by building cities and temples for them because they ruled over everything. However, human kings and rulers owned land and property.

"Words alone could not produce anything magical even by the gods who were always scheming, plotting, and conniving to perform deeds.

"Gods were good and evil, as were humans from the beginning."

Allison places her fork on the table, "*Ummm*, this cake sure is nummy. You probably grew the carrots in your garden. Carrot cake is my second favorite."

"Let me guess. Dark chocolate cake comes in first."

"How did you know?"

I roll my eyes, taste my confection, and say, "That *Silver Palate* cookbook has great recipes, but for technical perfection and ultimate information, use *Cooks*. Sandra, my daughter-in-law gave me both as gifts. She is a blue ribbon champ in Vermont for her blueberry pie. My mom used the *Boston Cooking School Cook Book* by Fannie Farmer."

"My mom likes Julia Child. She and I work together in the kitchen preparing food. She's a good teacher."

"My mother loved family gatherings. She was a great meat-and-potatoes cook. Not very courageous when it came to baking. We'd never heard of Julia Child, nor instant packaged foods, except for Jell-O and breakfast cereals. Yep, fresh-squeezed orange juice daily and locally produced milk delivered to our door by a friendly milkman. It was wonderful. We didn't have to choose between products with additives, and products that were natural. You betcha! The good old days." I sigh, raising my glass of mango tea.

Allison raises her glass, also, proclaiming, "Here's to good new days! Here's to fresh dark-roasted coffee beans from Fair Trade farmers! Far superior to Grandma's weak, tasteless, dried-up stuff from a can."

"Aho!" merrily we clink our glasses together.

"Allison, do you remember the Omamama creation story? Let's include that as we compare spiritual stories."

"Yup, that day," Allison looks into space, "when you told that story, we were in Loring Park. It was very chilly. We were huddled on a park bench, a blanket on our lap."

"And you brought me maple syrup. *Miigwech* again," I say.

"Why didn't you choose to tell me the stories of the Minnesota natives? What are their creation stories?"

"You can find those too, like I did. I chose the Canadian Cree story, because they're a hunter-gatherer tribe whose diet never depended on agriculture or domesticated animals. Therefore, their traditions date back to the Stone Age, reflecting a more continuous, still existing, oldest possible perspective of human interaction with nature in the north-central part of North America.

"Omamama created the earth and sky and life on earth. She was a single female who in turn created a male named Wasakayjack, a supernatural being who created male and female humans.

"Omamama had a personality. She was called 'beautiful, ageless, always kind and happy.' She is not a goddess. She's not worshipped like a deity in organized religion. She's a character symbol. By her will and example she creates and teaches. We do not know her exact words for there was no written language, because teachings were oral renditions. Nor do we know any exact dates when she existed for no attempt is made to place her in a historical perspective. She is not frozen in time. The same is true of Wasakayjack who is not quoted for every word, but cited as an example. Behavior is more exemplified by actions than by words.

"In the Cree story there's no sense of a single, dictatorial instructor imposing power discriminately over selected nations, nor the exertion of an absolute will framed by dated, historical evidence that attempts to prove without doubt the truth of everything. There are no universities where the Cree are trying to identify *who* created Omamama, or who created the Great Mystery. The Mystery is beyond human definition, and cannot be spoken of by humans, yet it does behave in specific ways that can be observed in nature-as-a-whole, not separately in human behavior.

"Omamama creates by divine will, then leaves or disappears from the story; however, she is Mother Earth in spirit. By observing the teachings of Mother Earth, creatures know their duties unique to each creation, which in turn defines relationships between the earthly and supernatural, and underworld and above-world entities.

"Like the Judeo-Christian God, the Great Mystery is omnipresent, omnipotent, and omniscient, and encompasses the one or the whole. However, the Cree believe that the One is an impartial bestower that cares for all equally, no matter race or belief, plant or animal. While each American native tribe or nation devises their own story, they all share the concept of a mysterious originator. They respect the rituals of all tribes that manifest those beliefs. No one tribe has exclusive power due to its relationship with a deity. Indeed, it was fortuitous to capture the power of another individual and turn it to one's own benefit. Among northern nations, spiritual power was inherent and could be earned individually. Contrarily, other more efficient, inventive societies inherited hierarchies such as the Incas, Mayas, and Southeastern or Mississippian cultures where birth class determined one's future. Individuals who were free to earn spiritual energy experienced an enhanced sense of freedom and confidence.

"In the Near East, only the self-appointed chosen few, like Moses, Jesus, Mohammed, and many other 'kings' would continue where the ancient priests had begun. There were many changes. Ordinary people could no longer be intercessors with a direct line to the biblical God, the non-mystery. This one-male god, bearing conflicting dictates for behavior in a book, is lord over all, only accessible by individuals like popes and bishops, priests and ministers, who claim exclusive connections due to their exceptional goodness and pious devotions."

"Wow," Allison says, shifting in her chair, "The pope really is a living relic, a walking museum piece, isn't he? So is Queen Elizabeth and all royalty, I suppose."

"Traditional Cree do not have gods, but rather messengers, or intercessors, such as Omamama, which are all spirits who they do not worship, but whom they respect, appease, and communicate with, so that they will intercede in their behalf to the Great Spirit, who is too great, or awesome to approach directly. Therefore, humility is required of one who hopes for respect in return. The Great Spirit has no one shape or form, sex or personality, but does ultimately regulate, and is the source of all life."

Allison asks, " Is the Great Spirit the same as the Great Mystery?"

"Yes, they are the same.

"For the Cree, there was no definite separation between spirit and matter for they were inextricably bound, like different degrees of one aspect of being. The mythical water serpents were as real as a frog or a human for they represented something extremely real, and that was forces of nature that brought death, while the great thunderbird brought life, or rain. Although I have never seen either with my own eyes, perhaps they really did exist in prehistoric times and to the natives, whose cyclic time frame begins millions of years earlier than the Bible's. Such creatures' bones and remains were surely found by early man, and explanations for them formulated. This speculation is purely hypothetical on my part.

"Allison, we do know that natives personified the forces of nature in imaginative, and highly intelligent ways, for the purpose of bringing meaning and understanding to bear upon society to create codes of conduct."

Oh. Oh. Allison's slumping in her chair like she's going to fall asleep. Her eye lids are drooping. I'm going on much too long. "Allison, where's that treat? We need some chocolate, don't you think?"

"I'm sorry," she says tiredly, "But I need a little break, too."

"Don't be sorry. You've been a great listener, I have an idea."

"What's that?" she replies, reaching in her cloth bag for a wee box wrapped in silver foil, setting it before me, gushing, "Open it. But watch out for the spirits. Surely, this chocolate is full of them."

Excitedly, we reach for one of four little chocolate mounds that appear like smooth, glazed breasts without nipples. We lick them, bite them, roll them on our mouths, savoring the creamy, rich flavor slowly. *Ahhh*, truffle ecstasy. *Ummm.* "Let's eat the others, too!"

Dramatically, I raise my cacao-stained fingers to the sky, "Listen up! The power of truth seems limited! Power of consensus holds promise! Do we gathered here agree that *real* women shed the evil hex of sin? That we hereafter eat of the sacred truffle? That we give sour apples to the less-fair sex?"

Allison jumps to her feet, raising her fist, "Here's to Eve, who we pity. If only she'd eaten of the sacred chocolate, women would not suffer so."

Giggling, flushed with flavonoids, we lick our fingers, slap our palms together, and shout, "High-five!"

Allison sputters, "Say! Didn't you say you had an idea for me?"

"Yes. I'm going indoors for a minute. You could hike to the mill pond and back for exercise. Look for the otter that lives there. Then, I'll tell you more about the Cree people."

"Omamama has no stone tablets, commandments, or parchments to hand down to Wasakayjack or humans. She doesn't personally control human behavior. She allows them limited free will which is tempered by greater-than-human natural elements, or forces. The wolf learned this the hard way, therefore sacrificing itself so people could benefit from its teaching, although it did not die willingly.

"While Omamama didn't dictate or write specific rules, she gave examples. Many trickster stories contain situational scenarios in which the culture hero must make choices which affect consequences in far-reaching, connective ways. Natives noted that only superhuman/man culture heroes, and mortal humans have to muse about morality and choices. The honeysuckle, iris, sweet fern, have spirits and life, yet seem to exercise no intelligent choice about their existence. With grace and integrity, they simply do their duty, like every butterfly, chipmunk, and crow is expected to do. They, too, are like intercessors with messages, or may be thought of as evidence of the existence of spirits within all that lives.

"The story of the Cree suggests that each creature on earth, under, or above the earth, has a unique gift, therefore has something special, or a gift to share in many forms, including a teaching. Man should not only eat other life, he should learn from it. Omamama obviously chose the frog to be a shaman due to certain characteristics she gave it. She did not choose a worm, or a sparrow. She gave the world's inhabitants roles, and responsibilities, and if those responsibilities were not met there were consequences, such as illness or starvation. I have heard a similar version of the Cree story in which the wolf does not heed Wasakayjack's warnings to never do such and such, and as a result the wolf must die, leaving Wasakayjack angry at the water serpents who killed the wolf. However, Wasakayjack is eventually given a gift to replace his loss and order is restored once more.

"The point here is important, for it suggests that there was a reason why the wolf died, and a moral lesson to learn from the disobedience of lessons; that there were consequences to poor behavior. Indeed, many stories that suggest such consequences may involve future generations."

"There must be," Allison suggests, "explanations in native tales for why nature behaves this way or that, such as why the kingfisher has red and grey on his back, or why rapids in rivers are respected."

"One lesson that Wasakayjack tries to teach primitive Cree people is that progress comes at a price if progress reaps foolishness. Being out of balance and foolish are the same thing. He foresaw that destiny is for wise men and fools alike in the great, birchbark canoe adrift on the sea. The human propensity to control the earth, sky, other humans, and even spirits is the trickster behaving foolishly within us: the uncontrolled will, desire, ego, pleasure of our instincts. Wasakayjack not only fought external monsters and natural elements, but his own internal striving. Within the Cree legends, just like Nanabush, the rabbit of the Ojibwe, the coyote for others, Wasakayjack often tries to manipulate other animals and plants but is always defeated. His foolish, short-sighted tricks fail. But that is how he and the Cree come to learn wisdom."

Allison says, "That's like I'itoi, the Tohono O'odham spirit man, too."

"Yes, Wasakayjack epitomized the Cree's attempts to live harmoniously. He was not an epic-hero-god like Gilgamesh, the Sumerian folk hero."

"I remember him! He became a hero by murdering the sacred cedar tree and conquering the wilderness. And the Bible has a symbolic tree, too—one of evil where those heroes become sinful by eating its apples. Both stories seem to symbolize the triumph of a leader. Gilgamesh was about civilization conquering nature and death. The Adam and Eve story was about God's power over mankind."

"Yes, Gilgamesh was a story that severed the earth-human relationship. Wasakayjack didn't set out on a quest that had a beginning and an end with the purpose of solving life's mysteries, or of discovering paradise, or of becoming immortal. Although he had the magic ability to slip in and out of life and death situations, he tried to live within life. He was understood by the Cree people as a mythological character with the same personality traits as themselves. He saw the world as already perfect, even with chaos in it, and not as something to be perfected by human intervention. His journeys were lessons to seek balance within a cosmos that changed very little and therefore had predictable qualities, including those with disastrous effects."

Allison comments, "In the Babylonian story there are many funky gods that behave like humans, but are there many that like to have the qualities of other animals? Like wolves, or bears?"

"In the Babylonian myth, Ea, a male god with human attributes, creates humans and possesses power over all Babylonian gods. Power is not greatest in the first deities, but is distributed unevenly among all gods. Little emphasis is placed upon the creations of humans who are created last, as is the case in the Cree story. In both stories, many things occur before the beginning of all other life. While the Babylonian story only mentions humans, the entire rendition is about god—human—like activities, or gods with human personalities and divine gifts, while animals are barely mentioned, similar to the biblical story, except for the one quite predominant one— the serpent of evil connected to the female. There is no idea, that I know of, that the Cree water serpents were female! The Bible story is quite different. Humans precede other animals, and quickly are given clothing!"

Allison giggles.

"None of the Babylonian gods, or the goddess Tiamat, are conceptually universal as is the Christian God. But no concept of a god is as ethereal as the Algonkian ultimate spirit.

"Allison, a little talk about good and evil here. It seems to me that in the Cree story there is no example of humans bringing evil to earth, just different human colors. It seems to me that there was no evil until humans came along and invented it. They created a perception that there were opposing elemental forces. They were only evil because they caused destruction or death. Yet without death, there could not be life. One had to have death in order to have life. In this wise system of reciprocity, mankind could never extinguish, or defeat, either. I die so you may live. Most natives practiced good medicine, but there were always some who used bad medicine.

"Wasakayjack was given the role of preparing the earth for the people who would come to share it with all that had come before, and he was given rituals to perform as a replacement for his wolf brother, as a gift to the people. The rites were intended to create health and longevity, not defeat human evil. In a sense, one may conclude that while the Cree idea was to accept and live with opposing forces, the Anglo idea became to defeat one at the expense of the other. There is nothing to defeat unless forces are perceived as unequal. I personally conceptualize earthly forces as good-good; yet I understand that human emotions, and suffering, demand a psychological explanation, therefore conceptions of evil serve a real purpose, but obviously those purposes vary widely from one cultural context to another.

"According to Algonkian mythology, like Ojibwe, Cree, and others, humans did not, like the Christians, cause the origin of evil upon earth exclusively by their personal, or radical actions. What they DID cause, was unbalance amongst earthly life forms due to their gift of cleverness. This was not evil, but could be used for evil deeds, such as evil magic. It never occurred to them that they could construct an evil bomb.

"Good and evil are essential components of Zoroastrian and Christian religions, but have a vastly different connotation for hunter-gatherer Cree ancestors or today's traditional elders."

Allison wonders, "What about the story of the flood? I've always thought that any observations of geological changes all over the earth could explain the universal theme of the great flood."

"Me, too. In the Cree story, there is no sense that the universe, while in constant change and motion, was a disorderly, or chaotic place that needed discipline or a 'strong hand' or a reordering by mankind. The explanation for the flooding of the earth is that the water serpents were up to their old tricks. Revenge for the slain father serpent? A reminder of where the real power lay? Man's deeds were not the cause of the catastrophe, for humans did not yet exist, and only animals were in the great canoe.

"The Bible, in Genesis, states: 'And the Lord said, I will destroy man whom I have created from the face of the earth; both man and beast, and the creeping thing, and the fowls of the air; for it repenteth me that I have made them. Also, The earth was corrupt before God, and the earth was filled with violence.'

"If God wished to destroy violence upon earth, it seems paradoxical that the Bible is about one thousand pages of violent activities perpetrated by men and women upon each other. It makes the short, oral Cree creation quite humble in comparison. A wolf, frog, and serpent die, not by the deed of man, but by a man-trickster, while behaving as a man.

"There is no moral evidence that the animals in the canoe are more good, or righteous, than those left behind; or no requirements of purity of character to enter the canoe, no contests for dominance between male and female humans—just between personified elements; no hierarchical, stratified class system, rather equal spiritual value; no clear value distinction between matter and spirit. No one power under the Great Mystery is superior forever, even when endowed with supernatural strength. Human and animal roles are flexible in some ways, and static in others, in relation to changes in nature.

"The elements in the Cree story represent the forces of energy, or creation of balance through motion of complementary—not necessarily competitive—forces. The water serpents challenge Wasakayjack over and over again, and he fights back knowing he cannot defeat *all* of them, yet neither is he impotent. He has magic, or cleverness that he can employ. He is stronger than the frog shaman, and the one who instructs the building of the boat. Yet, *he is not* the one who saves the earth from total lack of land mass. That role is given to the beaver, otter, and muskrat. In other Algonkian tribal stories, this role may be performed by a duck, or water bird. The man-trickster, with all his special attributes, still depends upon other, equally important creatures to assure the survival of the planet."

Allison nods in agreement, "We need the plant sisters and animal brothers more than ever. Honeybees are disappearing in a cloud of pesticides and polar bears are starving on melting ice floes. Soon, there'll be the mother of all floods, and it will be *real*. And not because Mother Earth wanted one—because stupid people believe in inevitable holocausts brought on by *themselves*! It makes me sick!"

"I know, I know. The Hebrew biblical version of the flood came out of Babylonian accounts, according to those who find parallels between the two traditions. The Babylonian one has little moral posturing. The flood seems to have occurred because the gods felt mischievous, not because they wanted to correct anyone's behavior. Everyone, good or bad, was affected by the flood.

"In the Hebrew flood story, god sent the flood himself, and although he says he's a just god, he punishes the sinners and by destroying the earth . . ."

"Destroying the earth!?" Allison proclaims, waving her arms, "Isn't that just a little extreme?"

I'm giggling at her.

"Oh, whatever." She rolls her eyes, settling down.

"Well, he does save the good humans, making the story a moral judgment. In the Cree story the animals and the earth simply begin life anew in the same manner as before. In the Babylonian one, the gods feel sorry that they destroyed man, and in the Hebrew one, God regrets creating man."

Allison adds, "He isn't sorry he destroyed them in a flood. So why should he be sorry if he does it again? If people can't escape their own human behavior, created by God, they're trapped by God in a doomsday! How depressing is that?" she pauses, "Why do children believe this stuff?"

"Because their parents do."

Allison registers a look of surprise, "Well, I don't. I am not going to teach this to my children. How would it feel to be a sensitive, thinking kid who's told by her parents, 'You're evil so the world will end. There is nothing you can do about it. After you are dead you'll be judged in heaven in the sky.' Geeze, a lot of good that will do my grandchildren!"

"Yeah, it's as if some people have a death wish, like they'll do or believe anything just to prove they're—the Bible's—right. Look at the crazy war, I mean, invasion-occupation of Iraq and Afghanistan!"

Allison scowls then says, "Well, I really don't know much about Islam."

"I know some. You can learn about that and teach me."

"Where's all the love and forgiveness the church is teaching?"

I smile, "I feel loved by Mother Earth and feel lucky to be here. An Indian never forgets the natural cycle of coming from the womb of Earth Mother, being nourished by her and Father Sun, and returning to her. The returning is one way to give back some of the caring we have enjoyed, and assures us that our children will be nourished also. Common sense tells the Indian that his destiny depends upon what he returns to the earth, not what he takes from it. He was happy to return to 'dust,' to the womb of the mother. The Cree were not ashamed to be born from the mud in Wasakayjack's clay pot.

"Animals are the outstanding characters in the world of the Cree. Their entire creation story pivots around their comings and goings, their environment, their diet, their habits, and relationships. The human figure is almost an innocent, imperfect anomaly in an otherwise harmonious world. He/she is the main character who constantly outwits himself or herself, behaves stupidly and generally creates chaos, *because* he has intelligence. Wasakayjack does many noble things also, such as organize the escape in the flood, and create men and women, but he is never the dominant figure who lords over all else

369

that exists. He entertains no notion that he knows what is right for the rest of the world. There isn't even the idea that one person or god would know what is right for another person. Therefore, there is no worshipping of gods or goddesses or of any other human form or figure. There is no sense that human endeavors could improve upon what the Great Mystery has already created. Human existence depended upon natural, undomesticated, uncultivated lifestyles. Humans depended upon Mother Earth and Father Sky. The sky and earth did not depend on humans."

Allison stares down at the brick walk, lost in thought. She looks into my eyes and softly said, "We don't need a savior to have a good heart."

Silence falls upon us. Again we hear the wren singing, the crow "cawing," a distant lawn mower. Feeling tired, I assume Allison feels the same way, but no. She's pondering things.

"One more thing," she adds, "What about Islam? You haven't told me their story."

"I don't know much, except that Mohammed lived from 570–632AD. Islam had a prophet named Mohammed. The followers believe in one god—Allah; in heaven and hell; in rules in a book, the *Koran*; in an uncontaminated god who created a supernatural order where man can gain entry by obeying the laws; in extending his domain; in being subservient. Abraham was father to the Arab Islamists, and he had an Egyptian mother. God created man from a blood clot. There are five pillars of Allah, duties to perform with absolute perfection. A monotheistic, hierarchical system much like Judaism. Mohammed, was not born until 570AD, however much of the character of Zoroastrianism can be found in the Koran, and also in the Bible and in other Hebrew scripture.

"The tragic Crusades, which were Christendom's war with Islam, from 1097AD to 1229AD began with Christians killing Jewish 'infidels' and continued as an attempt to reunite the Eastern Church with Rome, even though the Western pilgrims hated their Byzantine Christian brothers. Besides religious causes, there were economic and political reasons that gave justifications for war. European lords of little kingdoms and fiefdoms wanted the wealth of the Orient and Byzantium, and this meant conquest of Muslim territories. There were few avenues for a commoner to create wealth for himself, and going to war to kill and plunder possessions was one of the most lucrative options available to them. Soldiers were like slaves. They received no paycheck. Kings bought and sold their own serfs to fight for other kingdoms. The crusaders returned to Europe with ideas that eventually encouraged the Renaissance."

"Oh. Well, sounds to me like you know quite a bit."

"I read too much."

"Nothing wrong with that."

"Sure there is. Remember, it's often what you are not doing that matters, not what you are doing. Lots of people think that writing or the printing press was the best thing man ever invented, however, I think it was probably the most dangerous one."

"What about nuclear bombs?" she says, rising from her chair.

"You got me there!" We laugh, walking to the front of the house, making a date for our next meeting. I lean on one crutch, waving with one hand, as Allison drives away.

Back in the house, I bump on my fanny up the staircase from the living room to the second floor where I plop into bed, unable to fix dinner until I have a nap. But I can't sleep. I'm still thinking.

The Indians didn't trust written words from the beginning. Every promise made, every treaty signed was lies. What good could writing do? Many distrusted the Bible, an object of fighting among Protestant denominations, and between Protestants and Catholics, and between church and government. Education *was* biblical learning, or time away from nature where normal learning occurred. White education meant trusting written words. Religion or Christian history was not relevant to Indian experience. Why should the Ojibwe or Dakota trust the Bible when it was forcefully used to subvert, conquer, divide, and acculturate them? The white forked tongue was not only an oral one, but a written one.

I roll over in bed and reach for a favorite little book, *Touch the Earth*, by T.C. McLuhan; then turn to a quote taken from Tatanga Mani, a Stoney Indian:

Oh, yes, I went to the white man's schools. I learned to read from school books, newspapers, and the Bible. But in time I found that these were not enough. Civilized people depend too much on man-made printed pages. I turn to the Great Spirit's book which is the whole of his creation. You can read a big part of that book if you study nature. You know, if you take all your books, lay them out under the sun, and let the snow and rain and insects work on them for a while, there will be nothing left. But the Great Spirit has provided you and me with an opportunity for study in nature's university, the forests, the rivers, the mountains, and the animals which include us.

Long before laws were written in cuneiform, humans were inventing morals, but writing gave them new direction. In what ways are we better off today because we can read and write? Does it not depend upon *what* we choose to read and write? Are we any more wise, good, or kind because we read and write?

Writing had a profound effect on spirituality that we don't consider today. Judaic-Christian-Islamic traditions emphasize written dogma as morality and history "set in stone." Anything written became magically truthful and legal. Anything spoken lost meaning or was subject to misinterpretation and mistakes, as if something written could not be altered or changed. Many people revered writing, as if writing contained higher thoughts, like those of priests and scribes, higher than the thoughts of farmers or nomads, seamstresses or mothers.

Those who had access to books had access to influence and power. Interpreting laws for others became a profession. Saving those who didn't know the laws became another. Teaching laws in schools became another. Lawyers, ministers, teachers—that which family roles once provided, became specialized skills, then occupations, or jobs.

Like others, the Jews had used written scripture to their advantage by recording history as they wished it to be. Ancient oral stories were replaced by newer versions. We have God's laws, man's laws, and government's laws. Some are laws by decree, and some are by consensus. Some get to choose who makes them, and some don't, which is why it's good to vote.

Religious doctrines were, and are, used to manipulate people for political gain, territorial acquisitions, and monetary dominance. The Indians never had jails, partly because they never had writing or record-keeping of humans who were deemed good or bad, or a menace to society. It cost them nothing to correct one's behavior.

Judaism and Christianity hardened their attitude and hearts as they defined their spirituality. Along with Islam, the three great faiths of Semitic Near Eastern origins evolved out of the Bronze Age into the Iron Age with creeds encouraging good behavior through words, but in practice they lived by the sword, as their own technological prowess created greater and more extreme choices.

I believe that we have more to learn from native wisdom than natives have to learn from us. Native American spirituality lessons have too often gone unheeded by the vast majority of Americans. I was fortunate to discover indigenous stories which remain in the oral tradition, because that which matters needn't be written down.

I have more to learn. As I think inside the circle, on my spiral—spiritual path, there will be many more *Teachings from Mother Earth*.

Now for that nap . . . .

About the Author

Judith Carol Stern moved from Minneapolis, Minnesota to Grand Forks, North Dakota, with her husband and four children in 1971. She began her college career at the University of North Dakota in 1973, returned to Minneapolis and finished her education at the University of Minnesota with a double major in Applied Arts and American Indian Studies (Ojibwe language) with a minor in Elementary Education.

In Minneapolis she began a clothing design and production company, Judy Stern Inc., and the Judith Stern Gallery. Judith studied at The Playwrights' Center, under Lee Blessing. At the Guthrie Theater, under Maren Hinderlie, she joined a storytelling troupe, culminating in a one woman show at the Jungle Theater, Two Chairs Telling in 1993. In 1989 she moved to Marine On St. Croix, Minnesota and continued storytelling until 1996 with Kay Grindland and the St. Croix Storytellers. In 1994 Judith co-taught classes at Warner Nature Center, a Minnesota Science Museum outreach facility, with Ed McGaa (Eagle Man) author of *Mother Earth Spirituality*, and with Chuck Robertson, Ojibwe / Dakota teacher, administrator. The class was titled Exploring American Indian Spirituality in Contemporary Society. In 1995 she began a retail store in Marine On St Croix, selling designs for log-cabin-living including her own clothing designs, furniture, canoes and art.

Judith began writing a journal as soon as she could write, gathering boxes of notebooks, interviews and news articles about Native Americans, world theology and philosophy for future use. In 1990 she sat down to begin her 'big book', but was soon the owner of eleven commercial rentals in Marine On St Croix. In 2000 she published a children's book, *PJ Penguin, A Race to Save Penguin Land*. From 2006 to 2008, at the University of St Thomas in Minneapolis, she taught American Indian Art to Elementary Education majors, as a visiting instructor.

Judith has memberships in many volunteer organizations. Her strong interest in environmental preservation has been accented by involvement with The Superior Hiking Trail Association (three years as a board member), and the Parks and Trails Council of Minnesota. She is working with Save the Boundary Waters organization to prevent foreign copper mining companies from unearthing harmful sulfites which pollute our precious waters. The watersheds of the Boundary Waters Canoe Area Wilderness near Ely, Minnesota and Lake Superior could become irretrievable dead zones.

A note to my readers:

The events in this book are recorded to the best of my knowledge based upon actual happenings. However, Allison is a composite of all my beautiful University of St. Thomas students. Yet, there was one woman, not named Allison, who inspired me more than others.